SLOW TRAVEL

South Devon
& Dartmoor

cal, characterful guides to Britain's special places

Hilary Bradt & Janice Booth

South Devon & Dartmoor

Devon's combination of moor, river and sea is an invitation to travel slowly, whether on foot, bicycle, horseback or in a canoe. The less energetic can watch the scenery gently unfold from the comfort of a steam train or riverboat, or potter around a quintessential English village.

1 The medieval clapper bridge at Postbridge, Dartmoor. (TPC/AWL) 2 Walking the South West Coast Path at Gammon Head. (NS/SWCP) 3 Canoeing on the River Tamar. (TG/TV) 4 Mountain biking on Dartmoor. (WW/A) 5 The steam train between Kingswear and Paignton. (VB/DC)

DEVON ON THE WATER

South Devon is *the* place for messing about in boats, whether on a river or an estuary. And for swimmers there is a choice of family beaches and remote coves accessible only on foot.

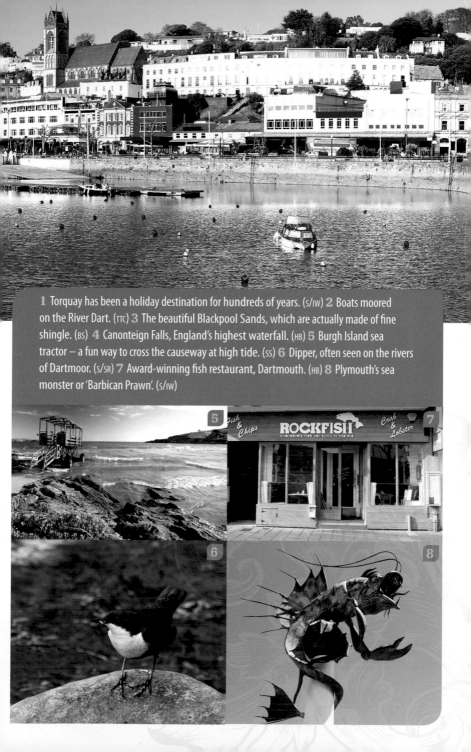

1 Torquay has been a holiday destination for hundreds of years. (s/iw) 2 Boats moored on the River Dart. (ttc) 3 The beautiful Blackpool Sands, which are actually made of fine shingle. (bs) 4 Canonteign Falls, England's highest waterfall. (hb) 5 Burgh Island sea tractor – a fun way to cross the causeway at high tide. (ss) 6 Dipper, often seen on the rivers of Dartmoor. (s/sr) 7 Award-winning fish restaurant, Dartmouth. (hb) 8 Plymouth's sea monster or 'Barbican Prawn'. (s/iw)

DARTMOOR

Dartmoor is one of England's last true wildernesses, where you can wander for hours without seeing a house or road. Its slopes are scattered with remnants of its prehistoric past. But the national park is not all high moorland; around the perimeter are small villages, cultivated fields and tumbling rivers.

1 Hiking the 102-mile-long Two Moors Way. (ss) 2 Wistman's Wood, one of Dartmoor's few remaining patches of forest. (ss) 3 Chinkwell and Honeybag tors, Widecombe Valley. (ac) 4 The jumble of rocks that is Hound Tor is also the site of a medieval village. (n/d) 5 Bowerman's Nose, a natural rock formation. (hb) 6 The tough Dartmoor ponies subsist year round on the moor. (gp)

AUTHOR

Hilary Bradt's career as an occupational therapist ended when potential employers noticed that the time taken off for travel exceeded the periods of employment. With her then-husband George she self-published the first Bradt guide in 1974 during an extended journey through Latin America. Since then she has seen Bradt Travel Guides grow to be an internationally recognised and award-winning

publisher. In 2008 she was awarded an MBE and in 2009 received the Lifetime Achievement Award from the British Guild of Travel Writers. Now semi-retired she writes regularly for the national press and travel magazines and currently has a monthly travel slot on BBC Radio Devon. She lives in Seaton, East Devon (🖰 www.hilarybradt.com).

CO-AUTHOR

Janice Booth's working life has included professional stage management, archaeology, selling haberdashery in Harrods, compiling puzzle magazines and travelling widely. She initiated and co-wrote the Bradt guide to Rwanda, has edited 25 or so Bradt guides to various far-flung places, and helps to judge Bradt's annual travel-writing competition. She moved to Devon in 2001 with

happy memories of childhood holidays, having tasted her first clotted cream here aged eight and ridden on Burgh Island's sea tractor aged ten, and lives within sight and sound of the sea.

Authors' note

The two authors researched this book both together and apart, so the 'I' could be either Janice or Hilary. Just so you know...

First edition published April 2014
Bradt Travel Guides Ltd
IDC House, The Vale, Chalfont St Peter, Bucks SL9 9RZ, England
www.bradtguides.com
Print edition published in the USA by The Globe Pequot Press Inc,
PO Box 480, Guilford, Connecticut 06437-0480

Text copyright © 2014 Hilary Bradt
Maps copyright © 2014 Bradt Travel Guides Ltd
Photographs copyright © 2014 Individual photographers (page 245)
Series Editor: Tim Locke
Project Managers: Maisie Fitzpatrick, Anna Moores and Laura Pidgley
Series Design: Pepi Bluck, Perfect Picture
Cover: Pepi Bluck, Perfect Picture

ISBN: 978 1 84162 552 2 (print)
e-ISBN: 978 1 84162 852 3 (e-pub)
e-ISBN: 978 1 84162 848 6 (mobi)

British Library Cataloguing in Publication Data
A catalogue record for this book is available from the British Library

Front cover image Dartmoor pony at Sheeps Tor in the Dartmoor National Park (CJ/AF)
Back cover image Bantham Bay viewed from Bigbury Bay (PS/A)
Title page image Colourful hotels on the seafront at Paignton on the English Riviera (SS)

Photographers
See page 245 for details.

Maps Pepi Bluck, Perfect Picture & David McCutcheon FBCart. S
Typeset from the author's disc by Pepi Bluck, Perfect Picture
Production managed by Jellyfish Print Solutions; printed in the UK
Digital conversion by the Firsty Group

ACKNOWLEDGEMENTS

The authors would like to thank Imogen Vignoles and the Mais Estate for kind permission to use extracts from *Glorious Devon* by S P B Mais. Thanks are also due to Kate Mault for additional local information for the Dart area, and Noel Hughes, of Berry Head, for his patience in sorting out a natural history query. Special thanks to author and ornithologist Tony Soper who is always ready to answer all sorts of questions about South Devon, and whose boxes on birdwatching are retained from *Slow Devon and Exmoor*. Philip Knowling provided prompt answers just when we needed them, and gave permission for some of his boxes on follies to be reused, while Dave Clegg brought us up to date on the Dartmoor Railway. Editor Tim Locke gave the text his usual meticulous and knowledgeable attention, showing admirable patience throughout the process, and the Bradt editorial team beavered away during the holidays to meet a tight deadline.

Thank you all.

AUTHOR'S STORY

Hilary Bradt

I bought my little house in Devon in 2005, but it was a while before I could tear myself away from my roots in Buckinghamshire. Now I wonder why on earth it took me so long. It's always fascinating to look back at the process of getting to know a new place; I've done it often enough. It begins with your immediate neighbourhood then gradually radiates out, like ripples, as locals tell you about, or show you, their favourite places. Devon has been different. Because the predecessor of this book, *Slow Devon and Exmoor*, was researched within a year of moving here, the process has been more like one of those speeded-up nature films where the greening of my knowledge has quickly spread from one point to cover the whole landscape. It's a process that never ends, nor does the excitement at finding something new ever diminish. I remember the sheer elation when we discovered Kenn and walked on a spring day down its main street past the thatched cottages and library in a phone box, marvelling that no-one seemed to know about such an enchanting village. Conversely, our pleasure at experiencing the paddle-steamer on the River Dart – a well-known tourist attraction – was just as fresh and untarnished by expectation.

I feel so lucky to live here, and to have such a good reason to keep exploring.

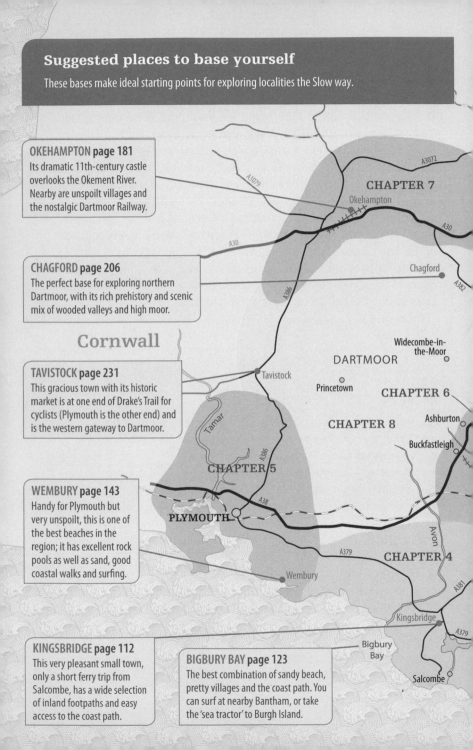

Suggested places to base yourself

These bases make ideal starting points for exploring localities the Slow way.

OKEHAMPTON page 181
Its dramatic 11th-century castle overlooks the Okement River. Nearby are unspoilt villages and the nostalgic Dartmoor Railway.

CHAGFORD page 206
The perfect base for exploring northern Dartmoor, with its rich prehistory and scenic mix of wooded valleys and high moor.

TAVISTOCK page 231
This gracious town with its historic market is at one end of Drake's Trail for cyclists (Plymouth is the other end) and is the western gateway to Dartmoor.

WEMBURY page 143
Handy for Plymouth but very unspoilt, this is one of the best beaches in the region; it has excellent rock pools as well as sand, good coastal walks and surfing.

KINGSBRIDGE page 112
This very pleasant small town, only a short ferry trip from Salcombe, has a wide selection of inland footpaths and easy access to the coast path.

BIGBURY BAY page 123
The best combination of sandy beach, pretty villages and the coast path. You can surf at nearby Bantham, or take the 'sea tractor' to Burgh Island.

Cornwall

CHAPTER 7

CHAPTER 6

CHAPTER 8

CHAPTER 5

CHAPTER 4

DARTMOOR

Okehampton

Chagford

Widecombe-in-the-Moor

Princetown

Tavistock

Ashburton

Buckfastleigh

PLYMOUTH

Wembury

Kingsbridge

Bigbury Bay

Salcombe

A3072

A3079

A30

A386

A382

A386

A386

A38

A379

A379

A381

Tamar

Avon

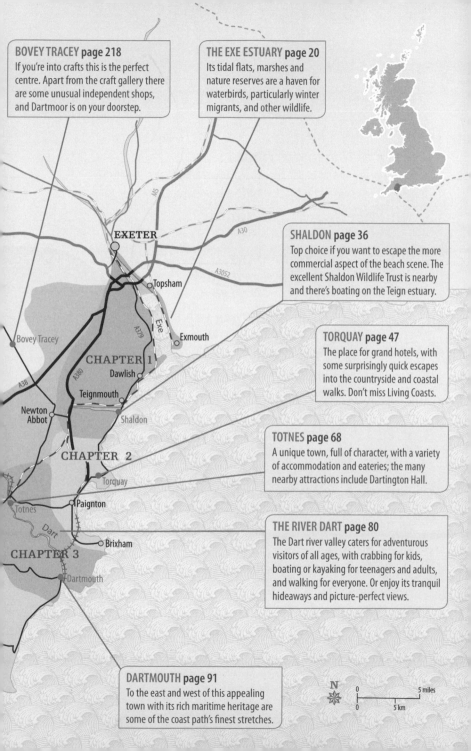

BOVEY TRACEY page 218
If you're into crafts this is the perfect centre. Apart from the craft gallery there are some unusual independent shops, and Dartmoor is on your doorstep.

THE EXE ESTUARY page 20
Its tidal flats, marshes and nature reserves are a haven for waterbirds, particularly winter migrants, and other wildlife.

SHALDON page 36
Top choice if you want to escape the more commercial aspect of the beach scene. The excellent Shaldon Wildlife Trust is nearby and there's boating on the Teign estuary.

TORQUAY page 47
The place for grand hotels, with some surprisingly quick escapes into the countryside and coastal walks. Don't miss Living Coasts.

TOTNES page 68
A unique town, full of character, with a variety of accommodation and eateries; the many nearby attractions include Dartington Hall.

THE RIVER DART page 80
The Dart river valley caters for adventurous visitors of all ages, with crabbing for kids, boating or kayaking for teenagers and adults, and walking for everyone. Or enjoy its tranquil hideaways and picture-perfect views.

DARTMOUTH page 91
To the east and west of this appealing town with its rich maritime heritage are some of the coast path's finest stretches.

EXETER

Topsham

A3052

A30

A35

A379

Exe

Exmouth

Bovey Tracey

CHAPTER 1

A380

A38

Dawlish

Teignmouth

Newton Abbot

Shaldon

CHAPTER 2

Torquay

Totnes

Dart

Paignton

Brixham

CHAPTER 3

Dartmouth

N

0   5 miles
0   5 km

CONTENTS

SOUTH DEVON
& DARTMOOR

INTRODUCTION

[The holidaymaker] comes to Devon for what he cannot get anywhere else, clotted cream the colour of cowslips for breakfast, lunch, tea and dinner, scenery as rich as the cream, contact with a glorious past history and a very pleasant type of modern people. The way, and I think the only way, to see Devon, is to go slowly in and about her, to keep moving, but to keep moving at snail's pace.
S P B Mais, 1928

One thing that has been a constant pleasure when researching this book – and its predecessor, *Slow Devon and Exmoor* – is the way that early guidebook writers like S P B Mais so wholeheartedly endorse our new appreciation of the Slow movement. Indeed, there's nothing new in Slow, it's a rediscovery of the perfect way of appreciating the most beautiful and fascinating parts of our country. It's about taking the time to visit a church, or watch the scenery unfold from a bus window, or observe a peacock butterfly fluttering from flower to flower, or sit gazing out to sea from the coastal path, or plunging from the moor into one of those deep, wooded valleys we call combes. Indeed, that's where the county gets its name: Dyfnaint was the Celtic name for Devon, and means 'dark and deep valleys'.

NGS GARDENS & OPEN STUDIOS

Each year householders from all over England and Wales open their gardens for the **NGS Gardens Open for Charity** scheme (⌂ www. ngs.org.uk ✆ 01483 211535). Since this guide aims to get under the skin of Devon, a visit to one of these open gardens is the perfect way of understanding Devonians or – if you are a visitor from overseas – the English. We are the most passionate gardeners in the world and Devon, with its rich soil and mild climate, makes enthusiasts out of even reluctant horticulturists. The gardens that are open in this scheme come in every size, from manor-house grounds to the kitchen gardens of semi-detached cottages. And it's not just the gardens you'll enjoy. Almost every householder taking part in the scheme adds to the money raised by offering coffee and tea with a wonderful array of cakes. I'm writing this stuffed to the gills with lemon drizzle cake and apricot slice. And full, too, of ideas of how to transform a small garden into a blaze of colour.

The NGS publishes *The Yellow Book* annually which lists all the participating gardens in England and Wales, but there's one for just Devon, which can usually be picked up free at tourist offices or through their website. There are gardens to be visited throughout the year, from January to December, although more, of course, in the spring and summer months. Some open only for one weekend a year so you need to plan ahead.

One NGS participant in Devon is Heather Jansch, whose sculptures inspire awe and admiration in anyone who sees them. Using curved or chunky pieces of driftwood collected from Devon's estuaries and beaches, she builds horses that prance and leap through her acres of meadow and woodland near Newton Abbot. She is just one example of the county's artists who invite visitors to see them at work and to buy their art at lower prices than in a gallery. She also has a small shop in Ashburton. Her studio is open to the public, under the name of her property, Sedgewell Coach House, during both the NGS scheme and the **Devon Open Studios** fortnight which takes place annually in September. This is an initiative of the Devon Artist Network (🖰 devonartistnetwork. co.uk), a non-profit organisation set up in 2004 to promote the visual arts and create opportunities for local artists; participating studios are listed on its website.

EXCEPTIONAL CHURCHES

S P B Mais wrote: 'We are now beginning to discover in a quickly-changing England that almost our only link with the past lies in our churches... [They] bring back memories of our ancient stock. I make no more apology for turning aside into every church than I do for exploring every stream and river.'

We have turned aside into a lot of churches and described them with enthusiasm for the same reason that so moved Mr Mais. From their monuments and tombstones to the present day's flower rota and village-life kneelers, they represent an unbroken link with the past. Churches are also repositories for important art (just how important is illustrated by the recent theft of Torbryan's treasures). Devon's intricately carved wooden screens (which divide the nave from the chancel) with their panels of painted saints are exceptional; there are more complete ones here than in any other county, so we can be forgiven for describing them with such affection. Likewise, carved bench ends and stained-glass windows which show us the mind-set of a medieval craftsman whose life was dominated by the twin fears of God and the law, as well as his deep understanding of the rural life he was familiar with. And when asked to portray an animal he had never seen, he did his best.

Some of our favourites are Combeinteignhead and Haccombe (pages 38-9), Bere Ferrers (page 145), Doddiscombsleigh (page 157) and Higher Ashton (page 159).

THE SLOW MINDSET

> We shall not cease from exploration
> And the end of all our exploring
> Will be to arrive where we started
> And know the place for the first time.
>
> T S Eliot 'Little Gidding', *Four Quartets*

This series evolved, slowly, from a Bradt editorial meeting when we started to explore ideas for guides to our favourite country – Great Britain. We wanted to get away from the usual 'top sights' formula and encourage our authors to bring out the nuances and local differences that make up a sense of place – such things as food, history, nature, geology, or local people and what makes them tick. So without our realising it at the time, we had defined 'Slow Travel', or at least our concept of it. For the beauty of the Slow movement is that there is no fixed definition; we adapt the philosophy to fit our individual needs and aspirations. Thus Carl Honoré, author of *In Praise of Slow*, writes: 'The Slow Movement is a cultural revolution against the notion that faster is always better. It's not about doing everything at a snail's pace, it's about seeking to do everything at the right speed. Savouring the hours and minutes rather than just counting them. Doing everything as well as possible, instead of as fast as possible. It's about quality over quantity in everything from work to food to parenting.' And travel.

So take time to explore. Don't rush it, get to know an area – and the people who live there – and you'll be as delighted as us by what you find.

ANIMALS & WILDLIFE

There are some who are bored with birds but adore zoos, and others who abhor zoos but would happily spend all day in a hide. We love both, so have catered for both enthusiasts.

Exceptional spots for **birdwatching** include the Exe Estuary (page 20), Dawlish Warren (page 32), Berry Head (page 62) and Slapton Ley (page 106).

Birdwatchers and other wildlife enthusiasts should check out the **Devon Wildlife Trust** (✆ 01392 279244 ⌂ www.devonwildlifetrust. org), an active, 50-year-old charity with wildlife reserves and other conservation projects throughout Devon. The RSPB (⌂ www. rspb.org.uk) also manages several reserves here and organises birdwatching events.

Foremost among the area's **zoos, aquariums and farm attractions** are: Shaldon Wildlife Trust (page 36), Living Coasts, Torquay (page 52), Paignton Zoo (page 58), Totnes Rare Breeds Farm (page 70), the National Marine Aquarium, Plymouth (page 133), Dartmoor Zoo, Plymouth (page 142) and the Miniature Pony Centre, Dartmoor (page 213).

MEDIA: NEWSPAPERS & LOCAL RADIO

The *Western Morning News* (⌂ www.westernmorningnews.co.uk) has been published six days a week since 1860 and is an excellent paper for Devon-based visitors, with lots of information and reports on local events as well as politically unbiased international news. Taking the longer view is the monthly magazine *Devon Life* (⌂ www.devonlife. co.uk) with in-depth articles on a range of town and country issues.

Radio Devon (103.4MHz FM), broadcast since 1983 from the stately BBC studios in Plymouth, is one of the most listened-to of the BBC's local radio stations. Tune in to hear traffic news as well as local-interest stories and interviews.

FURTHER READING

We've enjoyed these books and found them useful, and hope you may too. Those that are out of print can be picked up in secondhand bookshops around the county or bought online; a useful website is ⌂ www.abebooks.co.uk. You will find that the list is heavy on churches, because Devon's little village churches are such an integral part of its history and that of its people.

IN PRINT

A Cloud of Witnesses: Medieval Panel Paintings of Saints in Devon Churches
Wilks, Diane. Azure Publications, 2011, updated 2013. Many of Devon's churches contain historically important paintings of saints; some of the finest are illustrated here, with intriguing background details of the saints themselves, many of whom had unexpectedly colourful lives.

Devon Food Heroes *Gorton, Peter* (text) & *Oakes, Adrian* (photos). Halsgrove, 2012. Interviews and profiles of 13 Devon food producers, their products ranging from honey to apples, chillis to mussels and sheep to goats, along with tempting recipes by Peter Gorton as used in his Tavistock restaurant.

Devon *Hoskins, W G*. Collins, 1954; reprints 2003 & 2011, Phillimore & Co. Hoskins is *the* authority on Devon. No place is too small or insignificant to merit an entry in the gazetteer.

Devon's Fifty Best Churches *Gray, Todd*. The Mint Press, 2011. Some fine photos of the churches and their carvings, accompanied by location maps and informative text.

England's Thousand Best Churches *Jenkins, Simon*. Penguin, 1999. The essential companion for any churchphile: knowledgeable and atmospheric descriptions of the churches (33 of which are in Devon) and their locations, in Jenkins' seductive prose.

The Pilgrim's Guide to Devon Churches Cloister Books, 2008. A practical, helpful little handbook, small and sturdy enough to carry in a backpack, systematically listing all of Devon's Anglican churches, with a small photo and brief description of each. Location maps are included.

The South Devon Coast *Harper, Charles G* Chapman & Hall, 1907. A lengthy and often entertaining look at Devon a hundred years ago. Reproduced 2013, Hardpress Publishing.

OUT OF PRINT

A Book of Dartmoor *Baring-Gould, Sabine*. Methuen, 1900. The prolific Reverend Sabine, who was living in Lewtrenchard at the time (see page 185), gives first-hand descriptions of much of Dartmoor and its people, and wanders off into some entertaining stories.

A Perambulation of Dartmoor *Rowe, Samuel*. Gibbings & Co, 1848 (updated 1896 and reprinted 1985). Meticulously researched and fascinating for its detail, including lists of birds

FEEDBACK REQUEST

Devon is stuffed with people who have specialist knowledge of their part of the county, and although we've done our best to check our facts there are bound to be errors as well as the inevitable omissions of really special places. You can post your comments and recommendations, and read the latest feedback from other readers, online at www.bradtupdates.com/southdevonanddartmoor.

and plants. However, Sabine Baring-Gould (see above) wrote only 50 years later (perhaps from professional jealousy?) that Rowe's 'mind was steeped in the crude archaeological theories of his period'.

Crossing's Guide to Dartmoor *Crossing, William*. 1909 and various updated reprints; a 1990 paperback (Peninsula Press) is currently available. Remains one of the most practical guides to the moor ever published: authoritative and informative rather than literary, with a good index.

Devon: A Shell Guide *Jellicoe, Ann & Mayne, Roger*. Faber & Faber, 1975. The erudite research and literary style that you would expect in a Shell Guide.

Early Tours in Devon and Cornwall *Pearse Chope, R (ed)*. James G Commin, 1918; reprinted 1967, David & Charles. A fascinating look at how early travellers in Devon saw the county. The writers include John Leland (travelling 1534–43), Celia Fiennes (1695), Daniel Defoe (1724) and Robert Southey (1802).

Glorious Devon *Mais, S P B*. Great Western Railway Company, 1932. A human and affectionate account, in Mais's masterly style, bringing the scenery and the people enjoyably to life.

Some Old Devon Churches *Stabb, John*. Simpkin, Marshall, Hamilton, Kent & Co, 3 vols, 1908–16. Careful descriptions of many of Devon's finest churches, arranged alphabetically, with grainy old black-and-white photos of their notable features.

The King's England: Devon *Mee, Arthur*. Hodder and Stoughton; various editions since 1928. Arranged alphabetically as a gazetteer, Mee's descriptions of the places are affectionate and his style is very readable. He includes some unusual details and a sprinkling of old tales and legends.

The Worthies of Devon *Prince, John*. 1701, reprinted 1810. In quaintly archaic English Prince chattily describes eminent Devonians and their families from the 11th century onwards. Copies are hard to find, but it has been digitised; for CDs see ⌐ www.parishchest.com or read it online at www.geni.com.

PLANNING YOUR VISIT

WHEN TO GO

Most of you will know that spring and autumn are the best times to visit any popular region in Britain. Our little island can't cope with the summer surge of cars that squeeze their way down lanes created by hoof and foot rather than design. So if you can avoid the school holidays, do. Come to Devon as soon as the Easter holidays are over for coastal hillsides awash with purple and yellow from the violets and primroses, and new-leafed trees not yet obscuring the sea views. Most National Trust properties open at Easter, as do museums and other managed attractions. Even as early as February you'll find carpets of snowdrops as white as hoar frost, and March gives you snow-like drifts of blackthorn and, in places, expanses of daffodils – or wait until May for the bluebells and tender new beech leaves. Autumn offers quiet, sunny days and the changing leaf colours. Of course many people go to this region for the beaches and swimming in the sea; early September, when the school holidays are over and the sea can still be tolerably warm, may be the best time for this.

We're so used to complaining about the weather forecast we often forget just how accurate it generally is. And most visitors have access to a television or at least a radio or some online device, so you just need to plan ahead for wet days. I know people who set out determinedly, booted and waterproofed, into horizontal rain but I'm not one of them. This part of Devon has some of the best walking country in England and it deserves to be seen through slanting sunshine, not slanting rain. For wet days there are some wonderful country houses, excellent museums and other interesting indoor attractions. Even zoos and wildlife parks can be rewarding on a rainy day, because the animals also hate rain so tend to come inside, nearer the viewer, if they have that option. We have listed our suggestions for *Wet-Weather Activities* near the beginning of each chapter.

"This part of Devon has some of the best walking country in England and it deserves to be seen through slanting sunshine, not slanting rain."

HOW THIS BOOK IS ARRANGED

If you look at a map of Devon, you'll see that you can extract an Africa-shaped chunk from the Exe estuary and the A30 and A386 roads that run around the northern perimeter of Dartmoor to Plymouth. This is what we have (mostly) done in *South Devon and Dartmoor*, though some villages north and west of the main road have been described – because they deserve to be. The chapter divisions are relatively arbitrary, with the largest (final) chapter covering Dartmoor National Park and some villages beyond its perimeter. As an offshoot of our former *Slow Devon and Exmoor*, we have put the villages and attractions around the western and eastern sections of the national park – some still technically within the park but with a different character – in separate, shorter chapters. Divisions of the south of the county are more logical, with water (either the sea or the river Dart) dictating the coverage.

MAPS

Each chapter begins with a map with **numbered stopping points** that correspond to numbered headings in the text, and the relevant regional maps are listed under the *Walking* headings.

FOOD & DRINK

We've listed some of our, and other people's, favourite pubs, cafés and restaurants, favouring those places that serve local produce. The list is by no means exhaustive, and some exploration and curiosity will yield many other splendid eateries.

ACCOMMODATION

Accommodation has been recommended on the basis of location and because it embraces a Slow approach either in its 'green' ethos or its overall feel. Places to stay are listed under *Accommodation*, page 237.

GETTING THERE & AROUND

It goes without saying that Slow Travel favours public transport above the car, and in Devon this isn't just because it's better for the environment. Although Devon actually has more miles of road than the whole of Belgium, its roads are mostly car-unfriendly, many being single-track lanes with high banks and hedges so you rely on intuition rather than eyesight where oncoming cars are concerned. S P B Mais recognised the problem for drivers: 'If you keep to the road you will not see Devon at all, only a succession of whitewashed thatched cottages red with fuchsia clustered round a tall grey granite church tower at three- or five-mile intervals as you bore your way through green tunnel after green tunnel.'

It is entirely possible to enjoy a holiday in Devon without a car. Transport to the area is good, and there are usually local buses to get you to the places of interest (all are listed in detail in each chapter) and to allow you to sit back and enjoy the scenery without wondering what's around the next bend.

A useful organisation for **planning journeys by bus or train**, or a combination of the two, is Traveline (✆ 0871 200 2233 ♁ www. traveline.co.uk). It's particularly helpful if you are stuck at a bus stop with no bus and only an unsmart mobile phone. You can phone the number, bleat out your predicament, and the helpful staff will tell you where your bus has got to.

Local buses are a boon for bus-pass holders, but even for paying passengers there are often special deals. Bus stations are a good source of such information. For **planning local bus journeys** and checking the timetable, use ♁ www.journeydevon.info and click on to the interactive map. This allows you to see the bus routes in Devon and select the bus number to view the timetable. Very efficient.

Devon County Council publishes a series of regional bus timetables as well as a bus map of the county. Relevant ones are listed in each chapter and they can be picked up at most Tourist Information Centres (TICs).

GOOD TIDINGS

Devon has some beautiful stretches of coastline, particularly tempting for any visitors fascinated by cliffs, beaches and the shore. However, lifeboats are all too often called out to rescue people who've wandered too far and are trapped by the incoming tide. These call-outs can be dangerous and costly, and can be avoided by always checking the **tide tables** (available in local shops and TICs) before a seashore wander; used sensibly, they open up a wealth of safe exploring.

Non-seawise visitors don't always realise how much the extent and timing of a tide's ebb and flow vary with the phases of the moon. The fact that you could walk past the tip of that promontory yesterday at midday and return safely doesn't mean you can do the same tomorrow, even if you calculate the time correctly: the tide may not ebb so far, or may rise higher, and you'll be trapped. (If this happens, don't try wading, particularly in rough weather; there can be dangerously deep pools close to rocks.) These timings and differences vary from place to place and from day to day, throughout the year, so – better safe than sorry!

CYCLING

This part of Devon has a good range of dedicated cycle paths as well as 150 miles of the National Cycle Network being developed by the sustainable transport charity Sustrans (⊕ www.sustrans.org.uk), along with local organisations. All these are listed and described in the booklet *Cycling Trails in Devon*, available from TICs. Among the most popular cycle trails are Drake's Trail, the Dart Valley Cycle Way, the Granite Way and the Dartmoor Way. These, and others, are listed in the relevant chapter. A useful website is ⊕ www.cycledevon.info.

Most of Devon's lanes are narrow with high hedges. I asked Mike Harrison (⊕ www.croydecycle.co.uk) for his tips on safe cycling. His best advice is to make sure you can hear. Then if a vehicle is approaching you have time to pull in to the edge or be more visible. Lanes may be narrow but there is usually space for a slow-moving car to pass a stationary cyclist or pedestrian – after all, the lanes can cope with trucks and tractors. The back lanes carry very little traffic, but coastal roads can be busy.

WALKING

The scope of this book encompasses the **South West Coast Path** from Starcross to Plymouth, a distance of almost exactly 100 miles. Some of the best walks in all of Devon are here, with the most rewarding short stretches described in each relevant chapter. Those tackling the whole trail, or planning to walk for several days, would do well to use the services of a luggage transfer company so they can walk unencumbered. **Luggage Transfers** (⊕ www.luggagetransfers.co.uk) will also arrange walker-friendly accommodation for you. Likewise, Dartmoor is the starting/finishing point for the **Two Moors Way**, a stiff but hugely rewarding challenge linking Dartmoor and Exmoor.

Walking guides & maps

There are plenty of **guidebooks** for walkers. Some are listed in the relevant chapters; Pathfinder's *South Devon and Dartmoor* by Sue Viccars is particularly useful, covering as it does the same area as this book. The best guide to the South West Coast Path is Trailblazer's *Dorset and South Devon Coast Path*, by Henry Stedman and Joel Newton, which has detailed maps and suggestions for accommodation.

The 1:25,000 Ordnance Survey Explorer **maps** covering Dartmoor and South Devon are huge, double-sided affairs, prefixed OL (the scale means they are great for detail but very unwieldy – we dubbed them 'the table cloth'). Much more useful are the series produced by Mike Harrison under his Croydecycle imprint (⌖ www.croydecycle.co.uk) at a scale of 1:12,500 (about five inches to a mile). Personal (he walks or cycles every road and path), idiosyncratic (plenty of observations to help the walker, such as the condition of the footpath or little nuggets of history) and small-pocket sized, these cover most of the coastal areas in this book but not the moor. The relevant maps are listed in each chapter and are widely available from TICs and gift shops.

EXETER

M5

Topsham

1
Exminster

A38

RIVER EXE

Lympstone

3
Kenn

2
Kenton

4
Powderham
Castle

A38

CHAPTER 6
page 154

5
Starcross

Exmouth

A380

A379

6
Dawlish Warren

7
Dawlish

Holcombe

8
Teignmouth

9
Shaldon

RIVER TEIGN

10
Combeinteignhead
Stokeinteignhead
Haccombe

CHAPTER 2
page 44

0   5 miles   **N**

0   5km

1

THE EXE &
TEIGN ESTUARIES

This area may not hit the touristic headlines very often but it has some of South Devon's loveliest views and best birdwatching. Flatter than much of the county, it is friendly to walkers and cyclists, and its lack of main roads and of large, publicised 'attractions' makes it well and truly Slow. It is well served by buses and well scattered with accommodation of all types; you can pick up current local information in the tourist offices, often staffed by enthusiastic volunteers bursting to promote their home place.

In olden times Exeter and Topsham were important ports for the lucrative Devon wool trade; by the 17th and 18th centuries when activities were at their height, great ships frequently billowed their way up and down the Exe with their valuable cargoes. The river is peaceful now, with nothing larger than ferries and pleasure boats shuttling across, but a sense of history still lingers.

GETTING THERE & AROUND

The obvious gateway town is Exeter, with its airport, rail links and M5 motorway, but if you're coming from Cornwall then the area is equally accessible from Plymouth.

PUBLIC TRANSPORT

Slow **trains** between Exeter and Plymouth stop at Starcross, Dawlish Warren, Dawlish, Teignmouth and Newton Abbot (the expresses go direct from Exeter to Newton Abbot), and offer wonderful estuary views. **Buses** B from Exeter High Street and 2 from Exeter Bus Station between them serve all of the above as well as Exminster and Kenton; the number 11 runs from Dawlish Warren to Torquay via Shaldon daily; while on

WET-WEATHER ACTIVITIES

Exeter Cathedral and Royal Albert Memorial Museum (page 22)
Powderham Castle (Mar–Oct excl some Sats) page 28
Dawlish Museum (May–Sep) page 33
Teignmouth Heritage Centre (page 35)

Wednesday and Friday the 886 runs between Shaldon and Newton Abbot via Stokeinteignhead and Combeinteignhead. Additionally, the 366 runs Monday–Saturday between Exeter and Kenn. The Devon bus timetable that you need is *Teignbridge*; you can also download routes and timetables via the interactive bus map (www.journeydevon. info). Small **foot ferries** will carry you and your cycle across the Exe (between Exmouth and Starcross) and the Teign (between Teignmouth and Shaldon). An 80-year-old Ward Lock guidebook talks of 'the thrill of a steamer trip' from Exmouth to Starcross so goodness knows what they used for the 1½-mile crossing in those days.

CYCLING & WALKING

The new Exe Estuary Trail (see opposite) is a huge asset for this area – and is already being well used both on wheels and on foot. The stretches (some of them on tarmac) between towns are manageable, with a refreshing cuppa or something stronger never too far away. Hardier riders or hikers may feel inadequately challenged by such a flat and pleasant route, but they've plenty of scope for tougher exercise around Dartmoor.

BY CAR

If you're hesitant about Devon's single-track roads, you'll like this area, because there are very few – unless you're tempted to stray on to peaceful small lanes, with their freckling of wildflowers in the hedges.

THE EXE ESTUARY

The broad Exe estuary stretching south from Exeter is a haven of birdlife, nature reserves, easy trails for cyclists and walkers, and exceptional views across the water. Strictly speaking only the western side comes within the area of this book, but we're including some practicalities about the eastern bank in this section just to help you with overall planning.

GETTING THERE & AROUND

Buses serve towns along both banks. Seasonal **foot ferries** operate to/from Exeter, Exmouth, Topsham, Starcross and Exminster: see listing below. Do double-check current times and availability before planning your journey. When you buy bus, train or ferry tickets, ask about Exe Estuary Circular tickets allowing a linked trip on all three systems. **Walkers** and **cyclists** are spoilt for choice: between them they have parts of the South West Coast Path and the Exe Valley Way, as well as the new 26-mile **Exe Estuary Trail**, which runs around the estuary from Exmouth via Exeter to Dawlish. At the time of writing, the section from Turf Lock to Powderham Church isn't finished although it's walkable, and some minor work remains to be done on other sections, otherwise this valuable resource is well and truly open. You'll spot cyclists' heads bobbing along it if you take the train south from Exeter. Some sections (both on-road and off-road) are suitable for wheelchairs and pushchairs. OS Landranger map 192 covers the whole area; the larger-scale OS Explorer map 110 maddeningly just misses the estuary's start in Exeter.

From Exeter, two **train trips** either side of the Exe estuary are far more scenic than the same routes done by road. Both run close to the water, with some station platforms right on the edge. On the eastern bank, the tiny stretch to **Exmouth** is known as the Avocet Line – with good reason. In winter, around 15,000 waders and waterbirds come to the estuary, and the train windows offer a tremendous view. During the 30-minute journey you're likely to spot a variety of species – including avocets – and even the occasional peregrine as it seeks out its prey.

 TOURIST INFORMATION

Dawlish Tourist Information Centre The Lawn, Dawlish ✆ 01626 215665 ⏱ www.visitsouthdevon.co.uk. Open Mon–Sat summer, Thu–Sat winter.

Dawlish Warren ✆ 01626 215665 (Dawlish TIC, above) ⏱ www.dawlishwarren.info

Exeter Tourist Information Centre Dix's Field, Exeter (near main bus station) ✆ 01392 665700 ⏱ www.exeter.gov.uk. Open Mon–Sat year-round.

Shaldon Tourism Centre Ness Drive, Shaldon ✆ 01626 873723 ⏱ www.shaldon-village.co.uk and ⏱ www.shaldon-devon.co.uk. Open May–Sep.

Teignmouth Tourist Information Centre The Den, Sea Front, Teignmouth ✆ 01626 215666 ⏱ www.visitsouthdevon.co.uk. Open Mon–Sat year-round.

Numbers dwindle in summer, but the view is wonderful anyway. The little two-coach train shuttles along half-hourly by day, hourly at

A GLIMPSE OF EXETER

The city of Exeter is just outside the area covered in this guide, but if you're there for any reason then the must-sees are the **Cathedral** and the **Royal Albert Memorial Museum**. From Exeter's Central Rail Station the museum is only a couple of minutes' walk and the Cathedral about five minutes; from the central bus station they're both about ten minutes and you can take in the Tourist Information Centre on the way; from St David's Rail Station it's a stiffish walk uphill (20–25 minutes) but you can catch a city bus H to the centre. Here's a brief glimpse.

The **Royal Albert Memorial Museum** (Queen St ✆ 01392 265858 ⏏ www. rammuseum.org.uk, closed Mon) occupies an imposing gothic building, completed in 1868 and extensively redeveloped in 2010–11. In 2012 it was named the UK's Museum of the Year by Art Fund, the national fundraising charity for art, and described as 'quite simply a magical place'. It has also been called 'an exquisite jewel-box of a building; a Venetian casket; one of the most appealing treasures in Britain'. It claims to be the 'home to a million thoughts', and indeed its million-odd exhibits do cover a massive range. As you might imagine it's strong on the history of Devon and Exeter, from the prehistoric to the present; but also includes international cultures (with some rare West African art), ceramics, natural history (including various birds, bugs, mammals and seashells) the 18th- and 19th-century global explorers and many other changing exhibits. Wonderful for a browse – but allow plenty of time.

The great crouching bulk of **St Peter's Cathedral** (✆ 01392 285983 ⏏ www. exeter-cathedral.org.uk), with its massive carved frontage, was started by the Normans in 1114 and remodelled in decorated Gothic style in 1270–1369. It's hunkered solidly on the Cathedral Green, the weight of centuries pressing it into Exeter's earth; yet when you step inside your eye swings instantly up to the space and grace of its amazing roof: the longest unbroken stretch of Gothic vaulting in the world. When you've recovered from the impact of its size and splendour, you can focus on small, intimate details: animals on the choir stalls, sweet-faced angels playing musical instruments, sad swans with entwined necks, intricate roof bosses and the centuries-old hole in the door of the north tower to allow access for the Cathedral cat. (And just imagine how beautiful it can be at a Christmas service, by candlelight.)

You may want simply to gaze and absorb the atmosphere, but you'll gain far more from your visit if you get a guidebook from the Cathedral shop. There is an entrance fee, and personally I'm happy to help maintain this treasure-house of history and human faith.

evenings and weekends. Most tickets let you get off at intermediate stations and continue your journey later; for example you could visit historic Topsham or tranquil Lympstone, where villagers in homes bordering the estuary walk out on to the silt when the tide is low, hang their washing on tall lines there, leave it to flap above the water as the tide rises, and collect it a few hours later once the tide has ebbed! The train takes up to two cycles if there's room but can be jam-packed with Exeter commuters at peak times, so travel off peak if you can. From Exeter, sit on the right-hand side.

The line to **Teignmouth** (sit on the left side if travelling from Exeter) gives similar views from the western bank: Lympstone nestling between its red cliffs, colourful yachts scattered against the distant backdrop of Exmouth and estuary turning gradually to English Channel. In Dawlish (page 33), probably best known as the town where the railway runs so close to the sea that trains get seriously splashed in winter storms, the station is right by the beach; from here to Teignmouth (pronounced Tin-mth; see page 34) views are across the open sea. At Teignmouth the train turns right to travel along the northern bank of the river Teign (pronounced Teen) to Newton Abbot; there are peaceful views across the water. Then from Newton Abbot to Plymouth the scenery becomes more gently rural, allowing you at last to read your newspaper or indulge in a snack from the catering trolley.

FERRIES & BOAT TRIPS

Exeter Cruises ✆ 07984 368442 🖰 www.exetercruises.com. From Exeter Quay to Double Locks Inn. Apr to end Sep.

Exmouth/Starcross Ferry ✆ 01626 774770 🖰 www.exe2sea.co.uk. Runs daily (hourly) from Apr to late Oct; carries cycles. Also runs trips round Dawlish bay, coastline cruises, cruises on the Exe and mackerel fishing.

RSPB ✆ 01392 432691 🖰 www.rspb.org.uk. Runs birdwatching cruises from Topsham.

Topsham Ferry ✆ 07801 203338. Topsham to Topsham Lock Cottage (for Exminster Marshes). Also water taxis. Run by Exeter City Council. Daily in summer except Tue; weekends and bank holidays in winter. Times depend on tide; phone for details or to book water taxis.

Topsham to Turf Ferry (*Sea Dream II*) ✆ 07778 370582 🖰 www.topshamtoturfferry.co.uk. From Topsham to Turf Locks for Turf Inn, also RSPB birdwatching cruises. Carries cycles. Times/dates variable: check beforehand.

White Heather Ferry ✆ 07884 164255. From Double Locks Inn to Turf Inn. Connects with Exeter Cruises (above). Times flexible; phone for details.

CYCLE HIRE

Braking Wind Cycles Dawlish & Dawlish Warren ℡ 01626 865161 ⊕ www.
brakingwindcycles.co.uk. Open Easter–Sep.
Exeplore Limited Exeter ℡ 01392 271426 ⊕ www.cyclehireexeter.co.uk
Saddles and Paddles Exeter Quay ℡ 01392 424241 ⊕ www.saddlepaddle.co.uk

1 EXMINSTER

> There some time lived in this parish one Stone, who was of so
> hard a grit that he lived to the age of a hundred and twenty
> years; he served King Henry the eighth in his chapel, King
> Edward the sixth, Queen Mary and Queen Elizabeth . . .
>
> Tristram Risdon – *A Chorographical Description or Survey of the County of Devon.*

Longevity apart, the points of interest here are the RSPB's Exminster
Marshes Nature Reserve (on the Estuary Trail) and Powderham Marshes.
You can also walk or cycle to one of the few pubs in the country that
can't be reached by car: the **Turf Inn**, on the edge of the Exeter Ship
Canal, which has been providing refreshment to lock keepers and
passing vessels since 1827.

Powderham Marshes are accessed (courtesy of Palmers Ales) via a
track from the car park of the **Swan's Nest Inn** just south of Exminster;
the turning to the Swan's Nest is clearly signposted from the A379, at a
roundabout. It's a cheery pub, working hard under new management;
you should call in for a drink or snack if you park there. The one-mile
trail leads through arable fields managed for farmland birds, including
the rare cirl bunting. Brent geese gather there, and finches, including
goldfinches and linnets, flock to feed in the stubble in winter. From the
viewing platform at the end of the trail you can look across the estuary;
bring binoculars.

Exminster Marshes are on the cycle trail; or by car continue along
the Swan's Nest turning until the narrow road crosses the railway, then
almost immediately there's a sharp turn right to the free RSPB car
park. It's at the start of a 2½-mile circular trail that takes you through
fields alongside the railway – occasional trains whoosh by unnervingly
– to the wonderfully positioned Turf Inn (see above and opposite):
a good excuse for some mid-walk refreshment. At The Turf Inn you
turn left on to the cycle trail for a train-free and wonderfully peaceful
return beside the Exeter Ship Canal, the silence broken only by fish

breaking surface, coots scuttling through the water and the occasional bird-call. The estuary is very close – this was all a part of its shore until the canal was dug in the early 19th century – and there are fine views across the water to the Exmouth bank. An observation platform part-way along gives you a view inland; binoculars are helpful here, to identify birds in the fields and ponds, possibly lapwings, kestrels, buzzards, herons, egrets, Brent geese, finches and more. Along the canal, watch out for kingfishers and, in spring and early summer, hairy dragonflies (*Brachytron pratense*). Almost a mile from The Turf Inn, at a small private car park on your left (visitors' parking is allowed, in the marked bays), you can rejoin the lane that led past the RSPB car park or continue a little further to the Topsham ferry.

¶¶ FOOD & DRINK

The Turf Inn Exeter Canal, Exminster ☎ 01392 833128 ⏚ www.turfpub.net. Closed roughly from late Nov to Mar. This popular pub is known locally as The Turf Inn or just The Turf, but the sign on its wall says Turf Hotel. The location is amazing, right on the edge of the estuary mudflats and looking straight across the wide stretch of boat-speckled water to Exmouth. It's a rambling old place, with thick walls and a feel of the sea about it, accessible to visitors only by kayak or boat (the *Sea Dream*, Topsham Ferry or White Heather Ferry; see page 23) or by foot and/or cycle – from the RSPB car park or private car park mentioned above, or along the footpath from Powderham Church (about 25 minutes). You may spot a small tarred road, a continuation of the lane from the Swan's Nest, but it runs through private land where parking and unauthorised access are strictly forbidden. Virtually all the food is homemade from local ingredients, and there's a good wine list. Despite the isolation it can get busy in summer and at weekends. Very popular locally are its DIY barbecues: order your food a week in advance from a choice of six different meat and vegetarian options and it'll be ready, with salad, for you to cook up when you arrive. Camping and B&B are also available; see page 237.

2 KENTON

This is not a dramatically picturesque village but some of the lanes and old houses are attractive and worth a brief stroll. The car park in the centre is handily near the 14th-century **Church of All Saints**, an impressive listed building of red sandstone whose 120-foot tower is the second tallest in Devon. (St Nectan's in Hartland, north Devon, beats it by eight feet.) It incorporates walls from two earlier churches and was described by Leland as 'a right goodly church'. Don't be put off by the modern entrance; the interior includes a fine rood screen (mentioned in Simon Jenkins' *England's Thousand Best Churches*), some attractive carving and an unusual wooden 15th-century pulpit that was rescued from a cupboard, in pieces, by the ubiquitous Sabine Baring-Gould

BIRD RESERVES AROUND THE EXE ESTUARY

If you're walking or cycling round the estuary, you'll pass some of the best mudflats and wetland habitats in Devon.

Spring is a good season: you can see lapwings and redshanks and – if you're a serious twitcher – listen for the rare Cetti's warbler. But winter is the most rewarding time when, at high tide, there are thousands of waterbirds including black-tailed godwits, widgeons, shoveler ducks and Brent geese.

The ace in the pack, however, is the avocet and you have a good chance of seeing some in the winter (in spring they go to East Anglia and the Netherlands to breed), especially if you take a special RSPB cruise from Topsham, Exmouth or Starcross (see below). Bird cruises are also run by the Stuart Line.

The **RSPB** has four reserves along the estuary. On the eastern side is **Bowling Green Marsh**, in the pocket of wetlands south of Topsham between the River Clyst and the Exe; a summer ferry from Topsham (Topsham Ferry, above) connects it to **Exminster Marshes and Powderham Marshes** on the western side. The smaller **Matford Marsh** is close to the A379 in the surprisingly green outskirts of Exeter, on the edge of the floodplain. Other wetlands include the evocatively named **Old Sludge Beds** near Countess Wear, where old sewage waterworks have been turned into a wildlife haven and the old sewage pumphouse into a roost for bats, and the extensive and accessible **Exmouth Local Nature Reserve**, one of Devon's largest, with its constantly changing tidal mudflats and sands. Finally there's the **Dawlish Warren National Nature Reserve** (see page 32), centred on a 1½-mile sand-spit at the estuary's mouth. And all within easy reach of a major city: not bad!

Devon Wildlife Trust ✆ 01392 279244 🖰 www.devonwildlifetrust.org
Exe Estuary Management Partnership ✆ 01392 382236 🖰 www.exe-estuary.org. Their leaflets *Exe Wildlife*, *Exe Explorer* and *Exe Activities*, available online and from tourist information centres, are excellent, providing maps and useful details of walks, birds, ferries etc. However, double-check website information as it is sometimes out of date.
RSPB ✆ 01392 824614 🖰 www.rspb.org.uk/exeestuary. Details of bird cruises are on the website. The RSPB shop at Darts Farm near Topsham (✆ 01392 879438) runs nature walks (normally at 14.00 on Sat) and other events.
Stuart Line ✆ 01395 222144 🖰 www.stuartlinecruises.co.uk. Birdwatching and other cruises, including guided winter bird cruises which contribute to the work of the Devon Wildlife Trust.

(see page 180) in 1882 and reconstituted by Herbert Read to designs by Bligh Bond. It's said to be the model for pulpits at Ashprington (also by Herbert Read, see page 84) and Lewtrenchard (page 186). From the outside this church is strikingly similar to – and shares the same vicar as – St Andrew's in Kenn, which is only a few miles' drive inland from Kenton along country lanes.

3 KENN

Sometimes there's no alternative to the cliché of 'best-kept secret'. How did Devon manage to keep this village to itself when I have been committed to finding its hidden gems for *Slow Devon and Dartmoor*? The tiniest hint of the attractions of Kenn in *Devon's Churches* made us decide to take a look and resulted in a great dollop of serendipity.

Only five miles from Exeter, and perhaps a mile from the A38 heading south from Exeter, Kenn presents itself as the perfect Devon village. Well, almost perfect; there's no village shop, but the library, housed in the phone box, makes up for this! Villagers are invited to borrow a book, read it and return it, and to add to the selection.

A little brook runs past thatched cottages ending with the **The Ley Arms**, also thatched. Opposite the pub a mature chestnut tree, speckled with red 'candles' or dropping conkers, depending on the time of year, shares a grassy circle with a white wooden signpost. Up on a hill, and framed by trees, is the tall tower of the red sandstone church. An illustrated board by the graveyard points out the flora and fauna found there, and its ancient yew tree is utterly splendid. Huge, and cathedral-like with its pillars of surviving trunk around a hollow centre.

The church smells right – and that's important – that indescribable scent of old oak, flowers and mildew that defines our country churches. Part of the font comes from Oberammergau, there's a fine barrel roof with painted bosses, and some hand-hewn dark-oak benches and pew shelves. But the glory of this church is the wooden screen. Lavishly carved with entwining foliage, the niches contain some of the best-preserved painted saints in the county. There's St Sebastian, so cluttered with arrows that it's hard to make out his body; St Appolonia, patron saint of dentists and toothache (see page 159); and the four evangelists, who are so holy even the

"The church smells right, that indescribable scent of old oak, flowers and mildew that defines our country churches."

animals at their feet have halos, including a very cute lion. Most unusual is St Mary of Egypt, one of only two depictions in the country (the other is in Norfolk). Mary had a colourful life in the fleshpots of Alexandria, but repented her sins and wandered off into the desert with only three loaves of bread to sustain her and her long hair to keep her warm.

4 POWDERHAM CASTLE

Kenton EX6 8JQ ✆ 01626 890243 🖱 www.powderham.co.uk. Castle and grounds open Mar–Oct, closed some Sats for weddings. Powderham Country Store and Food Hall open year-round except over Christmas.

Entered from the A379 in Kenton, Powderham Castle, dating back to 1391, is the home of the Earl and Countess of Devon; the Earl's family have lived there for over 600 years. Like so many stately homes, it now earns its keep by being open to the public for part of the year. Guided tours of the interior (which has majestic rooms and some attractive art and furnishings) are held regularly throughout the day and prove very popular in summer; one of the guides told me that he barely has time to draw breath. The well-kept grounds offer scenic strolls and various family-friendly attractions, and during school holidays a tractor-trailer carries groups on 'safari' to the surrounding **deer park** with its 600-odd fallow deer and other wildlife. There are three nature trails for younger visitors, and the licensed Courtyard Tea Room has children's meals and lunchboxes as well as more adult temptations like cream teas, fresh baking and light lunches.

The peaceful and appealing little **chapel** was originally built around 1450 as a 'grange' or accommodation for visitors to the medieval castle. The 16th-century carved pew ends come from St Andrew's Church in South Huish near Kingsbridge, which is now a ruin looked after by (this sounds so sad) the Friends of Friendless Churches. In 1866, when parts of it were already 500 years old, the parishioners of St Andrew's decided that the repairs it needed were far beyond their means and it was abandoned. The pew ends were given to the 11th Earl of Devon, who converted the Powderham grange into the present chapel in 1874; while the 14th-century font went to a new church being built in Galmpton, near South Huish – so some of the old church's 'organs' were given new life elsewhere. Outside the chapel is a large mulberry tree with a notice warning visitors that the fallen fruit underfoot can be messy – and also saying 'help yourself', which I did and they were delicious. Manna from Heaven?

THE DEVIL'S FOOTPRINTS?

Deep snow fell all over Devon that night, and when folk in Topsham and elsewhere along the Exe estuary awoke in the morning of 7 February 1855 an unaccountable sight met their eyes. In the snow, stretching along roads, gardens and even roofs, were strange hoof-like footprints. Once it became clear how widespread they were, people armed themselves with whatever implements were to hand and set off to track the intruder – but found nothing. Based on reports it received (which may well have been considerably embroidered) *The Times* wrote up the event the following week. News had come in from other areas, reporting footprints around Teignmouth and Dawlish too. Altogether their alleged trail stretched for around 100 miles. Some, near Powderham, appeared to cross the Exe estuary (there's no record of whether it was frozen over). They were about 2½ inches wide, 4 inches long and 8 inches apart, generally travelling in a straightish line, apparently made by a biped rather than a quadruped. Individual stories – whether true or false – emerged, as of dogs in Dawlish backing away from them in terror. A local vicar claimed them as 'the devil's footprints' in his sermon the following Sunday, and this became their nickname.

There have been a few reports of similar phenomena around the world at different times, but none so comprehensive. The chronicler Ralph of Coggeshall, who was Abbot at Coggeshall (Essex) from 1207 to 1218, wrote of an occurrence in a small area after an electrical storm in July 1205. Many suggestions have been made as to the origin of the Devon prints, the strongest being that a weather balloon accidentally pulled loose from Devonport Dockyard and drifted over the area, its tether lines trailing so that they scratched the snow; but the route of the footprints apparently didn't match the direction of the prevailing wind. To this day, no explanation has been satisfactory – so perhaps they were indeed those of Old Nick on some grumpy nocturnal ramble.

The castle can be busy in summer; the assistant in the small shop told me that sometimes she has had 50 customers crammed in there, although at 2pm in October I was her first customer of the day. For Slow visitors, an off-season visit is recommended.

¶ FOOD, DRINK & SHOPPING

In the grounds before you reach the castle is the **Powderham Country Store**, a complex of local and fair-trade shops including the huge Powderham Trading Co, run by Bovey Tracey's House of Marbles (✆ www.houseofmarbles.com; see page 220). Apart from (of course) displays of multicoloured, multi-sized marbles there are old-fashioned toys and games of all sorts, together with wonderfully soft alpaca knitwear, 'ethnic' and other clothing, books, jewellery, toiletries, furnishings, bags and souvenirs. Two food places are:

Orangery Restaurant ✆ 01626 891639. Run by the House of Marbles, this covers the whole range from breakfasts through lunches to cream teas and is popular locally. It was bustling when I last looked in; and the lunch menu included homemade leek and stilton quiche and flaked salmon and dill fishcakes.

Powderham Food Hall ✆ 01626 891883 ⌂ www.powderhamfoodhall.co.uk. For food shopping, this is a treasure-house of local goodies – cheeses, preserves, patés, wine, baking (fresh from Ryder's Homemade Bakery in Kenn, which also bakes muffins for the Blueberry Brothers – see page 216), organic fruit and vegetables from nearby Bickham, meat from Pipers Farm in Cullompton and treats from further afield too, depending on the season and availability.

5 STARCROSS

The Exe Estuary Trail from Powderham church (from the A379 the signpost indicates the church and the 'SYC' which is the Starcross Yacht Club) to Starcross is a tarmac road, so if you're driving it's a peaceful alternative to the A379. There's a speed limit of 20mph and local residents get extremely fed up with visitors (and other locals) who don't respect it. It's just inland of the railway, which runs along the very edge of the estuary; on its other side is the Powderham deer park, so it's worth pausing for some stag-spotting.

Starcross has two pubs and a handful of small shops and businesses, plus – importantly – the **Exmouth–Starcross Ferry** (✆ 01626 774770 ⌂ www.exe2sea.co.uk). This runs daily from April to late October, and carries bikes as well as pedestrians. It docks just a stone's throw from the railway station; walk down the platform and along a pier and you're there. With it you can do a variety of circular trips (combinations of train, bus, cycling and walking) around the two shores of the estuary, linking up with National Route 2 of the cycle network. See *Ferries and boat trips*, page 23.

The reddish building with a tower, opposite the garage, was the old pumping station of Isambard Kingdom Brunel's **atmospheric railway** (see box opposite). The chimney was once much taller, but was damaged in a storm in the 1890s. **The Atmospheric Railway pub** (✆ 01626 890335) has – appropriately – some related memorabilia around the walls: old photos, newspaper cuttings, lamps, models and so forth. As the manager pointed out, apart from the tower it's all that remains of Brunel in Starcross now, since the small museum closed a few years ago. Opening hours vary.

¶¶ FOOD & DRINK

Anchor Inn ☎ 01626 890203 ⏚ www.anchorinncockwood.com. A mile or so south of
Starcross, by Cockwood's small harbour, is this deservedly popular inn, specialising in seafood.
It can get very busy so, if you're eating there before catching the Starcross Ferry, leave plenty
of time as it'd be a shame to rush your meal.

THE ATMOSPHERIC RAILWAY IN DEVON

The possibility of using air pressure to provide propulsion for a vehicle or train came to life early in the 19th century. In 1812 George Medhurst of London proposed somehow blowing passenger carriages through a tunnel but unsurprisingly the idea didn't catch on. In 1838 gas engineer Samuel Clegg and marine engineers Jacob and Joseph Samuda jointly took out a patent for a new improvement in valves and at this point atmospheric propulsion became feasible. They set up a working model in Southwark in 1839, and ran a half-mile demonstration track at Wormwood Scrubs from 1840 to 1843. Things were moving fast, with many top-level railway engineers expressing both interest and criticism; the first atmospheric railway opened in Ireland in 1844, followed by one on the outskirts of Paris. Another was started in 1846 on five miles of the London and Croydon Railway, but it encountered too many problems and in 1847 was scrapped.

Among engineers keeping a close eye on progress was Isambard Kingdom Brunel, who then recommended the use of the system on a much longer stretch, planned to run from Exeter to Torre and Totnes. The trains literally ran on air, with a combination of partial vacuum and atmospheric pressure; they were practically silent, and with no nuisance of steam or smuts. At stations along the route, including Exeter, Turf, Starcross and Dawlish, pumping houses were built and steam-driven pumping engines were installed in them. The first train ran in September 1847, between Exeter and Teignmouth.

There were always difficulties. Among others, the pumping engines used far more coal than expected, communication between pumping houses was poor, and the leather flap valves sealing the traction pipes deteriorated from use and the salty atmosphere. Treated with oil to prevent this, they then attracted hungry rats and mice, which got sucked in to the tube and thus jammed the piston — at which point third-class passengers might have to dismount and push the train to the next station. At the system's peak, nine trains a day ran between Exeter and Teignmouth at up to 70mph; but for reasons of cost and many operational problems it just wasn't viable. The last train ran in September 1848. Gradually the machinery was removed and the pumping houses were closed and dismantled; the one at Starcross is the only one that has survived in situ, although its machinery has been removed long since.

DAWLISH WARREN & DAWLISH

Now we're moving from estuary to English Channel. I have a soft spot for both these small seaside resorts, just a couple of miles apart, despite their very un-Slow 'amusement' areas and tourist paraphernalia. Bustlingly busy in the summer, out of season they retain a flavour of old-time seaside, with long, wind-swept beaches, ice-creams, beach huts and promenades. Below the tideline (gritty sand at Dawlish, finer at Dawlish Warren) you can beach-comb for shells, bleached driftwood, cuttlefish 'bone', sea-smoothed glass and other salty treasures, and swimming is safe. The flat walk between them along the sea wall and cliff path is a constant pleasure – beware of waves in stormy weather – and you can do part of it on the beach at low tide. The railway runs close by but isn't intrusive: as you've no doubt seen on TV, during winter storms the trains can be soaked by waves. The waterside rail journey from Exeter is the most memorably scenic in this book (see page 21); bus B from Exeter High Street goes alternately to one or the other about every half hour; and Dawlish is also served by the number 2 from Exeter Bus Station.

"Here you can beach-comb for shells, bleached driftwood, cuttlefish 'bone', sea-smoothed glass and other salty treasures."

6 DAWLISH WARREN

The particular attraction of Dawlish Warren is its **nature reserve,** a wild, peaceful and wind-swept place where (out of season) I've wandered without spotting another soul. The long, sandy, dune-edged shoreline is superb and it's an internationally important area for wildlife: the main roosting site for the huge numbers of wading birds and wildfowl that spend the autumn and winter on the estuary. The reserve is also designated a Special Area of Conservation (SAC) for its dune grassland, humid dune slacks and the tiny, rare 'petalwort' that grows there. A small visitor centre (✆ 01626 863980) with information and displays is open most weekends, and more frequently during the summer season. About a mile beyond the Visitor Centre is a bird hide, excellent for watching wading birds and wildfowl in winter. Viewing is best two hours either side of medium-high tides.

To get to the reserve from the centre of Dawlish Warren go through the dark little railway tunnel by the station, turn left past the amusement area with its arcades and razzmatazz, and continue through the car park to the gate at the far end. Be aware that the last public toilets are near the tunnel; there's nothing in the reserve. You'll need to return the same way, as there isn't an exit at the far end.

In its defence, the amusement area does have a useful shop, Warren Trading Co, selling outdoor and indoor clothing. The town has a handful of other shops, including a branch of Braking Wind Cycles (see page 24), and there's an open-air market on Wednesdays.

7 DAWLISH

Half village, half town, it is – pleasant but smallish,
And known, where it happens to *be* known, as Dawlish;
A place I'd suggest
As one of the best
For a man breaking down who needs absolute rest,
Especially too, if he's weak in the chest.
R H D Barham, 1867

I wish I could, as apparently local residents do, come to terms with the garish amusement complex that dominates the main square, because without it Dawlish could be a pretty town. A brook flanked by gardens, Dawlish Water, runs through the centre, there are some pleasingly twisty streets and attractive buildings, the beach is long and mostly sandy between red sandstone cliffs and there's a friendly feeling of bustle. Oddities are appealing: Dawlish Community Transport runs a little red minibus called Rosie, black swans and various other exotic waterbirds live on Dawlish Water, and the busy railway station café, improbably named Geronimo's Diner, is decorated with Wild West artefacts.

Jane Austen holidayed here in 1802 and later complained about the 'particularly pitiful and wretched library'. Today she could feed her mind in **Dawlish Museum** (☎ 01626 888557 ⏚ www.devonmuseums.net/dawlish; open Wed–Sun, May–Sep), with its three floors of wonderfully miscellaneous memorabilia linked to Dawlish and Devon: anything from a penny-farthing bicycle to bagpipes and an ancient mouse-trap. In the early 20th century, Dawlish became famous for the popular perfume Devon Violets, and hundreds of varieties of violet were raised in market gardens – some still grow wild in the area. The **Tourist Information Centre** is in the centre of town.

Walking from Holcombe to Torquay

�֎ OS Explorer map 110; start: near Holcombe.

One of my favourite sections of the South West Coast Path is the stretch from Holcombe, a mile or so south of Dawlish, to Torquay, which can be comfortably walked in a day by a fit person (it's about 12 miles). It combines the paved stretch that runs between the sea and the railway north of Teignmouth with the ups and downs, woodland and meadow which characterise the more remote section to Babbacombe or Torquay.

Take the number 2 bus from Exeter towards Teignmouth and get off just past Holcombe where a narrow signposted lane connects the road with the coastal path, just south of Hole Head. Then it's an easy walk by the sea, in the company of other strollers, for less than two miles to Teignmouth where you can eat lunch or at least buy an ice cream before taking the ferry (operates all year; times vary) to Shaldon where the energetic part begins. Although you are rarely walking on the level, the variety and beauty of the scenery, with views of the sea and little coves at the bottom of the indented cliffs, help you forget your tired muscles. It may feel isolated but you are never far from the main road and bus services to Torquay or Teignmouth so you can give up and take a bus at any time.

The trail is well marked, but you should take OS Explorer map 110, Torquay and Dawlish, with you for reassurance.

South of the main beach (which you enter via a small tunnel under the railway) is the smaller Coryton Cove, sheltered and pleasant for swimming. In the days of segregated bathing this was the gentlemen's beach; the ladies had their bathing pavilion towards the other end. At the cove, information boards describe the area's geology and history, including the development of the railway and Brunel's involvement; a good outdoor café serves fresh snacks, toasted teacakes, cream teas and so forth. But at holiday time the whole beach and indeed the whole town can become uncomfortably busy.

THE TEIGN VALLEY

8 TEIGNMOUTH

Teignmouth was granted its market charter in 1253 and in the early 14th century was Devon's second-largest port, smaller only than Dartmouth. Now it's a well-laid-out and organised seaside resort with a range of facilities: hotels, Victorian pier (now given over to 'amusements'), gardens, clean sandy beach, heated lido and the excellent **Teign Heritage Centre** (✆ 01626 777041 🖰 www. teignheritage.org.uk; open Tue–Sat, Mar–Nov plus Sun in Jul/Aug), opened in an eye-catching modern building in 2011. Its extensive displays run from prehistory to the present, and include relics from the mysterious 16th-century shipwreck discovered on Church Rocks. You can also step inside an old-fashioned bathing machine and try your luck on old pier slot machines.

For me Teignmouth hasn't the endearing quirkinesses of some smaller resorts, but its classic Georgian crescents are attractive and visitors return year after year. An **International Folk Festival** is held in June and the **Teignmouth Regatta** in July/August. **Walks** are varied and plentiful, whether along the coast or up into the countryside; the **Tourist Information Centre** near the pier has maps and leaflets.

Ther is a **Teignmouth-to-Shaldon ferry** (✆ 07896 711822 🖰 www. teignmouthshaldonferry.co.uk) which has been running in various forms since at least the 13th century and is said to be Britain's oldest such service; it starts from Back Beach near the lifeboat station and runs year-round except over Christmas; times vary seasonally. Near its starting point are a couple of small huts selling seafood and snacks, so while you're waiting for it to arrive you could try the fresh seafood platter or crab sandwiches at the **Blue Hut**. An alternative to the ferry is to walk to Shaldon across the

"A Teignmouth-to-Shaldon ferry has been running in various forms since at least the 13th century."

bridge; when the first – a wooden one – was built in 1827 it had 34 arches and was said to be the longest in the country. A span at the Teignmouth end could be raised to let tall vessels pass through. The centre collapsed in 1838 having been eaten by ship-worm and again in 1893. The bridge was completely rebuilt in 1927–31, using steel for the piers and main girders and concrete for most of the deck, and allowing for subsequent repairs that's the one you see today. It's occasionally heard to whistle when winds catch it from a certain direction.

A couple of miles from Teignmouth, tucked away among fields, is the little ruined 13th-century Chapel of St Mary, protected by a rusty iron railing. I'm reminded of Tennyson's 'a chapel near the field, a broken chancel with a broken cross' from *Morte d'Arthur*, but this old story is far grizzlier: of a medieval monk living there who lured travellers to the chapel, murdered them and threw their bodies down a well. R H D Barham, son of the author of the *Ingoldsby Legends*, wrote a light-hearted poem about it (*The Monk of Haldon*) in 1867, by which time it was already the stuff of legend, so who knows what's true. Drive out of Teignmouth on the B3912 and, just after you've passed the golf course (on your left), a steepish footpath on the right leads down to it. The ground can be very muddy. It's marked on OS Explorer map 110, near Lidwell Farm; (✳ grid reference SX924762). There's not much to see – only the west wall is still standing and the rest has crumbled – but it's a pretty and peaceful place and a listed monument. The sign on the railing calls it Lidwell Chapel.

9 SHALDON

This appealing small village looks over the Teign estuary at its much larger partner, Teignmouth, and has several attractions. It's reached via the train to Teignmouth and then the ferry across the estuary, or by the number 11 bus between Torquay and Dawlish Warren.

There's a pleasant **beach** of sand plus shingle (though covered at high tide) which you approach through a tunnel – lots of fun for children – often called the Smugglers' Tunnel though I doubt if that was its actual purpose; it's a little too well built. The beach also has rock pools.

Towering over the beach is a red headland, Ness Point, and on this high ground is a delightful little zoo, the **Shaldon Wildlife Trust** (✆ 01626 872234 🖑 www.shaldonwildlifetrust.org.uk; open year-round except Christmas), which sensibly specialises in small animals such as marmosets and tamarins from South America, meerkats from Africa and lemurs from Madagascar. There is also a small collection of reptiles and invertebrates. The spacious enclosures are well designed and the animals well cared for. A keeper-for-a-day scheme allows visitors to roll up their sleeves and work hands-on with the staff; costing £75, it makes an original gift for a wildlife enthusiast.

"There's a pleasant beach of sand plus shingle which you approach through a tunnel – lots of fun for children..."

For such a small village there's a surprising amount going on: an international music festival in June, a horticultural show in July, a water carnival and popular nine-day 200-year-old regatta in August, various watersports on the Teign estuary and other local events to suit the season. On summer Wednesdays there's a Craft Fair, with craftspeople in medieval costume. The helpful **Tourism Centre** in Ness Drive is conveniently sited in the main car park, with the Wildlife Trust a short walk away.

If you take the road to the west along the estuary, you'll come to a tiny church tucked away at the end of an alley with its back to the Teign. This is the **Church of St Nicholas**, and it's officially in Ringmore but only about half a mile from Shaldon village centre. I'd read that it has a Saxon font, though the writer W H Hoskins dismisses it as containing 'nothing of note'. It was early evening, well after closing time, but the cleaners were busy hoovering. And Hoskins was right, there's really nothing of note inside the church, but one of the cleaning ladies couldn't wait to show me a special gravestone. It's to William Newcombe Homeyard who invented Liqufruta, a garlic-based cough remedy which was revered as a cure-all in the early part of the 20th century. When he died in 1927 his widow wanted the brand name of his great achievement to be put on his gravestone, but it was vetoed by the vicar as inappropriate advertising. She then asked if she could put a Latin inscription instead and that was approved. So forget the Saxon font and seek out the three-tier commemorative cross with Gothic letters proudly spelling out ATURFUQIL on the top stone, in the 'unfading' memory of its creator. No, it's not Latin, just Liqufruta spelt backwards!

"Homeyards Botanical Gardens: natural rather than manicured and pleasant for strolling, with some unusual shrubs and trees."

Shaldon's **Homeyards Botanical Gardens** (a stiffish climb up to the top of town) were created by the energetic Maria Laetitia Kempe Homeyard with the money made from her husband's invention. They're free of charge, natural rather than manicured and pleasant for strolling, with some unusual shrubs and trees and an Italianate garden. There's a substantial 'summer house' (now roofless), designed to look like a castle, where Mrs Homeyard used to entertain guests to tea – not to be confused with the limestone grotto where the local witch Old Mother Gum is said to come at dusk for a furtive cuppa. The disused gardener's hut is now a roost for swallows and lesser horseshoe bats. Volunteers work hard to look after and develop the gardens, and arrange various activities; you can follow their work on their website (⌐ www.shaldonbotanicals.wordpress.com).

¶¶ FOOD & DRINK

Food is taken seriously in Shaldon although, in common with other Devon towns, some tea-places do tend to shut at tea-time. It's well worth trying the sustainably minded **Café ODE** (✆ 01626 873427; open daily except Tue) up near the Tourism Centre (even the cutlery is compostable) and **ODE Restaurant** at 21 Fore Street (✆ 01626 873977; open Wed–Sat plus occasional Tue). Their motto (see ⌐ www.odetruefood.com) is 'Good food that doesn't cost the Earth'. Pretty much everything there is organic and local, from Riverford Farm milk and meat products to seafood from the bay, and the manager told us: 'If we're sent vegetables that weren't grown locally we just send them back'. They also support local charities and local activities, and are starting to hold occasional cookery 'masterclasses' which are proving popular. The Café ODE has a good range of hot and cold meals and snacks with indoor and outdoor seating. The ODE Restaurant offers regional food on its tempting menu (with items such as rare-breed pork belly, seared fallow deer, cured Crediton duck leg and oven-baked pollock).

Also recommended is the **Ferry Boat Inn** on The Strand (✆ 01626 872340), with good local seafood (try their pint of prawns) and traditional pub grub.

SOUTH OF THE TEIGN

10 STOKEINTEIGNHEAD, COMBEINTEIGNHEAD & HACCOMBE

The alternative spellings, Stoke-in-Teignhead and Combe-in-Teignhead, give a clue to the pronunciation, although I have also heard 'Stokeeintinny' and 'Combtinhead'. These two pretty villages, deep in the countryside yet a stone's throw from Teignmouth and Newton Abbot, have good pubs, thatched cottages, and interesting churches. Arch Brook, which runs into **Stokeinteignhead**, gives the village some extra charm which it has in bucketfuls anyway. There's a particularly pretty row of white houses lined up along the combe and the church has allegedly the oldest screen in the country. Certainly it seems to be a simpler design than usually seen, and there's a brass dated 1375 which makes it the oldest in Devon.

"These two pretty villages, deep in the countryside, have good pubs, thatched cottages and interesting churches."

Combeinteignhead also has an absolute treasure in its church, which you'd never guess when approaching its shocking pink door and seeing the even more inappropriate pink wall-tiles inside which make it look like a municipal swimming pool. It's only when you get to the north transept (to the left of the altar) that you see the carved bench ends. These date from Elizabethan times, and are fascinating in their subjects as well as the bold carving and beautiful dark oak. There are saints galore, including St Catherine with a big crown and her wheel, a very serious St Peter with exuberant flowing locks and a giant key, St George in full armour spearing a tiny, dog-like dragon, and one of those really obscure saints that turn up in Devon churches from time to time: St Genesius, dressed in a fool's costume of cap and bells. Two strange men, side-by-side, seem at first glance to be dressed in densely pleated costumes, but it's much more likely to be fur (the lion's mane is done the same way). Each is holding a club, or escutcheon, and has a mop of unruly hair. These are probably 'wild men' or wodwo (woodwose), which appear quite frequently in old church carvings, perhaps representing untamed nature. There is a recognisable lion, but what are we to make of the animal which looks like a lion until you notice its long back legs and huge feet clutching a branch? Could it be a baboon? An animal the carver had never seen but had described to him? There is also an utterly indefinable animal, or possibly it's a fox, carrying off a goose flung over its shoulder – an image that is quite often seen in churches. All in all, these are the most interesting carvings I've seen in any Devon church, so it's well worth braving the pink.

"These are the most interesting carvings I've seen in any Devon church, so it's well worth braving the pink."

Near the church are traditional almshouses built of red sandstone, given to the village by William Bouchier, Earl of Bath, in 1620.

Haccombe is worth the diversion, but only on a Wednesday (14.00–16.00) in April to September, when the little, peach-coloured church is generally open, or for a 09.15 service on most Sunday mornings. It's awkward to find; set your satnav to postcode TQ12 4SJ, or follow the helpful directions on ⌂ www.shaldonchurches.co.uk. Since medieval times the **Church of St Blaise** has been associated with the adjacent manor, originally lived in by the Haccombe family and later by the Carews. The original mansion was replaced by the present Georgian building at the end of the 18th century. Approaching the imposing house down the narrow lane, you have an uncomfortable feeling of trespass and expect His Lordship to emerge with a musket. However, it has long since been converted to flats.

The horseshoes on the door of the church are explained in the box opposite. Its tiny interior is a treasure-trove of memorials to erstwhile owners of Haccombe and other ecclesiastical goodies. To put you in the right frame of mind, there's a 'wool-comb' with fearsome nails; St Blaise was martyred by being flayed with a carding comb used to process wool, and then beheaded. Despite this, as a physician he managed to dislodge a fishbone from a child's throat, so is now patron saint of the wool trade and of throat ailments. He is also the patron saint of Dubrovnik, where a reliquary supposedly contains some of the saint's body parts – and a fish bone.

The biggest memorial is for Sir Hugh Courtney who died in 1425 and his wife Philippa, and nearby is a miniature alabaster memorial, possibly of their son, Edward, who died while a student at Oxford. Sadly the hands are missing, but the sculpture is otherwise in very good condition, including the charming dog on which his feet rest. The size suggests that this was a 'heart burial' and that the rest of the body was interred elsewhere. Had he not died the estate might not have passed to the Carews, for it was his sister who married Sir Nicholas Carew. Sir Stephen de Haccombe, the knight who built the church in gratitude for his safe return from the Crusades in 1233, is also there along with his wife Margaret. The stone carving was originally covered with plaster, and painted. Traces of the paint and plaster remain, most notably in the moulding of a chain. His crossed feet rest on a rather cute lion. Beneath the carpet by the altar is a fine set of Carew brasses. There's some good medieval stained glass in the windows, some from Haccombe Manor; the east window is 17th-century Flemish. Note, too, the lovely uneven, medieval floor tiles.

"The priest was appointed to the church when it was little more than a ruin, covered in ivy, with visiting birds the only congregation present to listen to his services."

The church is unusual in having an archpriest rather than a vicar. This dates from the founding of a college of six chantry priests, with an archpriest at their head, in 1335. He has the power to keep an eye on the local clergy and reports to the Archbishop of Canterbury rather than a bishop. He is also entitled to wear a fur stole. At the time of writing, the post was vacant and its future uncertain. One of the archpriests at Haccombe was the renowned botanical artist, the Reverend W Keble

Martin. He was appointed to the church when it was little more than a ruin, covered in ivy, with visiting birds the only congregation present to listen to his services. One such bird was a wren that nested in the pulpit. The nest is there today, and if you poke your finger into the obvious hole in the stone carving, and wiggle it to the right, you can still feel it.

THE HACCOMBE HORSESHOES

The horseshoes nailed to the door of St Blaise's church in Haccombe – only one and a half of them now, although there used to be four – are said to be relics of an ancient wager between a George Carew, Earl of Totnes, and Sir Arthur Champernowne of Dartington. A ballad attributed to an Exeter schoolmaster in the early 1800s tells how the two men attended a feast in Haccombe Hall, with many flagons of good ale. Sir Arthur wagered the Earl that he could beat him in a horse race; Carew accepted the challenge and suggested they see who could ride furthest out to sea in Torbay. Champernowne staked Dartington Manor while Carew put up Haccombe Hall.

Reaching Torbay, the two men galloped seaward, Carew just beating Champernowne into the breakers. Neck and neck they forged ahead, battered by the waves. Then Champernowne fell back; his horse was weakening and could barely hold its head above water. He cried out to the Earl to save him, promising him Dartington Manor in return. Carew grasped the reins, turned the horses about and guided them both to shore, then spurred his steed back to Haccombe, and in the church thanked God for his good fortune. He removed his horse's shoes and nailed them to the door, saying that the brave beast should work no more but live out its life in pasture.

The Carews at Haccombe date back some six centuries and the Champernownes at Dartington even longer, with many Georges and Arthurs among them. Some reports claim these two were cousins, but the time-line throws up discrepancies. In any case, since Champernownes lived on at Dartington until the 20th century, it seems that Arthur reneged on the bargain! In 1546 a Sir Arthur Champernowne married the widow of the Sir George Carew who captained the *Mary Rose* and drowned when she sank, so they may have known each other, but were they the subjects of the ballad? In fact did any Carew really plunge into Torbay's billows with a Champernowne – or did the Exeter schoolmaster invent the story to enliven history for his pupils? Were the horseshoes from Carew's horse – or fixed to the door to deter witches, as happened in other churches? Believe what you will! What's certain is that the processional cross inside Haccombe church today contains wood from the ancient *Mary Rose*. After she was raised in 1982, two small pieces of her timber were given to the church in memory of her final captain: a Carew whose wife became a Champernowne.

No one would dream of removing it! Keble came to Haccombe from a busy industrial parish and is reported to have been advised to find something else to do after complaints by his parishioners that he had visited all of them twice in one week. His great work, published in 1965 when he was 88, was *Concise British Flora in Colour*; it was anything but concise, containing 1,400 meticulous watercolours.

Church Farm, signposted as you approach the church, was formerly the Georgian coach house of the manor. Now, set in a secluded valley of woods and fields, it's the private country home of award-winning BBC TV wildlife producer and author Andrew Cooper and his wife Jeanne (✆ 01626 872310 ⏚ www.wildlink.org). The elegant house and its surroundings, rich in wildlife (including buzzards, barn owls, sparrowhawks, deer, glow-worms, badgers and bluebells) have featured in many TV programmes including the BBC's *Autumnwatch* and *The One Show*. It's not open or visible to the passing public but the Coopers offer (pre-booked) group talks and guided walks around their land. Andrew also runs wildlife video and photography courses of one day or longer – or you can opt for luxury B&B (see page 237) complete with badger-watching in comfort.

⅋ FOOD & DRINK

Church House Inn Stokeinteignhead TQ12 4QA ✆ 01626 872475 ⏚ www. thechurchhouse-inn.co.uk. In the spacious dining room of this 13th-century inn, you'll find a strong emphasis on locally sourced food: fish from Torbay, meat products from Shaldon. Good menu, loads of atmosphere.

The Coombe Cellars Combeinteignhead TQ12 4RT ✆ 01626 872423 ⏚ www. thecoombecellars.co.uk. Every old guide to Devon mentions this inn, even Harper's 1907 account where he quotes Keats as writing: 'And Coombe at the clear Teignhead/ Where close by the stream/ You may have your cream/ All spread upon barley bread.' It was then called Ferry Boat Inn, and the 'Cellars' were fish cellars. Recently modernised, it serves food all day; the waterside position is fantastic.

UPDATES WEBSITE

You can post your comments and recommendations, and read the latest feedback and updates from other readers, online at ⏚ www.bradtupdates.com/southdevonanddartmoor.

40 Years of Pioneering Publishing

In 1974, Hilary Bradt took a road less travelled and published her first travel guide, written whilst floating down the Amazon.

40 years on and a string of awards later, Bradt has a list of 200 titles, including travel literature, Slow Travel guides and wildlife guides. And our pioneering spirit remains as strong as ever – we're happy to say there are still plenty of roads less travelled to explore!

Bradt ...take the road less travelled

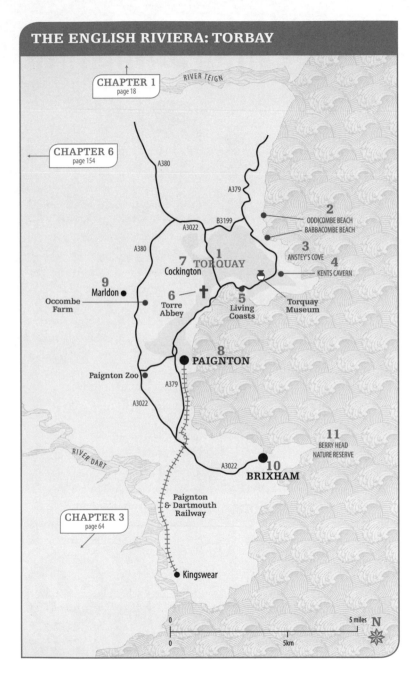

THE ENGLISH RIVIERA: TORBAY

CHAPTER 1
page 18

RIVER TEIGN

CHAPTER 6
page 154

A380

A379

2
ODDICOMBE BEACH
BABBACOMBE BEACH

B3199

A3022

3
ANSTEY'S COVE

A380

7 TORQUAY
Cockington

1

4
KENTS CAVERN

9
Marldon

6 ✝
Torre
Abbey

5
Living
Coasts

Torquay
Museum

Occombe
Farm

8
Paignton Zoo

PAIGNTON

A379

A3022

RIVER DART

11
BERRY HEAD
NATURE RESERVE

A3022

10
BRIXHAM

Paignton
& Dartmouth
Railway

CHAPTER 3
page 64

Kingswear

0   5 miles   **N**

0   5km

2

THE ENGLISH RIVIERA: TORBAY

The wide, curved deep-water harbour of Tor Bay has played a regular part in history, as well as attracting more recent visitors to its mild climate and sandy beaches. W G Maton, writing in 1794, reported: 'The bay appears to be about twelve miles in compass [four miles as the gull flies], and is reckoned one of the finest … for ships our coast can boast of. It was the general station for the English fleet during the whole time of William III's war with France, and here it was that this monarch arrived, when Prince of Orange only, on the memorable fifth of November, 1688.' The Napoleonic Wars (1799–1815) elevated the area still further, partly because the Channel Fleet was anchored in Tor Bay for a while, with Napoleon on board *en route* to exile on St Helena, and partly because the war in Europe prevented the nobility from doing the Grand Tour abroad so some used the Devon coast as a substitute. Indeed, Napoleon may have inadvertently promoted the area as a holiday destination. On seeing the bay for the first time he is said to have exclaimed: 'Enfin, voilà un beau pays!' Suddenly, **Torquay** was fashionable and once the Great and the Good started coming here, they never really stopped.

"Napoleon may have inadvertently promoted the area as a holiday destination. On seeing the bay for the first time he is said to have exclaimed: 'Enfin, voilà un beau pays!'"

The bay area with its linked towns is officially known as Torbay, but the marketing people prefer 'the English Riviera'. Torquay has its downside – big department stores and traffic jams – and much of **Paignton** is hard for Slow visitors to love, but if you know where to go and what to see there are all sorts of pleasures to be found: excellent art exhibitions, the spookily fascinating **Kents Cavern** (Torbay is one of UNESCO's

Geoparks – the term given to areas of exceptional geological interest), and surprisingly rural lanes folded into the hills behind the town. In fact Torbay has more peaceful walks and picnic places than you could justifiably expect. Tucked behind the craggy projections of **Berry Point** and **Hope's Nose** which contain the bay are quiet beaches and small, pebble-and-sand coves.

GETTING THERE & AROUND
PUBLIC TRANSPORT
It's horrid **driving** and parking in Torquay, and you can manage perfectly well here without a car, with a variety of enjoyable travel options. The **bus** service into the town and along the coast is excellent, particularly the number 12 which runs every ten minutes. Paignton and Torquay are accessible by **rail** from a branch line from Newton Abbot. A wonderfully picturesque alternative is the **steam train** which runs between Kingswear and Paignton, a perfect route for window gazing and a stunning introduction to the beauty of Torbay when approached from the south. A 'Round Robin' ticket enables you to include a cruise on the River Dart to Totnes, and return to Paignton by double-decker bus.

Ferries run regularly between Torquay and Brixham, also from both Brixham and Torquay to Dittisham and Greenway on the River Dart (✆ 0845 4890418 ◌ www.greenwayferry.co.uk).

TOURIST INFORMATION

Brixham Tourist Information Centre Hobb Nobs Gift Shop, The Quay ✆ 0844 474 2233
English Riviera Tourist Information Centre 5 Vaughan Parade, Torquay. ✆ 01803 211211 or 0844 474 2233 ◌ www.englishriviera.co.uk

CYCLING & WALKING

In Torbay itself a **bicycle** is an efficient means of transport rather than a means of enjoyment; it's ideal for covering the long, bleak stretch of waterfront between Torquay and Paignton, and gives you quick access to Cockington or Marldon. Bicycles can be rented in Paignton and Torquay (Paignton Bike Hire ✆ 01803 523118 or Simply the Bike ✆ 01803 200024).

For such a populated area there is a good selection of long-distance walking trails. Wending its way round the area for 35 miles, the **John Musgrave Heritage Trail** starts at Maidencombe, north of Torquay, heads inland following paths and lanes to Cockington, then continues to Totnes. The walk can end here, but the trail then joins the Dart Valley Trail to return to Torbay at Brixham. The most rewarding section of the **South West Coast Path** is round Berry Head to Kingswear and the stretch north of Torquay (see box on page 34).

TORQUAY & AROUND

1 TORQUAY

Visitors have been holidaying in Torquay for hundreds of years and, until recently, no one had a bad word to say about it. Dr W G Maton wrote happily in 1794: 'Torquay far exceeded our expectation in every respect. Instead of the poor, uncomfortable village that we had imagined, how great was our surprise at seeing a pretty range of neat, new buildings, fitted up for summer visitors, who may certainly here enjoy convenient bathing, retirement, and a most romantic situation.' A visitor burbled to Bishop Phillpotts that Torquay was like Switzerland, to which he replied: 'Yes, only there you have mountains and no sea, and here we have sea and no mountains.' There are, however, hills which give the upper town its attractive, layered look, and some splendid mansions overlooking the bay. The seafront and marina are attractive, and there is a sandy beach – at least until the high tide chases the sunbathers on to the esplanade.

Perhaps it all started to go wrong with the arrival of the trams, as predicted by Charles Harper in 1905. 'Presently there will be electric tramways at Torquay! Conceive it, all ye who know the town. Could there be anything more suicidal than to introduce such hustling methods into Lotus-land?' The hustling methods of the modern motor-car have anyway done for Lotus-land, but stick with it because there are plenty of escapes.

Take the advice of S P B Mais, writing in the 1920s: 'At the back of the inner harbour is the shopping centre. There will be time for this on a wet day. The wise tourist will cling to the coast to explore the outer edges before venturing inland.' I agree, and would add that the most attractive and interesting area of Torquay is the knob that includes Hope's Nose, north of the excellent marine zoo, Living Coasts. The number 32 bus runs to, or near, all the places in this area.

Torquay Museum
529 Babbacombe Rd, TQ1 1HG ☎ 01803 293975 ⌂ www.torquaymuseum.org.
There's a miscellany of permanent and temporary exhibits here, including a reconstructed Devon farmhouse, some artefacts excavated from Kents Cavern and an Agatha Christie gallery. It's a substantial place with some original exhibits; you could spend quite a while browsing. The number 32 bus stops outside.

2 BABBACOMBE & ODDICOMBE BEACHES

Charles Harper in 1907 found the walk down to the beach too challenging for comfort: 'There are winding walks down to Babbacombe, but for all their circumbendibility they are so steep that by far the easiest way to descend would be to get down on to your hinder parts and slide… the walking down jolts the internal machinery most confoundedly.' Now, fortunately for those worried about their internal machinery, there is a cliff railway to transport visitors up and down the steep cliff – at least in summertime (it is closed from early October to Easter). This deposits you on Oddicombe beach, which was once lovely but now is dominated by a fast-food outlet; it still has good swimming off the pebble-and-sand shore, however. In April 2013 a landslip

"Babbacombe is reached via a delightful walkway, hugging the jungle-clad cliff, with access to rocks for adrenalin-fuelled jumps into the sea."

deposited a large part of the cliff and a small part of a house on to the beach, and it's no longer possible to walk up to the road from Oddicombe. The more up-market Babbacombe is reached via a delightful walkway, hugging the jungle-clad cliff, with access to slipways and rocks for adrenalin-fuelled jumps into the sea. The Cary Arms (☎ 01803 327110 ⌂ www.caryarms.co.uk), which has been there for several hundred years, has an excellent menu, and there is also a more humble café.

BEACHES

There are beaches galore here, but it is the secluded coves that are the most rewarding for those looking for beauty as well as swimming. They can be divided into the mostly sandy stretches at the southern, Brixham, end of the bay, and the pebble coves north of Hope's Nose.

In the south, apart from the large and popular sandy beaches at Paignton and Goodrington, the most accessible smallish one is Broadsands, with reddish sand, colourful beach huts and rewarding rock pools at the southern end at low tide. There's parking here and most water-sports. But it's the little coves that can be reached only on foot which most appeal to me. Accessible from the South West Coast Path as you head towards Brixham is Elberry Cove (about 15 minutes' walk), a quiet pebble beach, and then Churston Cove, a delightfully secluded sand-and-shingle beach tucked into the wooded hillside. Fishcombe Cove is tiny, equally scenic and secluded, only 15 minutes from Brixham and has a summer-only café.

In the north, Anstey's Cove, Oddicombe and Babbacombe are the main beaches, scenic, accessible and notable for their unusually beautiful pebbles.

3 ANSTEY'S COVE

This tiny bay (TQ1 3YY) is an unexpected delight so close to Torquay and seems to have changed little, if at all, since 1907 when Charles Harper described the steep path leading to the beach and the café. Perhaps the walk from the (free) car park deters visitors since even on an August Bank Holiday, admittedly drizzly, we were the only people there until joined by an old fisherman and his dog, checking for mackerel. He told us that the nearby Redgate Beach, now closed because of the danger of rock falls, used to be connected to Anstey's Cove by a wooden bridge. Mind you, adventurous souls can still get round at low tide, or swim round at high tide, to enjoy an unspoilt beach backed by high red-and-green cliffs with the dramatic spike of Long Quarry Point at its northern end. This is manmade, our fisherman friend told us, the result of quarrying in Victorian times for the high-quality limestone, similar to marble, which was used to build some of Torquay's finest houses.

The beach at Anstey's is composed of pebbles as colourful as marbles, red and white mixed with greens. At high tide it disappears and, being so small, can get crowded on a sunny summer day when there are deckchairs for hire and a pleasant little café. You can also hire sit-on-top sea kayaks here in the peak holiday months.

4 KENTS CAVERN

89 Ilsham Rd, TQ1 2JF ✆ 01803 215136 ⌂ www.kents-cavern.co.uk. Open all year.

I've had quite a few depressingly commercial and dumbed-down cave experiences and feared that Kents Cavern would be all entertainment and no education. Well, I was wrong. It's wonderful! We were lucky to be on the last tour of the day, with only one enthusiastic family, so our excellent guide was able to match his commentary to our interests. He told us that they can have as many as 30 people, which would not only make it hard to hear the explanations but also diminish the genuine feeling of awe at being in a place inhabited by our human ancestors and animals for around 350,000 years, and where modern man, Homo sapiens, sheltered some 30,000 years ago. The prize find at the cavern was a fragment of *Homo sapiens* jaw bone which was recently dated to almost 40,000 years ago, making it the oldest fossil of modern man found in Britain. We learned about William Pengelly, the first cave scientist, and his work excavating and identifying the bones found here. There's a model of the great man, frock coat and all, which highlights the difficulty of maintaining Victorian decorum in these conditions. Among the animal remains found in the cave were the teeth of woolly mammoth and scimitar-toothed cat, as well as a large number of hyena bones. Recent evidence suggests that the humans using the cave may have been cannibals: marks from flints used to butcher animals were found on human bones.

"The prize find at the cavern was a fragment of Homo sapiens *jaw bone, the oldest fossil of modern man found in Britain."*

The stalactites and stalagmites make Kents Cavern visually superior to the caves at Buckfastleigh (page 166) and knowing that it took them 60,000 years to get that way adds to one's appreciation. There was once an almost complete pillar of stalagmite and stalactite. Now it's just a stub next to its taller companion. Charles Harper describes how this happened: 'It began to be formed when the world was young. It grew and grew with the drops of water, charged with lime, percolating from the roof, and being met by its fellow stalagmite with equal slowness rising from the floor. And stalactite and stalagmite had nearly met, and only wanted another three or four centuries to bridge the remaining interval of an eighth of an inch, when a visitor, falling accidentally against them, broke them off!' 'What did you say?' one asks the guide. 'What *could* you say?' says he.'

The explorers of Kents Cavern

There's nothing secret about Kents Cavern (except, perhaps, when and why the apostrophe was dropped). Humans have been living there, on and off, for around 40,000 years, and tourists have been visiting the caves since at least 1571. We know that because William Petre carved his name and the date into the soft limestone walls, and another visitor followed suit in 1615. 'Robert Hedges of Ireland' added his name and village in 1688 (the hamlet of Ireland is near Dartmouth).

By the time Dr W G Maton paid a visit in 1794 there was a guardian to prevent such abuses. Maton describes 'Kent's Hole' as 'the greatest curiosity in this part of the country'. He was guided by two women with candles and tinder-boxes. 'The lights, when viewed at a distance, gleaming through the gloomy vaults, and reflected by the pendant crystals, had a most singular effect. We began to imagine ourselves in the abode of some magician, or (as our companions were two ancient females, and not the most comely of their years) in the clutches of some mischievous old witches...'

Although William Pengelly is the name associated with scientific excavation of the caves, he wasn't the first to take an educated look. In 1824 a Mr Northmoore broke through the lime deposits on the floor to the clay below and recognised the bones of extinct animals. The following year the chaplain of Tor Abbey, the Reverend J MacEnery, finding himself with time on his hands, started three years of excavation and discovered 'the finest fossil teeth I had ever seen!' He also collected many bones and some flint implements. Both these men paved the way for William Pengelly's scientific exploration of Kents Cavern between 1865 and 1880, and his conclusion that 'man was, in Devonshire, the contemporary of the mammoth and other extinct cave-mammals; and that, therefore, his advent was at a much earlier period than has commonly been supposed; or that his extinct brute contemporaries lived much nearer to the present day than has been generally believed; or that both propositions are true.' After Pengelly had enlarged the caves and sparked worldwide interest, more people wanted to make a visit. Charles Harper took a look in 1805 or thereabouts. 'A limestone bluff, shaggy with bushes, trees and ivy, rises abruptly to the

"Tourists have been visiting the caves since at least 1571. We know that because William Petre carved his name and the date into the soft limestone walls."

A walk to Daddy Hole & Hope's Nose

✳ OS Explorer map 110; start from Imperial Hotel, grid reference SX927632.

A quick escape from Torquay is provided by taking the footpath to Daddy Plain (2½ miles round trip) and, if you have time, to Hope's Nose, a rocky headland that is one of South Devon's best fishing venues.

The path starts at the Imperial Hotel, on Park Hill Road, uphill from Living Coasts. Go through the hotel gate and you'll see the path on the left. It's a most agreeable walk, with good sea views including 'London Bridge', an eroded rock arch, benches to rest on, plenty of wild flowers, and peeps into the gardens of the millionaires' homes that overlook the sea.

Above the curiously named Daddy Hole (Daddy was a colloquial name for Devil or Demon who was allegedly responsible for the landslip which created the hole) is Daddy Plain, an expanse of flat grass, popular with families and their dogs, backed by a row of picturesque houses. It's a shortish walk back down St Mark's Road the road to Torquay, or there's a bus.

From Daddy Hole the path continues round the Nose, briefly joining Meadowfoot Sea Road, before climbing above it to pass through Lincombe Wood on the South West Coast Path. This is a proper walk, with ups and downs, and gorgeous sea views. Soon it splinters off to take you to the tip of the Nose where you have a fine view across to the other horn of the bay, Berry Head. On the rocky shore below there are fossils, but it's strictly forbidden to damage or remove any; this is a Site of Special Scientific Interest, managed by Torbay Coast and Countryside Trust.

right of the road, and in the side of it is a locked wooden door, upon which you bang and kick for the guide, who is guide, proprietor, and explorer in one. When he is not guiding, he is engaged in digging … The freehold of the famous cavern which ever since 1824 has been the theme of more or less learned geological treatises was recently sold at auction for a trifling sum; not to an institution or a scientific society but to the guide, who has conducted many geological pundits over it, and by consequence has acquired an air of greater omniscience than the most completely all-knowing of those not remarkably modest men of science.'

5 LIVING COASTS

Beacon Quay, TQ1 2BG ✆ 01803 202470 🖰 www.livingcoasts.org.uk. Open daily.

The surprise here is not that there should be such a good marine wildlife collection in a seaside resort but that it hasn't been done elsewhere. Living Coasts admirably achieves what it set out to do when it was first opened in 2003: conservation and education. One of the world's rarest species of seabird is here, the bank cormorant from Robben Island. Compared with the puffins and penguins it's pretty boring to look at, but that's not the point; the influx of tourist development on Nelson Mandela's former prison home is pushing its endemic wildlife towards extinction, and Wild Coasts has teamed up with the South African conservation group Sanccob to save these birds and other endangered species.

The place is full of surprises. The puffins are not the usual ones seen in Britain but exotic tufted puffins from the Pacific, and in addition to the familiar African penguins often seen in zoos there are flamboyant macaroni penguins which, with their golden headdresses, live up to their name (macaroni has nothing to do with pasta, it means 'dandy'). Mammals are represented by fur seals and otters, which can be viewed both above and below water. Look out also for the octopus. 'Very clever creatures' commented a member of staff. 'If they weren't so short-lived they'd probably run the planet.'

In the mangrove swamp you can see one of the marvels of evolution, the four-eyed fish, and it's worth describing what is so special about *Anableps anableps* in some detail. This little fish hails from Central and South America where it spends much of its time floating near the surface of the water, thus rendering it vulnerable to predators from both above and below. Evolution has come up with a neat solution: eyes that can see both above and below water at the same time. Each eye has two lenses and two retinas, to give perfect vision whether through water or air, and the fish is as happy breathing air for short periods as it is in the water. But that's just the start of its peculiarity. Whereas most fish have pretty unexciting sex lives, releasing eggs which are fertilised outside the female's body, the four-eyed male fish has an impressive reproductive organ called a gonopodium. But this can only move in one direction – sideways. The female has an appropriate genital opening, but with a sort of hinged lid to it, so she can only be penetrated from one side. Thus for a successful coupling to take place, the fish has to find a compatible mate, either right-sided or left-sided. That accomplished, she pulls off a final trick: the birth of live young rather than the laying of eggs.

> *"Whereas most fish have pretty unexciting sex lives, this four-eyed male fish has an impressive reproductive organ."*

6 TORRE ABBEY

The King's Drive, TQ2 5JE ✆ 01803 293593 ⏱ www.torre-abbey.org.uk. Open year-round except Mon and Tue.

A great deal of thought, time and effort have gone into the restoration of Torre Abbey and it has succeeded admirably. The abbey was founded in 1196 and at the time of the dissolution of the monasteries was the wealthiest Premonstratensian house in England. Some of the ancient monastic buildings remain, including an early 14th-century gatehouse and a tithe barn, now known as the Spanish Barn because it rather improbably played a part in the Spanish Armada. In 1588 Sir Francis Drake, on board the *Revenge*, captured the 1,000-tonne Spanish man-of-war *Nuestra Señora del Rosario*. An oil painting of the Spanish captain surrendering to Drake is in Buckland Abbey. The crippled *Rosario* was towed into Torbay, where almost 400 of her crew were held prisoner in the tithe barn while she was repaired enough to be used as a floating prison. These prisoners are said to have included a young woman who had disguised herself as a sailor so that she could go to sea with her beloved husband.

"Prisoners included a young woman who had disguised herself as a sailor so that she could go to sea with her beloved husband."

During their two weeks of imprisonment in the barn she caught a chill and died; it's claimed that her ghost is sometimes seen and heard there, lamenting her fate.

After the dissolution, the abbey passed through many hands before being bought by Sir George Cary in 1653. It remained in the hands of this Catholic family until 1930 when it was bought by Torquay Corporation to be used as a museum and art gallery.

Most of Torre Abbey is now a museum, housing a very good collection of art, including ceramics. There is something here to appeal to everyone, well displayed and free from crowds. Treasures include William Blake's engravings for the *Illustrations to the Book of Job*, and paintings by Holman Hunt and Burne-Jones. Other rooms are preserved as they were when it was the Carys' private residence, with some of their loaned furniture. You can also see the secret chapel, used regularly through the times when Catholicism was banned.

Take time, too, to visit the peaceful and immaculately kept gardens and their palm and cactus houses.

7 COCKINGTON

I had a resistance to Cockington. With all the notable villages in Devon it seemed pointless to go to one that was more or less manufactured for tourists, especially one whose brochure claims it as 'South Devon's Best-Kept Secret' followed by 'Known the world over, the famous…'. However, I was wrong. Yes, Cockington is chocolate-box pretty, yes, it's packed with coach parties and tourists, but Cockington Court is also full of interest and to be able to escape Torquay within minutes and walk through spacious parkland beside a brook is not to be sneered at.

"A long stretch of lawn is shaded by trees and village cricket matches are still played there; spectators can enjoy the thwack of the ball on willow in idyllic surroundings."

Although you can drive here there are much better alternatives: the Cockington Tripper bus (number 62) runs every 30 minutes or so from Torquay Strand (Harbourside). It's also a very enjoyable 20-minute walk up Cockington Lane, opposite Livermead Beach; the lane crosses the railway line and Old Mill Road, then you'll see the Watermeadow Walk on the right, running parallel to the lane almost all the way to the village less than a mile away.

In 1935 Torquay Corporation bought Cockington and the town has owned it ever since, preserving the traditional thatched cottages and forge as in a time warp. Even the Drum Inn, designed by Sir Edwin Lutyens in 1934, is perfectly in keeping. The historic house and church are on the edge of the village, in a peaceful area of the old deer park. A long stretch of lawn in front of the house is shaded by trees and village cricket matches are still played there, on a delightfully uneven ground; spectators can enjoy the thwack of ball on willow in idyllic surroundings. But the main interest here is **Cockington Court** and its church. This elegant mansion was once owned by the Cary family, but for the last 300 years of its private ownership belonged to the Mallocks. It is now a centre for crafts, and very good ones too. In the galleries upstairs are some seriously fine jewellery and other 'light' crafts, while in the old stable yard there are seven workshops including glass-blowing. They were giving a demonstration while I was there, and turning out impressively good stuff in front of the clicking cameras.

When you've finished with the crafts there are the gardens to stroll in and the church to visit. S P B Mais commented in the 1920s: 'I do not know quite what draws such multitudes to see a church which is surpassed in beauty by many others in the neighbourhood. It must be its accessibility. It is at any rate good that one survival of the feudal system should be visited and appreciated by multitudes who do not ordinarily take the trouble to investigate the insides of churches.' He may say that. I couldn't possibly comment. The ornate and unusual pulpit is said to include decorated timbers taken from the Spanish flagship *Nuestra Señora del Rosario*, which was captured by Sir Francis Drake during the Armada (see Torre Abbey, page 54). It consists of various pieces of screenwork, some from the 15th century, others possibly from the early 16th and the book-rest from still later. Parts may be from the front of a rood gallery. The whole effect is colourful and a little bizarre. There seem to be cherubs with wings sprouting from the sides of their heads, bringing the disconcerting mental image of heads flapping around the Devon countryside. It is said that the originals may have been portraits of captains or clergymen with huge ears to show that they 'heard all', but were converted to something more appropriate for their new home. Maybe.

¶¶ FOOD & DRINK

As you would expect in the English Riviera, there are plenty of excellent places to eat in and around Torquay. This is just a selection of local favourites to suit all palates and budgets.

Angels Tea Room Babbacombe Downs Rd, Babbacombe TQ1 3LP ✆ 01803 324477. A very popular (so often crowded) traditional tea room with some of the best coastal views in the southwest. The jam and scones are excellent, and there is a good selection of teas. The ideal place to relax and watch the world go by.

Blue Walnut Café Walnut Rd, Torquay TQ2 6HS ✆ 01803 605995 ⏏ www.bluewalnutcafe. com. What makes this place special is that it is an arts café, with live music and performance poetry, and is also home to an original 25-seat nickelodeon, making it one of the smallest functioning cinemas in the world. There are occasional Friday-night film shows. They also host regular art shows.

The Elephant 3–4 Beacon Terrace, Harbourside, Torquay TQ1 2BH ✆ 01803 200044. This Michelin-starred restaurant is probably the best in Torquay, with two areas, The Room, which is the first floor 'gracious dining' part (closed in the winter) and the ground-floor Brasserie which is slightly less formal and open all year round. The menus are scrumptious and the prices high. The place for a special treat.

Hanbury's Fish Restaurant 24 Princes St, Babbacombe TQ1 3LW ✆ 01803 314616. Highly rated fish and chips; eat in or take away.

The Orange Tree Restaurant 14–16 Park Hill Road, Torquay TQ1 2AL ✆ 01803 213936. With prices on the high side this is not a place to rush; true Slow Food of the highest quality, and the wine list is very well chosen. The favourite restaurant of one resident who recommends it 'for a romantic evening and to sample the best Torbay has to offer'.

REDCLIFFE HOTEL
Philip Knowling

On the seafront where Paignton ends and Preston begins, the Redcliffe Hotel was built as a private residence in 1856 by Colonel Robert Smith. He had found success in India, and to mark the fact he built in the Indian style – or a fantasy version of it, known as Hindoo. It's a great grey confection of Eastern arches, exotic turrets, pointed windows and Arabesque crenellations. The Hindoo style stems from the Mughals of central Asia, descendants of Ghengis Khan who founded a golden age of science, arts and architecture; one of their greatest achievements was the Taj Mahal. Mughal architecture uses columns and courtyards, marbles and mosaics, arches, domes and turrets. To the Western eye it is romantic, evocative and elegant but in Torquay Smith's creation must have shocked and bemused the locals. When Robert Smith started work on his grand design in the 1850s Paignton was a small fishing village. He took an early 19th-century coastal defence tower set on an outcrop of red sandstone among the dunes and marshes and turned it into a sumptuous new home, Redcliffe Towers, with 23 bedrooms and five acres of gardens.

After Smith died aged 86 in 1873 the property changed hands; it was owned for a time by Paris Singer, whose father built nearby Oldway Mansion, and it took in troops during the Boer War. Smith lived an exotic life and left us an exotic legacy. A Torquay amusement arcade is perhaps the only other local example of the Hindoo style. Its proximity is surely no coincidence.

PAIGNTON TO BRIXHAM

Brixham is generally considered the most picturesque of Torbay's three resorts, and Paignton the least, but beyond that they simply appeal to different tastes.

8 PAIGNTON

It's hard for me to find a reason to linger in Paignton except for the steam railway, the beach (if you have children) and the zoo. The long stretch of sand hemmed in by the traffic-clogged main road and holiday complexes is not my scene, but some people come here every year so it clearly works for them. The website ⊕ www.visitpaignton.net promotes it energetically. Out of season the **beach** is much quieter, and a stroll along it on a peaceful evening at low tide takes you well away from the razzmatazz. The old pier (⊕ www.paigntonpier.co.uk), built in 1879, glitters with slot machines and 'amusements' nowadays.

For a bit of aesthetic therapy take yourself off to **Oldway Mansion**, now used as council offices and a wedding venue. It's open all year (check hours on ✆ 01803 207933). The original mansion was the creation of sewing machine magnate Isaac Merrit Singer, remodelled in the style of the Palace of Versailles by his architect son, Paris, who made it as magnificent as possible. In 1909 he invited his lover Isadora Duncan, the dancer and darling of US society, to Oldway, making much of its splendour. She went expecting, as she said, 'a glorious time'. It didn't happen. She wrote to a friend: 'I had not reckoned on the rain. In an English summer it rains all day long. The English people do not seem to mind it at all. They rise and have an early breakfast of eggs and bacon and ham and kidneys and porridge. Then they don mackintoshes and go forth into the humid country until lunch, when they eat many courses, ending with Devonshire cream.'

Meanwhile Paris had suffered a stroke; under the care of a doctor and nurses, he spent most of his time in his room on an invalid's diet of rice, pasta and water. Isadora was banished to the opposite end of the building for fear of 'disturbing' him. Isolated from her lover, she practised her dancing and entertained herself as best she could, soon ending up in the arms of the conductor and composer André Caplet. Shortly afterwards she returned to France, with very few happy memories of Paignton.

Paignton Zoo
Totnes Rd, TQ4 7EU ✆ 0844 474 2222 ✆ www.paigntonzoo.org.uk; open daily.

This distinguished zoo, which celebrated its 90th birthday in 2013, is one of England's best. It is the big sister of Living Coasts in Torquay (see page 52) and is a constant pleasure; however often you visit it, there is always something new to see. What I love about it is the feeling of space and greenery. It was the country's first combined botanical and zoological garden, not always an easy relationship: 'I hate animals,' the former head botanist once said, 'They eat all my plants.' Paignton Zoo has solid conservation credentials, helping projects in Nigeria, Zimbabwe and Malawi among others. It has some impressive African primates, including Hamadryas baboons and lowland gorillas. 'They're all males,' I was told. 'Because gorillas

> *"However often you visit it, there is always something new to see. What I love about it is the feeling of space and greenery."*

live in complex social groups, these chaps need to learn how to be gorillas here, before going to other zoos where they can breed.' Their spacious enclosure is as natural an environment as can be achieved in a zoo.

The Crocodile Swamp is as attractive to humans on a cold day as it is to warmth-loving crocs. You can book ahead to enjoy an after-hours demonstration of crocodile feeding, showing how these normally immobile animals can leap from the water. A new bug house follows the theme of 'what have the invertebrates ever done for us?' Quite a lot, is the answer. It's about how adaptations and behaviours in the insect world have inspired us humans.

THE PUDDEN' EATERS OF PAIGNTON

Paignton's inhabitants got that nickname after a giant pudding was made in part payment for the granting of the town's charter by King John, back in the 13th century. For a while the pudding was made annually but then the custom lapsed, and it was made only once every 50 years or so, if that. It was said to be seven years in the making, seven years in the baking and seven years in the eating, although the last of these sounds less likely! It was also called a 'white pot pudding' or 'bag pudding' – boiled in a cloth, with a recipe of flour, suet, raisins and eggs.

One such pudding was made in 1819 for the annual show; described as 'a messy pudding', it took 64 hours to boil and was paraded round the town on a wagon drawn by eight oxen. The largest – weighing one and a half tons – was made in August 1859 as part of a great feast to celebrate the coming of the railway to Paignton. It was shaped like a giant pyramid, 13ft 6in at the base and 5ft around the apex. Around 18,000 people turned up hoping for a piece, and fights broke out. As the crowd surged forward, the police tried valiantly to protect the pudding but were outnumbered: soon only the crumbs remained. Post-office workers reported that a number of squashy, greasy little parcels were dispatched the following day.

Smaller puddings continued to be made from time to time. One in 1968 commemorated the granting of the town's charter and almost 1,550 portions of it were sold for charity. In 2006 there was another, to mark the 200th anniversary of Isambard Kingdom Brunel's birth. Finally, in August 2009, one was made for the annual Paignton Regatta. A solid, seven-tiered pyramid weighing 70 kilos, it was chuffed into the town by the Paignton & Dartmouth Steam Railway then paraded in a 1947 Bedford lorry, as the town crier called on the inhabitants to come and eat. Present-day pudden' lovers take note! If your mouth's already watering, keep an eye on websites such as www. thisissouthdevon.co.uk to see when you too can sample Paignton's 700-year-old delicacy.

¶¶ FOOD & DRINK

The Harbour Light Restaurant Paignton Harbour ℅ 01803 666500 ⌂ www.
theharbourlight.co.uk. Family-run for over 55 years, with great views across Tor Bay or
Paignton Harbour. Fish is bought daily from Brixham market. Quite pricey.

9 MARLDON

Marldon merits a mention because of the welcome speed with which
you can lose yourself in the little lanes leading to it, for **Occombe Farm**,
with its nature trails, organic produce and animals, and for Compton
Castle, a splendid fortified manor house. The village celebrates an **Apple
Pie Fair** each July.

Compton Castle (℅ 01803 661906; open end Mar to end Oct; Mon,
Wed and Thu; National Trust) is sometimes cited as the finest building
of its kind in Devon. It certainly makes a dramatic impression when you
round a corner and find yourself suddenly upon it, its huge castellated
walls towering above you in an appropriately threatening way. The
house belonged to the Gilbert family from the 1300s to 1800, and
again in the 20th century. There are connections here with Sir Walter
Raleigh – Katherine Gilbert married Walter Raleigh in 1550, after her
first husband Otho Gilbert died, and gave birth to the little Sir Walter.
The run-down estate was purchased by a descendant of the original
Gilberts in 1930 and painstakingly restored before being handed over to
the National Trust. Only part of the house is open.

¶¶ FOOD & DRINK

Occombe Farm Preston Down Rd, TQ3 1RN ℅ 01803 520022 ⌂ www.occombe.org.uk. A
farm shop with a great choice of organic produce, both meat and vegetables, and a variety of
local ales and cider. Café particularly recommended for breakfast. Nature trail, regular events.
Open (almost) every day, all year round. Hourly bus service: 60/61.

10 BRIXHAM

Brixham pushes out towards Berry Head, the southern prong of Tor Bay,
and the start of one of the South West Coast Path's most spectacular
sections: to Kingswear. In the mid 1500s John Leland described it as 'a
praty Towne of Fischar Men, caullid Brixham'. It's still pretty – at least its
setting is – and it still has a flourishing fishing trade.

At my last visit I met two Scottish visitors who used to know Brixham
a decade or so ago. The elderly man shook his head: 'So much has

changed.' Indeed, so visitors need to be prepared for the extensive building and renovation needed to bring Brixham up to the standard that the fishing industry requires and visitors to the English Riviera expect. A new state-of-the-art **fish market** keeps the catch fresh, and David Walker & Son will provide a choice of take-home fish to satisfy your inner Rick Stein. There are also amusement arcades, fish-and-chip shops galore, and all the offerings that help separate visitors from their money. However, there is a quiet, reflective side to Brixham. Walk down the west side of the harbour and you will

"If you want to see the real Brixham you need to be an early riser. The fish auction begins at 6am."

find a row of benches facing the afternoon sun, where you can watch the harbour activities and observe the unusual little birds competing with the gulls for scraps. 'They're sandpipers' said one of the bench-sitters, not very confidently, so I sent a photo to bird expert Tony Soper (see page 3). 'Turnstones' he said. 'You find them on every beach all over the world except the poles. Chummy and hungry, they eat anything from carrion to ship's buns'.

Further along the walkway are lobster traps stacked neatly against the wall and other paraphernalia associated with the fishing trade. Here trawlers set out to catch the fish that end up in so many of the country's best restaurants. Indeed, Brixham has the highest-value catch in the country. If you want to see the real Brixham, unchanged for hundreds of years, you need to be an early riser. The fish auction begins at 6am with around 40 different kinds of fish on offer. The Fish Market Tour (✆ 07410617931) costs £8 including breakfast and must be booked in advance.

Among Brixham's visitor attractions is a replica of Sir Francis Drake's *Golden Hind* and a statue of William of Orange who landed here in 1688, and changed the course of history. Then there's the Coffin House, set back from the quay in King Street and thought to date from around 1640. It gets its name from its shape: that of a coffin standing on its end. The story goes that a young lady of the town had set her fancy on a young man who in no way met with her father's approval; in fact he had told the suitor that he'd sooner see him in his coffin than married to his daughter. So the young man bought the 'coffin house' and showed it to his sweetheart's father – who apparently relented in the face of such ingenuity and gave his blessing to their marriage. Coffin House has been tactfully renamed Destiny Lodge (well, it figures) as a self-catering place (see page 238).

One of the pleasures of Brixham is the variety of **transport options**. It's much nicer to visit without a car, and there is a frequent bus service from Paignton and Kingswear, allowing you to combine a visit here with the steam train from Kingswear. Ferries run from Brixham to Torquay and beyond.

(SEA)FOOD & DRINK

Beamers Seafood Restaurant 19 The Quay ☎ 01803 854777. In an enticing location overlooking the harbour, this has an extensive seafood menu.

Crab Quay House Fish Market ☎ 01803 858120. The best location in Brixham, with indoor and outdoor seating overlooking the harbour. Crabs, mussels, scallops and a variety of fish.

Poopdeck Restaurant 14 The Quay ☎ 01803 858681. Serves seafood, and only seafood.

11 BERRY HEAD NATIONAL NATURE RESERVE

Gillard Rd, near Brixham TQ5 9AP ☎ 01803 882619 ⌂ www.countryside-trust.org.uk/berryhead. Open year round, although visitor centre closes during quiet times.

This is a blissful oasis where nature and history are the focus, not commerce. The story of Berry Head begins 400 million years ago, when the tropical reef around this chunk of land started its slow progress from seashells to Devonian limestone. Heaved up by geological forces and further sculpted by ice and storms through millions of years, its exposed position left it free from human settlement until man had developed the means to blast his enemies with cannon-fire. It is the two fortresses from the time of the Napoleonic Wars that the visitor sees first, with picture-book crenellations and cannons peeping through the gaps. More blasting, this time for the quarrying of valuable limestone, left caves beneath the cliffs.

"The combination of the work of man and nature has made this a perfect environment for birds and rare limestone-loving plants."

The combination of the work of man and nature has made this a perfect environment for birds and rare limestone-loving plants and their accompanying wildlife. Twenty-eight species of butterfly have been recorded here, but it is the bird population that is the main draw, with around 200 species seen. A huge colony of guillemots nest on the cliffs; visitors can follow their everyday lives on the CCTV cameras at the visitor centre, or from the bird hide which has posters to help with identification and recent sightings. In the small auditorium in the visitor centre an excellent slideshow describes the geological and human history of the site as well as the wildlife. If your appetite for wildlife has been whetted by your visit here, Nigel Smallbone (℡ 07866202576 or 01803 856428 ✉ smallbone@supanet.com) runs wildlife boat trips or guided walks. See also the box by Tony Soper on page 99.

A path runs from the fort to the lighthouse at the end of Berry Head where you can admire the 360-degree view. The caves below are also an important roost for greater horseshoe bats (see page 167). Finally, the licensed **Guardhouse Café** serves teas and yummy snacks.

It's not easy to find your way here. I left my car at the (paying) car park below the Berry Head Hotel (see page 238) and walked up the lane to the signposted South West Coast Path which takes you through woods and out to the cliffs with a gorgeous view of the bay before you arrive at the fort. There is a closer (paying) car park, with a level walk to the fort and visitor centre, however.

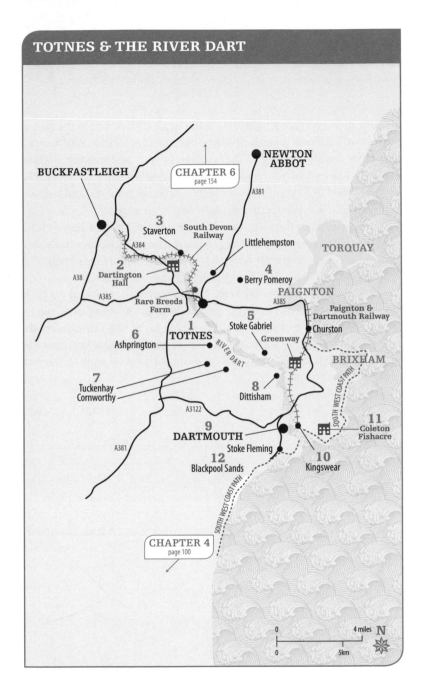

BUCKFASTLEIGH

NEWTON ABBOT

CHAPTER 6
page 154

A381

3
Staverton

South Devon
Railway

Littlehempston

TORQUAY

A384

2
Dartington
Hall

4
Berry Pomeroy

PAIGNTON

A38

A385

Rare Breeds
Farm

A385

Paignton &
Dartmouth Railway

5
Stoke Gabriel

Churston

6
Ashprington

1
TOTNES

Greenway

RIVER DART

BRIXHAM

7
Tuckenhay
Cornworthy

8
Dittisham

SOUTH WEST COAST PATH

A3122

11
Coleton
Fishacre

9
DARTMOUTH

Stoke Fleming

10
Kingswear

A381

12
Blackpool Sands

SOUTH WEST COAST PATH

CHAPTER 4
page 100

0   4 miles   **N**

0   5km

3
TOTNES &
THE RIVER DART

The **Dart** is arguably the loveliest river in England and, like the three other great rivers in Devon, the Exe, the Plym and the Taw, has played an important part in shaping the county's history. It rises in Dartmoor and meanders down to Dartmouth for 42 miles, with the lower 11 miles tidal. **Totnes**, at the upper navigable end, has been a prosperous town since at least the 10th century, and continues the trend thanks to the energy and creativity of its inhabitants. Of all the larger towns in Devon, this is perhaps the most rewarding to visit, so provides a perfect starting or finishing point for a walk or cruise down/up the Dart. Although Totnes is as far inland as you can go by passenger boat, the Dart is still a significant presence north of the town, and Dartington Hall, with its focus on sustainability and the arts, perfectly complements the spirit of Totnes. The **South Devon Railway** follows the river upstream as far as Buckfastleigh.

As the river snakes its way south, it passes small villages or grand houses which flourished as a result of their location and then subsided into tranquillity when water transport ceased to be viable. Now they are an ideal base for exploring this exceptionally scenic part of Devon, and for refreshment while walking the Dart Valley Trail. At the river mouth is **Dartmouth**, and its twin town **Kingswear**, which have been enchanting travellers for centuries, and to the east and west stretches the South West Coast Path.

GETTING THERE & AROUND

This region is easy to access by car and particularly well served by public transport, including river boats, as well as having one of the best short(ish) walking and cycling trails in the county.

PUBLIC TRANSPORT

Totnes is served by frequent **buses** from all parts of the county, and is on the mainline **railway** from Exeter to Plymouth. If you come from Exeter by train you're in for a treat since this line runs very close to the shore from Powderham right down to Teignmouth. Sit on the left to enjoy the view of the red cliffs and surf. The region is blessed with **two steam train** lines: the South Devon Railway between Totnes and Buckfastleigh, with a stop at Staverton, and the Dartmouth Steam Railway between Kingswear and Paignton. The original trains lost money so regularly that the line was closed in 1958 even before Dr Beeching axed his way through all the little unprofitable railways of Britain. It was reopened as a preserved steam line by Beeching himself in 1960.

The Slow way to see the River Dart & area

Round Robin and **Jubilee Pass** tickets are offered by the Dartmouth Steam Railway and River Boat Company ✆ 01803 555872 🖰 www.dartmouthrailriver.co.uk.

Take a tip from us. Leave your car in Totnes or Kingswear and spend a heavenly day enjoying Devon's best scenery rather than trying to find that elusive Dartmouth car park. The Round Robin ticket gives you the river, rail, and bus journey in one day, but the even more relaxing Jubilee Pass lets you take five days over it – and indulge yourself in multiple journeys.

In 2013 the paddle steamer *Kingswear Castle* was welcomed back to her original home, having spent time in the Isle of Wight and the Medway. Built in 1924, she spent the first decade or so of her life carrying up to 500 passengers between Dartmouth and Totnes, before the more efficient propeller boats took over. The *Kingswear Castle* is now the last remaining coal-fired paddle steamer in operation in the UK. All polished brass and wood, with sleekly pumping pistons keeping the wheels turning ('Nigel's down there shovelling coal', said the commentator) this is the best-looking boat on the river. Even the loo is gorgeous: almost literally a throne (raised on a platform, at any rate) with the white ceramic bowl and cistern decorated with blue flowers. We took the hour-long river cruise, which starts by doing a circle round the

WET-WEATHER ACTIVITIES

Elizabethan Museum Totnes (page 69)
Dartmouth Museum (page 92)

river mouth. Our guide pointed out the sights, including the two castles from where the great chain was stretched across the river in the 15th century to thwart invaders. Then up the river for a look at Greenway and Dittisham before heading back to Dartmouth. 'Look out for Danny the dolphin', said our guide. 'He's a real local celebrity – even has his own Facebook page'. We didn't see Danny but we did watch an indolent Atlantic grey seal which seemed as interested in us as we were in him.

The steam train complements the river trip perfectly. The brass is polished to mirror-shininess, and the trains wear their names with pride. Ours was *Hercules*. Most trains go via Greenway, over the Brunel viaduct, giving you a chance to visit Agatha Christie's former home (page 87). If you want to see the river views sit on the left, but for a real wow! experience find a seat on the right where you steam and toot past Longwood, with its sessile oaks, and on to Churston. It is shortly after this station that the train rounds a corner and, suddenly, there is Torbay. On the sunny October day that we did the trip, the sea was a Mediterranean blue and Broadsands Beach, contained within a semicircle of red cliffs, looked irresistible. Then on to Paignton and the option of taking the double-decker number 100 bus back to Totnes.

CYCLING

Totnes is full of enthusiastic cyclists, and using the bicycle as a means of transport is accepted practice. For recreational cycling, the **River Dart cycle path**, part of the NCN2 Coast to Coast Route, provides outstanding river views along largely traffic-free paths. The Totnes–Dartington stretch is 3½ miles in total, going to Dartington and on to Hood Barton in the direction of Staverton and Buckfastleigh. The three-mile ride from Totnes to Ashprington is largely traffic free, but quite hilly. Much of it runs along the old Sharpham carriage drive, and crosses the estate (see page 84) on the way to Ashprington. Cycles can be hired at **Hot Pursuit** (26 The Stables, Ford Rd, Totnes Industrial Estate ✆ 01803 865174; closed Sun).

WALKING

There's a wonderful variety of walks here, mostly with views of water: either river or sea. **The Dart Valley Trail** is described on page 82, and the **South West Coast Path** options on page 96. You can also walk the **John Musgrave Heritage Trail** from Totnes to Torbay. A look at the OS

TOURIST INFORMATION

Dartmouth Tourist Information Centre The Engine House, Mayors Av ✆ 01803 834224
⌂ www.discoverdartmouth.com
Totnes Information Centre Coronation Rd ✆ 01803 863168 ⌂ www.totnesinformation.co.uk

Explorer map OL20 will inspire other ideas, although by far the best maps for walkers are those produced by Mike Harrison (⌂ www.croydecycle. co.uk) at a scale of 1:12,500 (five inches to a mile). *Dartmouth* covers the coast path east as far as Coleton Fishacre, west to Slapton, and north, up the river, to the higher ferry, and includes the confusing streets of Dartmouth itself. *Dittisham & Cornworthy* continues up the river as far as Totnes. As in all these maps, not only is every geographical detail covered but there are helpful notes such as 'stone base' or 'grazed fields'.

The **South Devon Area of Outstanding Natural Beauty** (⌂ www. southdevonaonb.org.uk) has details of many local walks which can be downloaded.

TOTNES & AROUND

1 TOTNES

A few years ago a hand-painted addition to the town sign summed up the image of Totnes perfectly: 'Totnes, twinned with Narnia.' But Totnes is no fairy tale. Its success in creating a genuine alternative to 'clone towns' is built on the knowledge that the world's supply of oil is dwindling, and that a different, less consumerist life-style is not only inevitable but enjoyable. Transition Town Totnes, or TTT, is the result, outlined in *The Transition Handbook*, by Rob Hopkins.

Totnes is blessed with a perfect position. Its location at the navigable limit of the River Dart ensured its place in early history, with Brutus of Troy (see box, pages 72–3) allegedly making a rather giant leap for Britain here. Even the Totnes Pound, launched in 2007 as a means of boosting the local economy and still circulating locally (⌂ www.totnespound.org), isn't a new idea – the town minted its own coins in the 10th century. It grew rich on the cloth trade and in Tudor times was second only to Exeter in the wealth of its citizens. Daniel Defoe described it as having 'more gentlemen in it than tradesmen of note' and an 18th-century visitor wrote with approval that Totnes 'abounds in good shops to supply the country.' There are said to be more listed buildings per head of population here than any other town in England. This has helped ensure that it still abounds in good shops, mostly individual and quirky, since large chains look for large premises.

On my last visit the town was busy living up to its image; a 'soon to be opened' Time Traveller's Shop proclaimed 'The past is the future' and the town's notice board advertised 'Transference Healing, a Sacred Kingdom Event and Ecstatic Trance Dances'. While I was reading this a local resident spat out 'Utter rubbish!' which suggests that not all residents are Totnes-mellow.

Apart from shopping and spiritual pursuits there is plenty to engage visitors. The circular, crenellated **Norman castle** sits, like a child's drawing, on a hill and the 15th-century red sandstone **Church of St Mary** competes for attention. The rood screen here was carved from Beer stone, rather than the more usual wood, at the command of the town corporation who wanted it to rival Exeter Cathedral. **The Guildhall** started life as the refectory of the Benedictine Priory, but was rebuilt during the height of the town's wealth in the mid 16th century, for the Guild of Merchants. It has been the home of the town council ever since.

About halfway down the High Street on the left-hand side a flattish, rough stone is set into the pavement; this is the so-called 'Brutus Stone' (see box, pages 72–3). Legend apart, another possibility is that it was the *bruiter's* stone (to *bruit* meaning to report or proclaim, often by rumour) where news was announced by the town crier or equivalent.

One of the Tudor houses on Fore Street contains the **Elizabethan House Museum** (✆ 01803 863821 ⏚ www.devonmuseums.net/totnes; open Mar–Sep), whose 13 little rooms overflow with an eclectic mix of furniture, local history and childhood. Charles Babbage, credited with the invention of the first computer (see box, page 70), has his own room here. Nearby you can admire the ornate timbering on **Ann Ball's House**. She married Sir Thomas Bodley who founded Oxford's famous library. The plaque doesn't say whether she achieved anything in her own right.

At the north end of town is the **Steamer Quay** (TQ6 9PS) from where you can catch the river ferry to Dartmouth and, some way from the nearest car park, the station for the **steam train** to Buckfastleigh.

CHARLES BABBAGE, INVENTOR EXTRAORDINARY

Charles Babbage hated music, and was tormented by the barrel organs, buskers, fiddlers and other rough-cast musicians who enlivened London's 19th-century streets. He bombarded *The Times* with angry letters, and engineered a parliamentary bill to curb the noise. The objects of his fury retaliated by playing for hours outside his house; in his obituary in 1871 *The Times* commented that he had 'reached an age, [in] spite of organ-grinding persecutors, little short of 80 years'.

Street musicians apart, his interests were wide-ranging. Statistics fascinated him. His writings covered such subjects as how to lay the guns of a battery without exposing men to enemy fire, the causes of breaking plate-glass windows, and the boracic acid works of Tuscany. However, he is best known for the **Difference Engine** he invented in the 1820s: a massive calculating machine, designed to produce accurate results for logarithmic and other mathematical tables. For lack of funds it was never built in his lifetime, but a version built from his plans by London's Science Museum in 1991 worked as he had forecast. In the 1830s he followed it with his **Analytical Engine**, based on a punched-card system and the precursor of today's computers.

Born in 1791, Charles was from an old Totnes family, and Totnes proudly claims him as one of its 'sons'. The Elizabethan House Museum (see page 69) has a room devoted to him.

Apart from his 'engines' his many inventions included a prototype submarine, an Occulting Light, a system for deciphering codes, and more prosaically the cow-catcher on the front of American trains. In 1831 he founded the British Association for the Advancement of Science, and was also instrumental in founding the Royal Astronomical Society and the London Statistical Society.

In 1833 he met Ada Byron, later to become, Countess of Lovelace (Lord Byron's daughter, sometimes described as the first computer programmer); she was fascinated by his 'engines' and contributed to his work on them – but died in 1852. In 1864, the ageing and increasingly grumpy Charles wrote his obsessive *Observations of Street Nuisances*, recording 165 of them in less than three months, but achieved little else before his death. However, his name lives on in several university buildings and the Babbage crater on the moon. Since he loved trains, he might be happy that in the 1990s British Rail named a locomotive after him; also perhaps that his lunar crater is well out of reach of noisy street musicians. . .

The Totnes Littlehempston Steam Railway station & Rare Breeds Farm

The postcode for the mainline station is TQ9 5JR, but the car park is often full. There's more parking at the Pavilion (follow signs from the A385 roundabout at the northern end of town) but it's quite a long walk along the pleasant footpath towards Dartington to the station and Rare Breeds Farm. There is no free parking, so all in all it's better to arrive by train from

Buckfastleigh or Staverton, or by the main line. **Rare Breeds Farm** 📞 01803 840387 🖰 www.totnesrarebreeds.co.uk. Open early spring to Nov.

The station and this appealing little animal centre are all one entity. After walking to or arriving at the station you cross the tracks to the farm entrance. I was immediately captivated by the little Mille Fleur bantams scurrying around the paths. They did indeed look like animated speckled flowers, with their feathered feet and heads. The wonderfully named White Frizzle chickens, with their bad-hair-day plumage, were equally endearing. The centre doesn't try to do too much – it just does it small scale and very well. There are angora goats which look like gone-wrong sheep with floppy ears and stuck-on horns, pygmy goats, bouncy (caged) red squirrels keen to get their teeth into proffered peanuts, and nine species of gorgeous owls. You get the chance to gently ruffle the feathers of the owls and feel their density (one reason they can fly so silently),

"The wonderfully named White Frizzle chickens, with their bad-hair-day plumage, were equally endearing."

and learn their stories from the handler. Wizard, the European eagle owl, really did seem to enjoy this attention. I chatted to Jacquie Tolley over a cream tea in the café. 'Barrie and I bought the cottage and two acres of jungly land in 1999. We started clearing the land and acquired two goats and two pigs. Passengers on the train started looking at the animals and waving so, when the manager of the station pointed out that there was no nearby attraction, we decided that we could fill the gap – although I must say neither of us had professional experience with animals. We just loved them. Barrie, who thought he was retiring from his automobile repair business, designed the farm, and built all the cages and enclosures, and we gradually added more animals. I'm pleased to say that we're doing very well.'

🍴 FOOD & DRINK

Probably the most popular restaurant in Totnes is **Rumour** (30 High St 📞 01803 864682) all scrubbed wooden tables and cheery diners. The menu emphasises the locally sourced food with a map to show its provenance. For vegetarians the **Fat Lemons Café** (1 Ticklemoore Court, Ticklemore St 📞 01803 866888) is recommended – and it has the best tea and coffee in town. Another well-regarded vegetarian place is **Willow** (87 High St 📞 01803 862605) and, at the Dartington Shops (Cider Press Centre), there's a branch of **Cranks** (📞 01803 862388; vegetarian, self-service). Best for breakfast is the **Tangerine Café** (50 High St 📞 01803 840853).

EVENTS

Totnes carnival is held mid August, with fancy-dress parades, competitions and so on. Unique to the town, however, is the **Orange Race** which follows the carnival. Locals pursue the fruit down the hill, the speed (and danger) of the pursuit dictated by the age of the contestant; there are races for all age groups, from four to over 60. A stalwart supporter used to be a Mrs Pope, who ran her last race when in her late 90s. If you want to see the true definition of breakneck speed, watch the adult men's group. Apparently Sir Francis Drake started the ball rolling, so to speak. The **Totnes Festival** in September features music, performance literature and, this being Totnes, complementary therapies. Contact the Totnes

BRUTUS OF TROY – & TOTNES: A NEW TAKE ON AN ANCIENT TALE

As one version of the rather complicated legend goes, Aeneas (hero of Troy and of Virgil's *Aeneid*) had a son named Ascanius who had a son named Silvius who struck up an illicit affair with the niece of a princess, Lavinia, whom his grandfather had claimed in conquest. When the local soothsayer learned that the young woman was pregnant, he beat his not inconsiderable breast and launched into full prophetic mode, foretelling that the child would cause the death of both its parents and would then wander through many lands before gaining great honour. The mother did indeed die in childbirth, and the boy, named Brutus, later killed his father with an inadvertent arrow, mistaking him for a stag while he was out hunting.

For this misdemeanour Brutus was exiled to Greece, where, as he reached adulthood, he was lauded for his wisdom as well as for his courage and skill in battle. He persuaded the King, Pandrasus, to give him 324 ships, well stocked with food, so that he and a group of Trojans (who had been enslaved by the Greeks after the fall of Troy) could seek new horizons. After sailing for two days and one night they came to a green and wooded island, rich in game. At its heart was an abandoned city, with vines clinging to its crumbling stonework; and within the city, dappled with shade from the encroaching trees, was a shrine to the goddess Diana, where Brutus and his crew offered the appropriate libations and prayed for guidance. That night, the goddess appeared to Brutus in a dream. She told him of an empty island far away beyond the sunset, once peopled by giants, where he and his group could settle. They would breed a race of kings there, whose power would extend to all the earth.

Onward they sailed, westward and then north, fighting and pillaging as they went. On the Italian coast they were joined by Corineus, a fearless warrior, who became Brutus's right-hand man. But the earlier dream remained vividly in Brutus's mind; eventually he abandoned the conquest and set forth in search of his promised island.

Information Centre on Coronation Road (in front of Morrison's ☎ 01803 863168 🖰 www. totnesinformation.co.uk) for more information.

MARKETS

In the summer Totnes holds an **Elizabethan Market** every Tuesday, when the stall-holders dress up in Tudor costumes. On the same day 'Mistress Alice', a costumed guide, takes visitors (and local residents) on walks around town, putting it in its historical (16th-century) context. From June to August there's no need to book. Meet at Market Square at 11.30 and 13.00. The regular **weekly market** is held opposite the Civic Hall on Fridays and Saturdays.

Many weeks and many storms later their sails were tattered and their stomachs empty. Waking one day to sunlight and a calm sea, they saw ahead of them a rocky shoreline: grey cliffs towering above sandy bays. It was the coast of Cornwall, in the country then known as Albion. The breeze bore them northeastward to a river mouth; on the high tide they eased their ships inland, past low hills and wooded headlands, until they reached a narrow bay overlooked by a higher peak. Leaping from the deck, Brutus set off to survey the area – which is now Totnes. A boulder on which he placed his foot as he climbed can be seen to this day, in Fore Street; it's known as the Brutus Stone. Satisfied, he called his people ashore and they set up camp.

The goddess's earlier assurance that the area was free of giants proved wrong. For a while they kept their distance, but gradually drew closer. Brutus's fighters repelled them fiercely and finally wiped them out – the biggest, Gogmagog, a full 12 feet tall, was slain by Corineus in single combat; in reward, Brutus gave Corineus the part of his new kingdom now known as Cornwall, echoing his name. Next Brutus travelled far and wide, seeking a suitable site for the capital of his kingdom. Coming upon the Thames, as one does, he walked its banks for a while before selecting a location. There he built the rough wooden structures that would later become London. No longer Albion, his kingdom was now called Britain after his own name.

Twenty-three years after reaching Devon, Brutus died, and his three sons split his realm between them. Locrinus, the first-born, inherited what is now England. Kamber received Wales – hence 'Cambria' – and Albanactus, the youngest, inherited Scotland. It's said that Brutus was buried in London, in around 1100BC, no doubt with due ceremony and pomp: a far cry from his first windswept landing in Totnes. And so his story passed into local legend.

Source: Geoffrey of Monmouth's *The History of the Kings of Britain* (*Historia Regum Britanniae*), finished around 1136 and based on some earlier source(s); plus a dollop or two of 21st-century imagination.

2 DARTINGTON HALL

☎ 01803 847147 ⊕ www.dartingtonhall.com.

A footpath/cycle path runs close to the river at Totnes Bridge, heading to the Cider Press Centre and then up a little-used road to Dartington Hall. It makes a delightful walk of less than two miles; almost immediately you are under shady trees with the bustle of the town seeming far away.

These days Dartington Hall is a centre for the arts, but the estate dates back at least a thousand years. The FitzMartin family owned it in the 12th century and probably built the church, now ruined apart from the tower. By the mid 14th century it had reverted to the Crown and Richard II granted it to his half-brother John Holand who built the first great country house here.

In 1559 a prominent Devon family, the Champernownes, bought the estate and owned it for nearly 400 years. By the beginning of the 19th century, however, the family fortunes, and the buildings, were in ruins. Leonard and Dorothy Elmhirst saw Dartington's potential and bought it in 1925. He the son of a Yorkshire clergyman and she an American heiress, they shared a vision of rural regeneration through the arts. Leonard had done missionary work in India and studied agriculture in order to improve farming methods there. It was on his return to India that he became secretary to Rabindranath Tagore, the writer and social reformer, who had won the Nobel Prize for Literature in 1913, sowing the seed for the establishment of Dartington Hall as a place for 'experiment and new creation'. His wife shared his enthusiasm for radical causes, and together they aimed to bring 'economic and social vitality back into the countryside' as well as restoring the Hall to its former glory and creating one of the finest gardens in Devon. They also founded the progressive Dartington Hall School (now closed) and their interest in the arts made their house a magnet for artists and musicians from around the world.

"Leonard and Dorothy Elmhirst saw Dartington's potential. He the son of a Yorkshire clergyman and she an American heiress, they shared a vision of rural regeneration through the arts."

The Dartington Hall Trust (⊕ www.dartington.org) continues the Elmhirsts' work, supporting various projects and the Schumacher school, under the umbrella of sustainability and social justice. There are two annual summer festivals, literature followed by classical music, and a continuous programme of lectures, films and theatre. This is also a venue for the ten-day **Ways with Words** (⌁ www.ways-with-words.co.uk) literary festival in July, and as a frequent visitor I can hardly imagine a more enjoyable way of spending a few days. The combination of top-notch speakers throughout the day and the spacious grounds (equipped with deckchairs) brings an atmosphere of indolence mixed with intellectual stimulation which is completely addictive. There is always plenty going on – sculpture exhibitions, informal talks, book sales, and food.

Even when there are no events, Dartington is a wonderfully gentle, peaceful place to visit, just to stroll around the gardens, take a look at the Great Hall and any other buildings which are not being used, and eat at the **White Hart Bar and Restaurant** (✆ 01803 847100). It also has an independent cinema, **The Barn**.

For longer visits, Dartington Hall has 50 comfortable rooms (see page 239), and all profits from the accommodation go to the Trust to help their work. The Elmhirsts would be happy to see how their inspiration has lasted.

The Dartington Shops (TQ9 6TQ, formerly called the **Cider Press Centre**), is the commercial wing of Dartington, but all profits from the shops and restaurants go to furthering the Trust's aims. The crafts on offer include a wide range of high-quality glass, pottery and jewellery. It also supports the Totnes Bookshop.

After your visit, woodland walks will take you back to town or on to Staverton from where you can catch a South Devon Railway steam or diesel train to Buckfastleigh or Totnes. Bus 165 runs every two hours from Totnes to Dartington Hall.

3 STAVERTON

The village has a good pub, but its main attractions are the railway station and the ancient packhorse bridge nearby. The bridge, built in the early 15th century, is considered the best medieval bridge in the county. Staverton means 'the village by the stony ford'.

The South Devon Railway between Buckfastleigh and Totnes stops at this delightfully vintage station. It is how people like to remember the 1950s, although I doubt if the busy station in those days had so many flowers and so much birdsong. It is cared for by volunteers from the Staverton Preservation Group, and there is also a wagon repair workshop here to keep the rolling stock on the rails.

Trains run frequently enough for you to alight here and stroll up to the Sea Trout, or take a brisker walk to Dartington and thence to Totnes. Or, if you are having a day out with the children, there's a lovely safe swimming pool in the river.

'A SENSITIVE & EXEMPLARY RE-ORDERING'

Step inside St John the Baptist Church in Littlehempston, and all is much as you would expect of a 15th-century village church that justifiably found its way into Todd Gray's *Devon's Fifty Best Churches*: the wagon roof is in good shape, carving on the fine screen is delicate and detailed, the sandstone seven-sided Norman font is an unusual example of local workmanship, the old stone floor gleams gently and a satisfactory smell of furniture polish drifts from the Victorian pews. Three medieval effigies, one with an impressive moustache, doze on their windowsills; and the stained glass, thought to have been acquired piecemeal from St John's in Marldon in the 18th century, lets in slivers of coloured sunlight. Then suddenly something catches your eye at floor level, like a Victorian lady's instep peeping coyly from beneath her capacious skirt. There it is again – a tiny glint of silver – and you realise that the old pews have been mounted on very modern metal castors.

This was part of a makeover, completed in 2012, that included the unobtrusive addition of a kitchenette and lavatories at the back, underfloor heating and these mobile pews, which can be pushed into any configuration or cleared to leave an open space. (They do have brakes, so there's no risk of mid-service wheelies.) Since then the church – now doubling as the newly named Littlehempston Community Space – has been used for concerts, theatre, films, coffee mornings, exercise classes, produce sales, lunches, toddlers' group meetings and more, while still returning to its traditional and historic form for worship. It's not known if mobile pews have been installed elsewhere in the country but, if not, they surely should be, as a way of saving old village churches that might otherwise be declared redundant.

The work was endorsed, to their credit, by English Heritage, and it's their inspector who declared the result sensitive and exemplary. More remains to be done, as and when funds can be found; meanwhile Littlehempston church looks set to serve its community for many years to come.

Littlehempston (www.littlehempston.com) is off the A381 about 2½ miles from Totnes. Buses 177 from Newton Abbot and X64 from Exeter stop at Littlehempston Cross, a shortish walk from the village.

¶¶ FOOD & DRINK

The Sea Trout Staverton TQ9 6PA ✆ 01803 762274 ⌂ theseatroutinn.co.uk. A friendly
15th-century pub whose restaurant makes tasty use of fresh local foods, with an emphasis
on fish and seafood; look out for daily specials on the blackboard. It's open from 09.00 for
teas and coffees, also it has good en-suite accommodation (see page 240).

4 BERRY POMEROY

The village has been in the possession of only two families since the
Norman Conquest. The Pomeroys (Ralf de la Pommeraye) and Seymours
(Wido Saint Maur) both came over with William the Conqueror. Ralf
or Ralph Pomeroy was given the baronial estate by William I, and his
family owned it until 1548 when his fortunes collapsed and he was
forced to sell it to Edward Seymour, Duke of Somerset.

The Pomeroys built a defensive castle in the late 15th century, ideally
situated in a deer park so hunting could be enjoyed as well as a lifestyle
appropriate to their station. The Seymours considered themselves even
more elevated, not without reason, since the Duke of Somerset was the
brother of Jane Seymour, the third wife of Henry VIII, and the only one
of six wives to bear him a son. Jane died shortly after giving birth and
Edward VI, the boy-king, ascended the throne when he was only nine.
His uncle was appointed Protector until the boy reached maturity but
Edward died at the age of 15. The Duke, being Protector of the Realm
and king in all but name, was a man of immense power and wealth, but
his rise in fortune was followed by an abrupt fall: he was overthrown
as Protector by political enemies in 1549 and beheaded two years later.

His son, also Edward, made Berry Pomeroy his home and set about
building the finest mansion in Devon within the walls of the original
castle. The work was continued by a son and grandson, so four
generations of Edward Seymours have left their mark on the village, its
church and its castle.

Royalists like the Seymours had a difficult time in the Civil War (see
box, page 79) but their fortunes were restored, along with the monarchy,
and the 6th Duke welcomed William, Prince of Orange, to Berry Castle
after he had landed at Brixham in 1688.

Berry Pomeroy Castle

TQ9 6LJ ✆ 01803 866618. Open Apr–Nov and winter weekends; English Heritage.

My expectations were so high that inevitably I was initially a little disappointed by the castle. I'd read various descriptions of this romantic ruin, starting with an account by W G Maton writing at the end of the 18th century: '...the principal remains of the building... are so finely overhung with the branches of trees and shrubs that grow close to the walls, so beautifully mantled with ivy, and so richly encrusted with moss, that they constitute the most picturesque objects that can be imagined.'

"Berry Pomeroy is also famed as being one of the most haunted castles in Britain, and almost every year there are reports of someone seeing a ghost here."

S P B Mais, writing in the mid 1920s, refers to the 'exquisite' ruin with ivy covering every inch of the walls, confirmed by the accompanying photo, and W G Hoskins (1954) describes it as 'one of the most romantically beautiful ruins in Devon, almost buried in deep woods on the edge of a cliff.' It is still romantically beautiful and still almost buried in deep woods, but the ivy has now been removed and quite a bit of clearance must have been done by English Heritage to have brought the castle to its present rather austere state. So it's worth taking the time to explore properly, with the audio guide, to bring the ruin to life and imagine it in its heyday when a succession of Sir Edward Seymours were striving to make it the grandest mansion in Devon before running out of money, or enthusiasm, and abandoning it to the elements.

Berry Pomeroy is also famed as being one of the most haunted castles in Britain, and almost yearly there are reports of someone seeing a ghost here, usually the White Lady. For some first-hand accounts check out ⌖ www.ghost-story.co.uk. The **café** at the castle serves very good snacks.

The Wishing Tree

I first visited Berry Pomeroy with a friend who used to take her children to the Wishing Tree. 'We had to walk backwards – very tricky with three little children in wellies. They kept falling over. One year we made a special journey [from Guildford] because all three were about to take exams.' There is now no sign indicating the magical powers of this mighty beech, but it's still there, by the footpath that leads down to Gatcombe Brook, so we clambered round it, forwards, and made our wishes. Just in case. Later I found this description in a 1963 Devon guide: 'According to local tradition, to walk backwards round this tree three times will bring the fulfillment of any desire... [but] as the earth has fallen away

WORTHY OF BEING A WORTHY OF DEVON

John Prince was vicar of Berry Pomeroy from 1681 to 1723, during which time he researched the history of Devon's noble families. His book *The Worthies of Devon* was published in 1701 and makes delightful reading – for the language as much as the content. Here are some extracts from his description of the life of the third Sir Edward Seymour.

The occasion of his being born there [in the Vicarage] …was that Berry Castle…was then a rebuilding: and his Lady-Mother, not likeing the Musick of Axes and Hammers (this Gentlemans great delight afterward) chose to lay down, this her burthen in that lowly place.

He had no sooner passed the care and inspection of the Noursery, but that he was put abroad to School (it enervates youth to keep it too long at home under the fondling of a Mother)…[At Sherborne] he met with a severe Master, tho a good Teacher: the Memory of whom, would often disturb his sleep long after he was a Man.

…it pleased almighty God, in just Punishment of a Nation whose sins had made it ripe for Vengeance, to let loose upon it, a most dreadfull Civil Warr. A War founded upon the glorious pretences of Liberty, Property, and Religion. …And when matters brake out into open violence between the King and Parliament, this Gentlemans native Principles of Loyalty soon instructed him which side to take.

[Sir Edward, then a colonel, was taken prisoner at Modbury before making his escape] by fileing Off the Bars of the Window, and leaping down, upon the back of the Centinel that stood under; who being astonished by so unexpected a rancounter, the Colonel wrested his Musket out of his hand, and gave him such a sound Rebuke as hindered him, for the present, from following after him, or making any Discovery of him.

from the far side, the slope is now too steep to admit of perambulation round the tree – either backwards or forwards.' On revisiting the place in 2013 I found the tree had been pollarded, cut to about a third of its height, no doubt because it had become a risk to visitors. I had a special wish to make, however, so managed a half perambulation in reverse.

The church

The church stands on its own, overlooking a glorious view. The first thing you notice is the vaulted porch, with some interesting faces carved on the bosses. Inside, the exposed brickwork is unusual, and the finely carved gilded screen stretching the full width of the nave catches the eye. The saints painted on the panels have been literally defaced, presumably at the time of the Reformation, leaving their eloquent hands to do the talking.

There's a memorial stone to the Reverend John Prince, author of *The Worthies of Devon* (see box, page 79), but the glory of the church is its Seymour chapel with the memorial to Lord Edward Seymour, son of the Protector, and his son (another Edward) with his wife Elizabeth Champernowne who was not known for her chastity. John Prince referred to her disapprovingly as 'a frolic lady'. All are lying uncomfortably on their sides, with their heads propped on one hand. Elizabeth has two of her 11 children with her: a baby in a cradle at her head and at her feet a little girl, described as 'an imbecile child', sitting in a chair. Lined up below are the kneeling figures of the nine surviving children.

Getting there from Totnes

The tiny village lies only a mile from Totnes, with the castle a further mile away, so although there is ample free parking at the castle it's more rewarding to walk there, using part of the area's long-distance footpath, the **John Musgrave Heritage Trail**, and the ancient paths through woodland leading to the castle. Or, if you want a shorter walk, catch the hourly bus 149 to the village and walk along the leafy, single-track lane to the castle. There are also frequent buses along the Totnes–Paignton road at Longcombe Cross.

THE LOWER RIVER DART

The claim that the Dart is the loveliest river in England is not misplaced. Ancient oak forests line the banks (the name Dart is derived from the Old English for Oak, which is probably why there are two river Darts in Devon; the other one joins the Exe at Bickleigh), drooping their gnarled trunks towards the water. Where the trees end the hills begin, chequerboard fields of red earth and green pasture rising steeply up to the horizon. Sometimes the river widens so it feels more like a lake, and at other times it's so narrow you could throw a stone to the other side. Small villages of whitewashed cottages hide along the arms of creeks, and splendid mansions are just visible through the trees. Clusters of sailing boats lie moored at Dittisham and Stoke Gabriel, and a variety of passenger-carrying vessels use the river

"Ancient oak forests line the banks drooping their gnarled trunks towards the water."

as a highway. The perfect way to get to know the river is to walk from Totnes to Dartmouth, and take the river ferry back.

ON (& IN) THE RIVER DART
FOR TRANSPORT OR PLEASURE

The line between a pleasure cruise and transport is blurred on this river. Price is the main difference. The most elegant and expensive way of travelling between Dartmouth and Totnes is by the **paddle steamer** *Kingswear Castle* (✆ 01803 555872 🖰 www.paddlesteamerkc.co.uk – and see box, page 66), but there are cheaper boats (✆ 01803 555872 🖰 www.dartmouthrailriver.co.uk) and the transport-only, good-value **Greenway Ferry** (✆ 01803 882811 🖰 www.greenwayferry.co.uk).

Whichever boat you catch, the hour-long trip most delightfully combines getting from Dartmouth to Totnes, or vice versa, with an overview of the sights along the river. You'll see a reasonable amount of birdlife, including cormorants and herons, and if there's a commentary, you'll hear about the history of the houses and villages *en route*. S P B Mais, writing between the wars, described the journey as 'an hour of such intense delight that it is impossible to communicate it adequately.' I wouldn't contradict him today.

For your own **river taxi** contact Tim Burke (✆ 07814 954869) who has two boats, the *River Rat* (capacity ten people) and the *Otter* (up to a dozen), which he operates as taxis, taking you wherever you want to go on the river for a very reasonable price. His main business is transporting people from the steam train station in Totnes to Vire Island and Totnes Town Bridge. However, he will pick you up at any of the riverside places described in this chapter, depending on the tides. He can only operate in a three-hour window each side of high tide.

If you're a keen **swimmer**, you can sign up to the Outdoor Swimming Society's **Dart 10k** in September, from Totnes to Dittisham.

Paddling or sailing the Dart

What better way of getting to know this wonderfully unspoilt river than on a hired kayak or sailing boat? There is a good choice of companies offering everything from sit-on-top kayaks to stand-up paddle boarding, and from sailing dinghies to cabin cruisers. Operators offering kayaks and canoes are based in the small villages on the upper river, where there is a selection of pubs to visit (always an important consideration!) as well as the best scenery and quietest water. Six hours is generally considered a full day's hire.

BOAT HIRE

Canoe Adventures ☎ 01803 865301 ⌂ www.canoeadventures.co.uk. Guided tours exploring the Dart aboard Voyager 12-seat canoes starting from Tuckenhay and Stoke Gabriel.

Dart Adventures ☎ 0845 8810110 ⌂ www.dartadventures.co.uk. Operate from Dittisham. Guided or self-hire kayaks. Also motor boats, sailing dinghies and stand-up paddle boards.

Dittisham Boats ☎ 0845 8810110 ⌂ www.dittishamboats.co.uk. Motor boats, sailing boats, kayaks and stand-up paddle boards.

Dartmouth Boat Hire Centre ☎ 01803 834600 ⌂ www.dartmouth-boat-hire.co.uk. Boat hire for experienced sailors, from cabin cruisers to sailing boats.

Totnes Kayaks ☎ 07799 403788 ⌂ totneskayaks.co.uk. Operate from Stoke Gabriel. The kayak specialists, with sit-on-top kayaks. You do not need to be experienced to hire one of these for an hour or the day.

THE DART VALLEY TRAIL

This highly worthwhile walkers' trail links Dartmouth to Totnes, and Greenway to Kingswear. In total it's 17 miles, but is linked to buses, ferries and the steam train so is easy to do in sections. With some planning, you can take in all that is typical of the area: river views (of course), small villages with impossibly narrow streets (you'll be glad you're on foot) and ancient oak woods. The main options are: the lower Dart from Dartmouth to Dittisham and across the river to Greenway, then back to Kingswear (nine miles); ferry from Dartmouth to Dittisham and walk back on either side of the river (about five miles); Totnes to Dittisham, taking in the villages of Ashprington, Cornworthy and Tuckenhay, and take the ferry back (about nine miles). If these seem too long, the river taxi (see page 81) can drop you off or pick you up at any point along the river providing you plan for the tides.

5 STOKE GABRIEL

A village of confusingly winding lanes funnels traffic down to the riverside car park, where the salmon fishermen used to mend their nets, and where boat-hire people now ply their trade. The church is large and, for Devon, relatively uninteresting apart from the striking wooden pulpit which is partly painted in green and gilt, and the rood screen with its intricately carved leaf design. The glory of the church is the yew tree that stands – or rather sprawls – in the graveyard. It is reckoned to be between 800 and 1,300 years old and is feeling its age. It stands hunched and droopy, with every limb supported on a pillar or draped across a tombstone. In early May the graveyard was full of cowslips with a fine view down to the river. **The Rivershack**, right on the quay, serves very good local food and there is excellent crabbing for children at low tide.

The village is not on the Dart Valley Trail so driving is the easiest way of getting here. It's served by bus number 25 from the main Paignton–Totnes road, or the Friday-only bus number 2 from Totnes.

CAPTAIN PHILEMON POWNALL

Philemon Pownall (or Pownoll, or Pownell) was born in 1734 in Plymouth, the son of a master shipwright, so he naturally went to sea to seek his fortune. At the age of only 28 Philemon struck gold – literally. War between Britain and Spain broke out in January 1762 and His Majesty's sloop *Favourite*, to which he had recently been promoted captain, was one of several warships despatched to guard Cape St Vincent. On 15 May, *Favourite* and the frigate *Active* spotted the Spanish man-of-war *Hermione* returning home to Cadiz from Lima; she responded to their challenge with a broadside, so they let loose their guns and took her. It then emerged that *Hermione* was no simple warship: she had set sail from Lima before the outbreak of war and was carrying bags of dollars, gold coins, ingots of gold, silver and tin – and, more prosaically, a large stock of cocoa.

The prize money from this capture was a record for the time: in total over £500,000, of which Pownall's share was £64,872. Even the ordinary seamen from the two ships received around £480 each, a sum it would have taken them over 30 years to earn. More than 20 wagons were needed to carry the booty to London.

Pownall and his fellow captain from the *Active*, Herbert Sawyer, had earlier been courting the two daughters of a merchant from Exeter, who had refused their suits because of their inadequate financial status. Now they rapidly married their sweethearts and even settled an annuity on the merchant!

Pownall spent his money lavishly. He had his portrait painted by Sir Joshua Reynolds, and started building his manor at Sharpham. The estate has a river frontage of nearly three miles, with gardens designed by Capability Brown. It was their daughter, also Jane, who married the unfortunately named Edmund Bastard. They had no sons, so the Bastard line ended there.

Pownall remained in the navy, and in 1780 he was killed by cannon fire while engaging a French privateer. Admiral John Jervis wrote in tribute that he was 'the best officer, & most excellent kind hearted man in the Profession'.

6 ASHPRINGTON & THE SHARPHAM ESTATE

The picturesque village of **Ashprington** sits at the top of a hill, the tall, slender tower of its church dominating the scene and its pub a welcome sight for those who've walked or cycled the three miles from Totnes.

The church of St David was thoroughly done over in the 19th century, but still retains some interesting features. Even before entering the graveyard I was struck by the lychgate which has a resting slab for the coffin – often considered to be a medieval feature, although this one dates from the 19th century. The tower, too, is unusual. Probably dating from the 13th century, it is constructed in four sections, each slightly smaller than the last, giving it a tapering appearance, and there's an external staircase to the belfry. On entering, the first thing you notice is the wooden pulpit. This is by the noted Devon woodcarver Herbert Read (or his son, also called Herbert), and is intricately carved with all manner of flora and fauna: vines, birds and even a snail, as well as the Virgin Mary and other biblical Marys (it was given in memory of Mary Coltam Carwithen of Ashprington House). The monuments are eye-catching. Three generations of Bastards are commemorated without shame: it was the surname of the family that inherited Sharpham Estate in the 19th century, following the death of Captain Philemon Pownall whose monument is in the church (see box, page 83).

"The first thing you notice is the wooden pulpit: it is intricately carved with all manner of flora and fauna."

Captain Pownall's former house and estate, enfolded in a loop of the river, were purchased in 1961 by Maurice and Ruth Ash. She was the daughter of Dartington Hall founders, the Elmhirsts, so it is no surprise that development of the estate took a spiritual and sustainable path, with quality food production just part of their work. It is now owned by the **Sharpham Trust** which runs weekly **Buddhist Meditation Retreats** at The Barn (✆ 01803 732661 ⁂ www.sharphamtrust.org). There could not be a better place to experience the inner stillness that the Slow concept is all about.

Sharpham Vineyard

✆ 01803 732203 ⁂ www.sharpham.com.

Open all year, Sharpham Vineyard offers a variety of tours in addition to a shop selling wine and cheese. The estate is not generally open to the public so this is one way of taking a proper look at the glorious landscape. Tours range from a self-guided or guided walk round the vineyards followed by an 'instructed' wine tasting, to a full-blown half-day Sharpham Wine Experience.

The views over the Dart from the long, steep lane down from Ashprington are such that drivers will need real concentration to stay on the road. **Walk** or **cycle** there from Totnes (about three miles) and you'll be enjoying the most rewarding trails in the Totnes area. Both the Dart Valley Trail and NCR2 pass the entrance to Sharpham Estate before reaching Ashprington. Walkers can call the river taxi operated by Tim Burke (see page 81) who can drop you or pick you up at Sharpham.

¶¶ FOOD & DRINK

The Vineyard Café ✆ 01803 732178 🖰 www.thevineyardcafe.co.uk. Serves light meals in this delightful setting using produce from the Sharpham Estate, mostly free-range and organic.

7 TUCKENHAY & CORNWORTHY

The tiny, elongated village of **Tuckenhay**, squeezed between the River Wash, Bow Creek and a steep hillside, makes an agreeable and peaceful base for exploring the middle section of the river. It's hard to believe that until 1970 this was an important industrial centre, with the paper mill providing local employment, and ships plying the river to transport its high-quality paper throughout the realm. It was used, among other things, to make banknotes. During wartime, when the raw materials were hard to get, local people were asked to save their rags and printed paper for the factory. They had to divide them into three bags: wool, cotton and paper – an early version of today's coloured bins. The mill and its outbuildings have been converted into luxury self-catering accommodation (see page 238).

I stayed at Riverside House (see page 240) and woke to find an Egyptian goose making a speech from a river bollard. Within an hour of leaving the guesthouse I knew that this was the essence of Slow Travel. Crossing the river on a tiny bridge, I followed a well-used footpath along Bow Creek, past benches for the weary, picnic places for the hungry, and a rope swing suspended from a high branch for energetic youngsters. The tide was low and kelp looked incongruous piled against the red earth of the river bank. In April, primroses brightened the footpath and the hazel catkins suggested rich nutting in the autumn.

A steep track took me to **Cornworthy** which is bypassed by most tourist traffic because it has 'no places of interest': a huge advantage. It has a great feeling of community and village pride. Notices were pinned on the board outside the church, and the houses and gardens were tended with love.

The church is a rewarding mixture of old and new. There's a simple screen, all worm-eaten, and a parish book detailing the history of the village and the Tuckenhay paper mill. Representing the present day are two modern sculptures: an angel's wing by Jilly Sutton and the feet of Christ, pierced by nails, by Robin Williams, son of a church warden. They are a walker's feet, with skinny shins and knobby, crooked toes. On the prayer board was a note 'Please help Mirabelle get her other leg strong again.' Adding, as an afterthought, 'My tortoise'. On the way back to Tuckenhay I passed the ruined Augustinian priory of St Mary, reportedly founded for seven religious women. It was a victim of the Dissolution of the Monasteries and abandoned in 1539. Nothing much remains except the gatehouse with its rather splendid arch, large enough to allow the passage of horse-drawn carriages, framing Cornworthy in the valley below.

"Nothing much remains except the gatehouse with its splendid arch, framing Cornworthy in the valley below."

Nearby is a more humble doorway for pedestrians.

¶¶ FOOD & DRINK

Maltster's Arms Tuckenhay TQ9 7EH ✆ 01803 732350 ⌂ www.tuckenhay.com. Very popular riverside pub with good food.
Waterman's Arms Bow Bridge (between Ashprington and Tuckenhay) TQ9 7EG ✆ 01803 732214 ⌂ www.thewatermansarms.net. A hotel and restaurant in an idyllic riverside setting.

8 DITTISHAM & GREENWAY

The river is at its narrowest between these two places, a delightful village and Agatha Christie's holiday home, and a motorboat acts as a ferry from one to the other. There's no particular schedule, you just ring a large bell when you're ready to cross and by and by the boatman will appear.

Dittisham

This sailing centre is reminiscent of Cornwall, with a hillside of tightly packed, steeply stacked white cottages with slate roofs. If you arrive here by car, avoid heading down to the quay; you'll regret it – there's no parking and your car may end up in the Ferry Inn or the river. Look for the car park in the upper town (the Ham) which overlooks the river. Once you have admired the cottages and speculated which one changed hands for over eight million pounds, there's not a whole lot to see here. The church is unexceptional, but has an interesting 15th-century stone pulpit, intricately carved, gilded and painted, entwined with fruit and foliage, with some very gloomy saints or apostles in the niches. This caught the eye of Richard Pococke, travelling in 1750:

> I...crossed the river Dort to Ditsham, a village with a little street in it, and a large ancient church new modelled, where I first saw one of those carved stone pulpits, of which sort there are many in this country.

Sightseeing as such may be limited but there is plenty to enjoy. Dittisham is said to be the best place on the Dart for crabbing (off the pontoon) or just pottering.

The village is self contained with a shop, the pub and The Anchorstone Café. North of the village is the blunt peninsula, Gurrow Point, which you can walk right round (with some difficulty) at low tide. Gurrow Point Cottage, a self-catering place (see page 240), is superbly located at the southern end of the peninsula.

If approaching from the river, look out for the typical thatched Devon longhouse, on the southern side of town.

Plonked in the river opposite Greenway's boathouse is the Anchor Stone, which doubled as the site of a ducking stool for disobedient wives.

Greenway

Galmpton TQ5 0ES ✆ 01803 842382; National Trust; opening times vary seasonally: see website. It's closed completely in Jan/Feb. Parking is limited and must be prebooked.

The Georgian house was built in the late 18th century, but its predecessor, Greenway Court, was the home of Sir Humphrey Gilbert, half brother to Sir Walter Raleigh. The young Walter spent holidays there as a boy, and as an adult, so they say, he sat by the river smoking his silver pipe with the first tobacco seen in England. Understandably, so legend has it, this act was misinterpreted by a servant who, seeing his master apparently on fire, threw a jug of ale (or maybe water) over him.

AGATHA CHRISTIE

Dame Agatha Christie – born Agatha Miller in Barton Road, Torquay, in September 1890 – is the best-selling novelist of all time, with sales of her work (novels, plays, short stories) topping two billion, in more than 60 languages; only Shakespeare, the Bible and the Koran have achieved higher figures. Her play *The Mousetrap*, which opened in London's West End in 1952, is now the longest-running theatre play in history.

The play came about because the BBC asked the late Queen Mary, a devoted Christie fan, how they might best celebrate her 80th birthday on radio. She requested something by Agatha Christie – who obligingly wrote a short sketch, *Three Blind Mice*, which was broadcast in 1947. Christie then adapted it for the stage as *The Mousetrap*.

On Christmas Eve in 1914, as World War I was breaking, Agatha Miller married Captain Archibald Christie of the Royal Flying Corps; they honeymooned in Torquay's Grand Hotel. During the war Torquay Town Hall served as a hospital and she worked there, gaining useful information about poisons and meeting Belgian refugees, the blueprints for Hercule Poirot. Her Torquay connections are commemorated in the Christie Gallery in Torquay Museum (see page 48), and the one-mile Agatha Christie Trail around the town.

The marriage was not happy, and in December 1926 Britain's newspapers were buzzing with the news that she had 'disappeared'; there were murmurs of foul play, a massive search was mounted and rewards were offered for information leading to her return. Ten days later she was spotted: it turned out she had travelled by train to Yorkshire and checked in to the Swan Hydro Hotel in Harrogate, using

Agatha Christie bought the house in 1938 for £6,000. She took a break from writing while on holiday here, but the sloping grounds, with glimpses of the river through the trees, provided settings for some of her murder mysteries. If you are an Agatha Christie fan you'll love your visit to the house, marvelling that you are looking at the actual Steinway piano she played, and appreciating the papier-mâché tables that she collected. Or an archaeology fan, since Christie's husband, Max Mallowan, organised digs in Iraq and other Middle Eastern sites and his collections are more interesting than her bits and pieces. Perhaps my lasting impression was of coupledom. The Mallowans clearly loved doing things together and Agatha was an enthusiastic helpmate on Max's

"If you're an Agatha Christie fan, you'll love your visit to the house, marvelling at the actual Steinway piano she played."

the surname (Neele) of a woman who was currently her husband's mistress. She claimed amnesia, but more probably had been reacting to her husband's affair. After some months they separated, and divorced two years later.

In 1930 Christie married archaeologist Max Mallowan, later to be knighted, and for the next 30 years travelled happily with him to his various excavations in the Middle East. *Murder on the Orient Express* was inspired by her train journey on one of these trips. Asked what marriage to an archaeologist was like, she is said to have replied 'Wonderful – the older you get, the more interested he is in you'. In 1938 they bought the Greenway estate on the River Dart.

Burgh Island Hotel in Bigbury Bay (see page 124) is the setting for her best-selling novel (and the world's best-selling mystery) written in 1939 as *Ten Little Niggers*, but later renamed *Ten Little Indians* and/or *And Then There Were None*. The 'writer's hut', reputedly built for her there in the 1930s and where she wrote *Evil under the Sun*, was rebuilt in 2007; it's now called 'The Beach House' and is one of the hotel's luxury bedrooms. Kents Cavern in Torquay appears as Hempsley Cavern in her novel *The Man in a Brown Suit*: her father helped to finance excavations there and was an enthusiastic volunteer on William Pengelly's dig (see page 51).

Agatha Christie died in 1976, but the many new television adaptations of her work have boosted her audience still more. In 1991, Royal Mail produced a commemorative Agatha Christie stamp book, and an Agatha Christie Week and Agatha Christie Festival are held annually in Britain (see ✆ www.agathachristie.com). Like *The Mousetrap*, the 'Queen of Crime' is nowhere near her final curtain.

archaeological trips. And it would be hard not to be happy in such a setting. The garden is worth a visit for its peacefulness and some unusual plants.

Visitors are encouraged to come to Greenway a green way if possible: on foot, bike, bus, steam train or boat. This is no great hardship when a large part of the house's attraction is its position overlooking the river and gorgeous surrounding scenery. The walk here from Dartmouth or Kingswear is particularly rewarding, passing as it does through the oaks of Longwood. Alternatively you can park on the approach lane and follow the well-signposted Greenway Walk, or take the steam train (it doesn't always stop at Greenway but you can walk from Churston). For a door-to-door service, take the 1940s bus, 'Barnaby', from Torquay, Paignton or Brixham operated by Greenway Ferries (✆ www.greenwayferry.co.uk). Or there's the river ferry from Dartmouth. In fact, you're spoilt for choice.

¶¶ FOOD & DRINK

The Anchorstone Café Dittisham ✆ 01803 722365. More of a licensed restaurant than a traditional café. Serves excellent food on a terrace overlooking the river. Very popular so booking recommended in the summer.

The Ferry Boat Inn Dittisham ✆ 01803 722368. Renowned for its location, right on the waterfront with views across to Greenway, and good pub food. The gents' loo is in a converted chapel, inviting patrons to 'spray and pray'.

DARTMOUTH & KINGSWEAR

It is rare for a town to combine a rich and interesting history with present-day beauty. Usually the accidents of geography that gave it strategic importance a few hundred years ago also caused its later industrialisation. Dartmouth and Kingswear, placed either side of the steep-sided estuary, have escaped this fate and the mouth of the River Dart is exquisitely picturesque. The writer W G Maton, although sometimes given to hyperbole, describes his arrival in the late 1700s in words that could still be used today:

> We were in some measure prepared for the enchanting scene which our passage across the Dart opened to us... On our left appeared the castle, which stands at the mouth of the river, surrounded by a rich mass of oak, and the steeple of an adjoining church just peeps above the branches. Opposite to us was the town, situated on the declivity of a craggy hill, and extending, embosomed in trees, almost a mile along the water's edge... The rocks on either side are composed of a glossy purple slate, and their summits fringed with a number of ornamental plants and shrubs. Enraptured with so lovely a scene, we arrived insensibly at the quay of Dartmouth.

A couple of centuries later, S P B Mais, arriving at night, wrote: 'As you step onto the cobbled quay and dimly glimpse the medieval, richly carved, gabled houses bending courteously to greet you, you feel that you have been transported not merely to another land but to another century.'

Kingswear is equally attractive in a smaller way, and the walk from here to **Coleton Fishacre**, or to **Brixham** if you can manage the 11 miles, is one of the best on Devon's South West Coast Path.

9 DARTMOUTH

Present-day visitors should endeavour to arrive, as Maton and Mais did, by water, or via the coastal path or steam train to Kingswear, for the enchanting view across the Dart. Arrival by car, in the summer, may only result in frustration and the inevitable backtracking to the park-and-ride car park which may be the only place you can leave your car for longer than four hours. If you do drive into the centre of town, ignore your satnav or you could find yourself wedged in one of those impossibly steep, narrow, and oh-so-picturesque approach lanes. Off-season parking is easier: free along the riverfront and there's a short-stay car park near the little inner harbour. One time you definitely don't want to drive into Dartmouth is during the annual August Bank Holiday **Regatta**.

Seen across the river the view is much as Maton describes it, with the castle at the furthest point of the cliff, and white houses dug into the hillside among dark trees contrasting with the terraces of multi-coloured houses arranged along the waterfront. On a sunny day it is one of the loveliest sights in Devon. And on a wet day you can happily fill a couple of hours under cover.

At the time of the Domesday Book (1086) the River Dart was under the control of the Lord of Totnes, Dartmouth coming into its own only with the arrival of decked sailing ships. The Second and Third Crusades sailed from here in 1147 and 1190, and, for the 300 years that Bordeaux was under English rule, trade was brisk between the two countries, with wine the main import, and wool, carried down the river from Totnes, the export. John Hawley (see box, page 93) built up his business through this two-way trade. Royal favour was guaranteed to this maritime town when privateers could fight the King's battles for him and enrich both themselves and their monarch. Richard II, a weak, effete king, if we are to believe Shakespeare, seems to have been particularly grateful for the services of Hawley and his followers to protect the shores from French invasion. In the 15th century the town was kept safe from invaders by a chain which was raised across the harbour mouth during the night, from Gommerock, south of Kingswear where the hole can still be seen, to Dartmouth Castle where remnants of the hoist still exist.

After England lost Bordeaux in 1453, Dartmouth's prosperity declined; but the great explorers of the Elizabethan era revived it, and from 1580 it profited from the cod fishery in Newfoundland.

The Civil War took its toll, and the town sank into relative obscurity until the building of the Royal Naval College in 1899–1905. Its strategic importance in World War II ensured that it was extensively bombed; the town sent 485 ships to Normandy for D-Day. The planned railway never reached Dartmouth so industrialisation also passed it by. We can be thankful for that.

Much of the Dartmouth you see today is on reclaimed land. Even before John Hawley's time the industrious inhabitants were harnessing the tides to provide power to their mill. Sea water ran into an inlet, known as the Mill Pool, through an artificially narrow entrance. Then at high tide a sluice gate was dropped, diverting the receding water to turn the mill wheel. The former Mill Pool now provides the only flat land in town.

Dartmouth was the birthplace of **Thomas Newcomen** (1663–1727), whose Atmospheric Engine was one of the forerunners of the Industrial Revolution. It was used to remove water from flooded mines, which hitherto had been hauled out by teams of horses. There's a plaque in the central gardens and the museum has some Newcomen exhibits, but more interesting is the reconstructed engine near the tourist office. And if you really want to understand how it worked, look at the neat animation on ⏚ www.animatedengines.com/newcomen.

Dartmouth Museum
Butterwalk ✆ 01803 832923 ⏚ www.dartmouthmuseum.org. Open daily, year-round, except over Christmas.

Dartmouth lost some of its finest medieval buildings in a road-widening scheme in the 1800s, but the timber-framed Butterwalk, dating from 1635, is still there, still bending courteously towards visitors, and rich with enigmatic carvings. It now houses the little Dartmouth Museum, which is well worth a visit. Staffed, as are many Devon museums, by volunteers it contains a variety of maritime exhibits. Model ships illustrate the history of Dartmouth from the wine trade to Drake's *Golden Hind*, and the *Mayflower* which put in for repairs before taking the Pilgrim Fathers to America. Look out, too, for the exquisitely carved ivory boat from China and the even more amazing man-of-war carved from bone by Frenchmen incarcerated in Dartmoor Prison during the Napoleonic Wars. There is also an extensive collection of ships in bottles, and some hands-on exhibits for younger visitors.

St Saviour's Church

If you do no other sightseeing in Dartmouth, go to St Saviour's Church and look at the door inside the south entrance. It's thought to have been made

JOHN HAWLEY, A 'SCHIPMAN OF DERTEMOUTHE'

John Hawley was one of those hugely successful entrepreneurs who shaped the history of England and who ensured that their name lived on in brass. Born around 1340 into a prosperous Dartmouth family, Hawley built up his ship-owning business until he had about 30 vessels, an asset which came to the attention of Edward III, who was involved in the interminable wars with France which later became known as the Hundred Years' War. He was granted a privateer's licence by the king in 1379. This meant that he could attack enemy ships, which might just happen to be carrying valuable cargo, and share the proceeds with the king. The arrangement worked well on both sides, and Hawley clearly gained the respect of his fellow citizens, since he was elected mayor of Dartmouth a total of 14 times, and also served twice as the town's MP.

Of course sometimes the line between 'enemy' and 'valuable' became a bit blurred and, as the description of Hawley in St Saviour's notes, 'There seems little doubt that he was also a pirate'.

Hawley is believed to be the inspiration for Chaucer's 'schipman of Dertemouthe', a somewhat shady character. He will have met Chaucer when the latter was customs officer for Edward III. Any illegal business of Hawley's was far outweighed by the benefits he brought to Dartmouth, however, during his tenures as mayor. He successfully kept the strategic port safe from enemy attack by building fortresses on each side of the mouth of the Dart and stretching a huge chain across the harbour to repel enemy ships.

The story goes that after a particularly successful sortie into French waters, from which he returned laden with booty, he declined to accept any personal reward, asking that the King's generosity be visited on his native town instead. Hence Dartmouth has a particularly charming coat of arms: Edward III, flanked by two lions, all perched precariously on a very small boat.

Hawley's last battle was fought in 1404, not on sea but on land, on Blackpool Sands (see page 98). England was having a little war with the Bretons at that time, under the leadership of William du Chatel. He had an army of 2,000 knights and their support troops, whereas Hawley's force was mostly farm labourers armed with bows and arrows, plus their wives who were expert with the sling-shot, yet they routed the French in a Shakespearian triumph against the odds. Henry IV was so delighted by this victory that he ordered a Te Deum in Westminster Abbey. Hawley died in 1408, in his late 60s. His huge, elaborate memorial brass in the chancel of St Saviour's is not excessive given his larger-than-life contribution to the town's prosperity and status. And anyway, he built the chancel.

in 1372 but the vigour and artistry of the ironwork would be amazing even for 1972. Two slinky lions leap through leafy branches, claws out, eyes bulging, mouths snarling. Equally impressive

"Two slinky lions leap through leafy branches, claws out, eyes bulging, mouths snarling."

and dramatic are the huge brasses near the altar, sometimes hidden under the carpet but often on display. A print taken from a brass rubbing is on the west wall, so you can examine them as a whole. They commemorate John Hawley and his two wives. He is in full armour, with his feet on a feisty lion, chastely holding the hand of one wife (he outlived them both). Often church brasses and memorials are of people whose deeds have been forgotten, but not so John Hawley. Privateer, pirate, MP and 14 times mayor of Dartmouth, he shaped the history of the town (see box, page 93) and paid for 'his' end of the church.

Other notable features are the splendid screen, with its fan vaulting, painted in muted gold and charcoal grey, and the early 16th-century painted Devonshire carved stone pulpit covered with bold clumps of foliage. The figures of saints were hacked off during the Reformation, to be replaced by secular emblems of the Kingdom: England, Scotland, Ireland and Wales.

More Dartmouth diversions

Other sights are **Bayard's Cove**, a picturesque cobbled quay, and **Dartmouth Castle**, built in 1488 on the site of one of John Hawley's fortifications, to guard the narrow opening to the estuary. The church of St Petrock is incorporated within the castle grounds. The castle, owned by English Heritage, is open daily except between November and March when it's open weekends only. It's a pleasant one-mile walk from the centre of town, or there's the Castle Ferry from the centre of town.

The imposing **Britannia Royal Naval College** (where the Queen first met Prince Philip) is open daily for group tours (✆ 01803 677787 🖰 www.brnc.co.uk).

Car ferries connect Dartmouth and Kingswear. You can take the Lower Ferry or the Higher Ferry less than a mile upriver, designed to carry cars from the A3122 to the A379, its continuation on the Kingswear side. Both ferries carry cycles and foot passengers as well as cars. River cruises to Totnes or to the castle are booked at one of the kiosks along the quay.

¶ FOOD & DRINK

In October is the **Dartmouth Festival of Food** ⌂ www.dartmouthfoodfestival.co.uk.
Alf Resco's ✆ 01803 835880 ⌂ www.cafealfresco.co.uk. Famous for its breakfasts and brunches.
Dolphin pub 5 Market St ✆ 01803 833698. A very good, traditional pub.
Rockfish 28 Lower St ✆ 01803 839182 ⌂ www.rockfishdevon.co.uk. Great fish and chips.
The Seahorse Restaurant 5 South Embankment ✆ 01803 835147 ⌂ www.
seahorserestaurant.co.uk. Terrific seafood from Mitch Tonks. Very popular, so book ahead.
The Singing Kettle Tea Shoppe 6 Smith St ✆ 01803 832624. Seriously good cream teas,
and lunches too.

10 KINGSWEAR & THE COAST

Kingswear is little more than the ferry terminal, a pub, a village shop, and
a car park (at the Kingswear Marina, up the steep hill towards Paignton).
Like Dartmouth, it has multicoloured terraced houses backed by green
cliffs up which the road towards Brixham climbs in a series of hairpin
bends. It is also the starting point for a particularly worthwhile, though
strenuous, stretch of the coast path. When I did it in April the cliffs were
splashed with purple and yellow from violets, primroses and gorse, and
new-born lambs were gambolling in the fields. But any time of year it
would be lovely if you're fortunate with the weather.

11 COLETON FISHACRE

Brownstone Rd, TQ6 0EQ ✆ 01803 842382; National Trust; closed Fri; check website for
off-season opening.

The National Trust acquired this house and garden in 1982, initially to
link the unconnected sections of the South West Coast Path which now
runs through the lower garden. It was built in the 1920s as a holiday
home for Sir Rupert D'Oyly Carte, the son of Richard D'Oyly Carte who
struck up such a lucrative friendship with the lyricist W S Gilbert and the
composer Arthur Sullivan. The contrasting personalities of the barrister
Gilbert and the young composer meant that if the partnership were to
survive, they needed a manager of great diplomacy. Richard D'Oyly
Carte was that man, encouraging them to follow their one-act operetta
Trial by Jury with others which combined witty words, outrageous plots
and catchy tunes, founding the D'Oyly Carte Opera Company in 1878.
Richard moved from one successful enterprise to another, building the
Savoy Theatre (specifically for the eagerly awaited Gilbert and Sullivan
productions) and the Savoy Hotel.

Walks from Kingswear

✳ OS Explorer map OL20; start: Kingswear, grid reference SX884509.

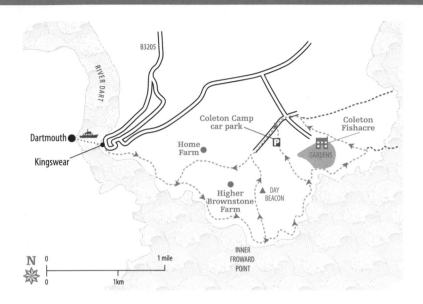

From Kingswear (✳ OS Explorer map OL20; grid reference SX884509) the coast path plunges almost immediately into woods, past Kingswear Castle, now Landmark Trust self-catering accommodation (see page 240), and on round the coast as far as Brixham if you have the stamina. You can make this a circular walk by following the coast for two miles to Inner Froward Point, then taking the track inland that leads past the **Day Beacon**, or Day Mark Tower. This looks like an unfathomable folly, but in fact it was built in 1856 as a 'day lighthouse', providing a 'mark' or 'beacon' for ships that otherwise might miss the concealed Dartmouth harbour. You return to Kingswear by turning left at the T-junction and taking the footpath that runs past Higher Brownstone Farm and Home Farm. The total distance is a bit over four miles, but it will feel more because of the up-and-down nature of the path.

The best walk of all is to park at the **Coleton Camp** NT car park (✳ Explorer map OL20; grid reference SX910513; honesty box, free for NT members), and visit Coleton Fishacre house and gardens (and café) before walking back to Kingswear. You'll be bowled over by the view of Dartmouth as it gradually appears through the trees, particularly if the sun is shining on those multicoloured houses. The sign at the entrance of Coleton Fishacre says there is no access to the coastal path but it crosses the bottom of the gardens.

VILLAGE COMMUNITY

Village life in Devon still revolves largely round the church and the pub, as it has for centuries, and limited amenities are no bar to ingenuity.

1 The 15th-century pub at Lustleigh, Dartmoor, where food is exceptional. (VB/DC) 2 The 'library' in the small village of Kenn, one of Devon's hidden gems. (HB) 3 Harvest Festival at Bere Ferrers. (HB) 4 Creative marketing at one of Devon's locals. (HB)

Husband ⇨
Creche

Leave him here while you
shop in peace..
deposits taken..

New for 2013..
The Dolphin phone in sick
service'
Gooble for him or her..

RELIGIOUS ARCHITECTURE

The county's churches are storerooms of history, with their medieval screens, stained-glass windows and enigmatic carvings.

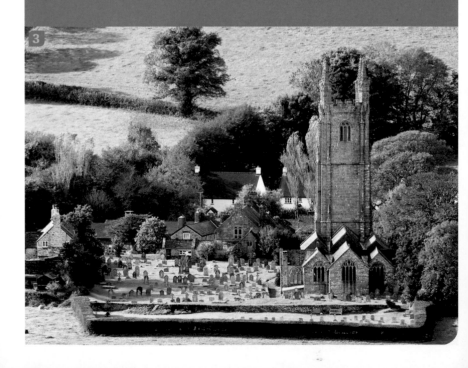

1 The little church of St Peter at Buckland Tout Saints. (HB) 2 The belfry of the tiny chapel in South Zeal. (HB) 3 The church at Widecombe-in-the-Moor, often called the Cathedral of the Moor because of its exceptionally high tower. (SS) 4 Brentor, the highest church in England. (S/HH) 5 St Paul, pictured in one of the medieval stained-glass windows in Doddiscombsleigh. (HB) 6 The hare-lipped devil carving in the same church. (HB) 7 St Apollonia, patron saint of dentists, proudly holds one of her extracted teeth (Higher Ashton). (HB)

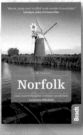
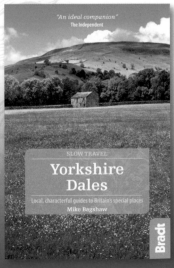
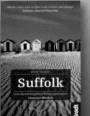

Richard D'Oyly Carte died in 1901 a very wealthy man, and that inheritance allowed his son Rupert, who took over the business, to continue to make money – and to build Coleton Fishacre. His architect Oswald Milne, formerly assistant to Sir Edwin Lutyens, was influenced by the Arts and Crafts movement which, at the turn of the century, highlighted the skill of individual craftsmen as an antidote to mass production.

"The garden of Coleton Fishacre is absolutely gorgeous. It slopes steeply down in a series of terraces to Pudcombe Cove, where the D'Oyly Cartes had their private bathing pool and jetty."

You need to be something of a connoisseur to fully appreciate the inside of the house. Only the built-in features are original – Bridget D'Oyly Carte, who inherited the house from her father and sold it in 1949, left very little furniture, and the replacements are unremarkable, though authentically Arts and Crafts style. It's worth taking time to read about the fixtures that remain from the original house – like the Art Deco Lalique uplighters in the dining room, the tide-indicator in the hall, and the splendid Hoffman painting of Coleton with an accompanying wind-dial in the library. The polished limestone fire surround in the sitting room is also fascinating: the stone comes from Derbyshire and is impregnated with fossils. I was also intrigued by the 1930s map of the Great Western Railway network in the butler's pantry: it would be the job of a Gentleman's Gentleman to look up the guests' trains.

The garden of Coleton Fishacre is absolutely gorgeous. It slopes steeply down in a series of terraces to Pudcombe Cove, where the D'Oyly Cartes had their private bathing pool and jetty. Stone was quarried from the grounds to use in the building of the house, allowing for the dramatic use of level areas and steep descents. Lady Dorothy was a keen gardener and plant enthusiast, and the grounds are an appealing mixture of native, untended vegetation and exotics such as tree ferns and the Persian ironwood. A stream runs down to the sea, providing a natural water feature. Even in rain this garden is special; in the spring sunshine, when the bluebells are out and the trees have that misty haze of green, it is magical.

The house is not directly accessible by bus; numbers 22, 24 and 120 run along the main Brixham–Kingswear road, a 1½-mile walk away.

SOUTH OF DARTMOUTH

The South West Coast Path lures you away from the town to the castle, and then along the cliffs to a pretty little shingle beach, Compass Cove, where you can swim. Continue round the cliffs or take the short cut via Little Dartmouth, until you pass the delightfully named cluster of rocks, the Dancing Beggars. **Stoke Fleming** is the next village. It has an interesting church whose tall tower used to be an aid to guide ships into Dartmouth harbour, and one of the oldest brasses in Devon, dated 1361. The great grandfather of Dartmouth's Thomas Newcomen was rector here in the 17th century. Beyond the village is the surprisingly named beach of **Blackpool Sands**, scene of John Hawley's last battle.

The walk here from Dartmouth is about six miles – but only three by road. Bus number 93 runs hourly back to Dartmouth.

12 BLACKPOOL SANDS & GARDENS

✆ 01803 770606 ⌂ www.blackpoolsands.co.uk

Blackpool Sands is a deservedly popular privately owned beach. Like Slapton, the 'sands' are actually fine shingle, but there is a sandpit for children with the real stuff. The bay is exceptionally beautiful, framed in a semicircle of woods, cliffs and green pasture. There are no junk-food outlets here, just the elegant **Venus Beach Café**, which serves high-quality organic food and wine. There's an area under cover, an outdoor terrace, and a takeaway hatch so you can eat your picnic on the beach. Toilets, showers, shop, watersports, lifeguards… this is firmly geared towards upmarket holidaymakers, and does it extremely well. No dogs are allowed in the holiday season.

"The owner understands the allure of a secret garden: you enter through a green door, overhung with fuchsia."

Behind the beach is a sub-tropical garden of the type that grows so well on Devon's south-sloping shores. Sir Geoffrey Newman, owner of Blackpool Sands, understands the allure of a secret garden: you enter through a green door, overhung with fuchsia. Subtropical plants from the southern hemisphere thrive in this sheltered place, as does native vegetation. The gardens are open from April to the end of September.

BRIXHAM TO DARTMOUTH BY SEA:
A GUIDE FOR BIRDERS

Tony Soper

A pleasure-boat cruise of Devon's south coast from Torbay (Torquay or Brixham) offers a great opportunity to observe seabirds and other wildlife, even if the cruise is for general interest. If you are a birder, don't forget your field guide, and a pair of binoculars is recommended for everyone.

As you leave Torbay behind you, the massive limestone cliffs of Berry Head loom on your starboard hand. Perched on the outermost clifftop you'll see the diminutive tower of the highest lighthouse in the British Isles. Tucked in around the corner and behind a few sentinel islets is a stretch of near-vertical cliff, some 200 feet high, pierced by seabird ledges and a fine cave: it's home to a thriving colony of kittiwakes and guillemots. Keep a sharp eye open for a possible peregrine power-diving on a hapless newly fledged chick. Many years ago puffins bred on the cliff slopes here; now we see just the occasional solitary one paddling a few miles offshore. Shags will keep station as you cruise. On a calm day there may be swarms of jellyfish decorating the surface of the sea, there may be the lazy fins of a basking shark cruising for plankton, there

may even be a turtle. On a wild day clouds of gannets will be looking for shelter and a shoal of mackerel to indulge their plunge-diving. This open-sea part of the cruise may offer anything from a healthy slice of discomfort to a Mediterranean-style tan.

Dartmouth is guarded by a typically shaped mewstone, a giant lump of rocky cheese, as you approach its entrance. On the exposed seaward side the steep slope is colonised by cormorants, a secret cove is a favoured seal pool and the jungle of sea-kale is home for herring gulls. Great black-backs favour the very top of the island. A chain of rocks, some barely submerged, leads across to the mainland.

Your final approach takes you between the much-photographed twin castles of Dartmouth and Kingswear as you enter the sheltered harbour. Now you have the choice of jumping ship to join one of the River Link ferries which will take you up the winding waterway to Totnes; crossing the harbour by way of the Lower Ferry to Kingswear and the steam railway back to Paignton; or getting a quick cream tea and reboarding for the return passage to Brixham. The perfect day.

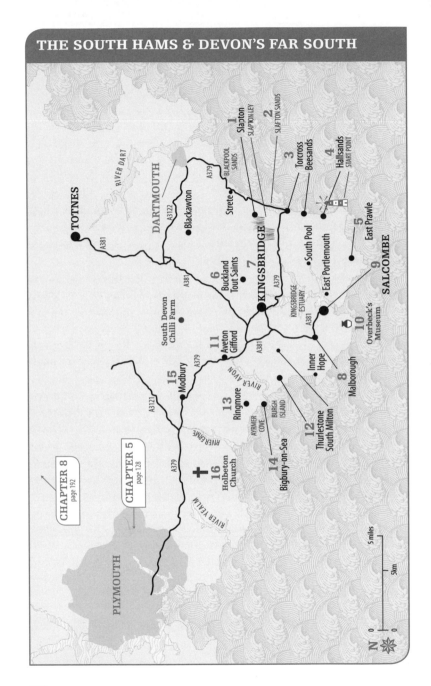

CHAPTER 8
page 192

CHAPTER 5
page 128

PLYMOUTH

RIVER YEALM

A379

A3121

RIVER ERME

16
Holbeton Church

15
Modbury

A379

A381

A379

SOUTH DEVON CHILLI FARM

TOTNES

A381

RIVER DART

DARTMOUTH

A3122

Blackawton

A379

BLACKPOOL SANDS

Strete

1
Slapton
SLAPTON LEY

2
SLAPTON SANDS

3
Torcross
Beesands

4
Hallsands
START POINT

5
East Prawle

6
Buckland Tout Saints

7
KINGSBRIDGE

South Pool

East Portlemouth

9
SALCOMBE

KINGSBRIDGE ESTUARY

A381

10
Overbeck's Museum

11
Aveton Gifford

RIVER AVON

13
Ringmore

AYRMER COVE

BURGH ISLAND

14
Bigbury-on-Sea

12
Thurlestone
South Milton

Inner Hope

8
Malborough

N

0   5 miles
0   5km

4

THE SOUTH HAMS &
DEVON'S FAR SOUTH

The name **South Hams** probably derived from the Saxon *hamm*, which meant peninsula but also a homestead or village. Some take it literally, and there are plenty of piggy references in the coastal landscape here: Pig's Nose, Ham Stone, Gammon Head.

The extreme south of Devon described here has its roots planted firmly in the sea; the coast and all it can offer is the magnet for visitors here, with **Salcombe** its epicentre. From here you can hire a boat and putter around the estuary, select some of the most scenic stretches of the South West Coast Path, or spend the day on a few of the prettiest sandy beaches in the county. With sea and sand and endless rock pools to investigate, it's an enduringly favourite family destination.

Coming from Dartmouth in the east, the first place of special interest is **Slapton**, with its long beach that played the part of Normandy during the war (see box, pages 108–9). But hereafter visitors gravitate south, beneath an imaginary horizontal line drawn through Kingsbridge. Here, in the South Hams, Devon points two knuckles towards Brittany, bifurcated by the estuary up which a weekly steamer used to carry merchandise to and from Kingsbridge, and which is now served by a passenger ferry.

Among a clutch of likeable and highly photogenic villages on the west coast are **Thurlestone** and the enchantingly named **Inner Hope**. Then cross the River Avon, with its trick pronunciation (see page 119), to reach **Bigbury-on-Sea** and walk or take the sea tractor to **Burgh Island**.

GETTING THERE & AROUND

There is really only one main road in the region (the A379 from Dartmouth to Kingsbridge and on to Plymouth, connecting with the A381 to Malborough and Salcombe). The narrow lanes that link the villages south of this line evolved through foot and hoof traffic and are not designed to transport holidaymakers. If you are visiting the area in July and August you would do well to leave your **car** at home, or at least drive as little as possible. You can access the area by public transport by taking the train to Totnes or Plymouth and then **bus** 164 from Totnes to Kingsbridge, the 'capital' of the region, or the 93 from Plymouth to Kingsbridge or Slapton. From Kingsbridge there are regular buses to Salcombe, and much of the western part of its peninsula. The most satisfying mechanised way of arriving in Salcombe is by **ferry** from Kingsbridge: the *Rivermaid* runs several times a day from June to October, dependent on the tides (✆ 01548 853607).

PUBLIC TRANSPORT

This is not a good area for committed users of public transport since buses rarely venture south of the A379. When they do, they are utterly delightful, and can be used for bus-assisted walks as well as just the pleasure of riding in them. A bus from Kingsbridge to Malborough and Hope Cove gives the opportunity to take the coastal path to Salcombe; the same service runs to Thurlestone, opening up another stretch of coastal path. Full details are given in the relevant sections.

The bus timetable for the area is *South Hams*, which you can pick up at Tourist Information Centres or access on line (⌂ www.journeydevon.info).

With so few buses available, you may need to use taxis if you are without a car. Local firms include **Eco Taxis**, Kingsbridge (✆ 01548 856347), **Moonraker Taxis**, Malborough (✆ 01548 560231), **John Edwards**, Modbury (✆ 01548 830859 or 07967 374502) and **Tim Craig**, Holbeton (✆ 01752 830225).

CYCLING & WALKING

A maze of small lanes meander up and down the relentlessly hilly, switchback South Hams, and the gradients can make it tough and slow-going for **cycling**. The National Cycle Network barely covers this area, although it's planned that NCN2 will eventually go from Salcombe to Plymouth. However, the section from Ashprington, south of Totnes, to East Portlemouth is finished. It runs via Blackawton, using quiet lanes.

You can take your bicycle on the passenger ferry between East Portlemouth and Salcombe, and cycling is the best way of exploring the East Portlemouth prong thoroughly since there's no public transport. A

WET-WEATHER ACTIVITIES
Paint your own pottery in Kingsbridge (page 114)
The South Devon Chilli Farm (page 115)
Overbeck's Museum (page 118)
Slow lunch at Burgh Island hotel or **Bigbury's Oyster Shack** (pages 125 and 126)

bicycle is also ideal for exploring the other southern lumps and bumps which are isolated between river estuaries connected only by bicycle-carrying passenger ferries.

Most **walkers** will head for the South West Coast Path and this southern stretch is certainly one of the very finest, being far from a main road yet with enough accessible refreshments to keep body and soul together, and enough accessible beaches, some sandy, to encourage you to carry your swimsuit. The coast path between Thurlestone and Hope Cove is broad and pushchair-friendly, while sections by Bolt Head, Soar Mill Cove and around Prawle have significant ups and downs. Fewer walkers do the more isolated rugged stretch of the coast path west from Thurlestone, partly because of the lack of public transport. There are no buses until you reach Newton Ferrers, a tough 13 miles or so away. The additional challenge on this part of the path is working out the timing so that you cross the rivers when the ferries are running or, in the case of the Erme, at low tide when you can paddle across. Carry a tide table.

Walk This Way (⌂ www.walk-this-way.co.uk ✆ 07759728245) is run from Thurlestone by Jackie Humphries and gives the choice of guided walks (great for meeting other like-minded people) or self-guided walks, long or short distance, with accommodation and luggage transfer an option.

Walking maps, guides, information & websites

The two-sided OS Explorer map OL20, scale 1:25,000, covers all this region. However, by far the best maps for walkers are the Croydecycle maps (⌂ www.croydecycle.co.uk) produced by Mike Harrison at a scale of 1:12,500 (five inches to a mile). They cover most of the coastal area of the South Hams: *Bigbury, Avon & Erme, Salcombe & Hope*, and *Prawle & Beesands*. Not only is every geographical detail marked in, but so are helpful footpath notes for walkers, such as 'can be muddy' or 'grassy and rutted'. Walking guide books include *The South West Coast Path* official guide (⌂ www.southwestcoastpath.com) and the excellent *Dorset and*

TOURIST INFORMATION

Kingsbridge The Quay ✆ 01548 853195 ⌂ www.kingsbridgeinfo.co.uk
Modbury 5 Modbury Court ✆ 01548 830159 ⌂ www.modbury.org.uk
Salcombe Market St ✆ 01548 843927 ⌂ www.salcombeinformation.co.uk

South Devon Coast Path (Trailblazer). Also useful is *Shortish walks: the South Devon Coast* (Bossiney Books). Another handy publication is *Holiday Times*, a free A3-format magazine listing events in the South Hams (available in most Tourist Information Centres). The website for

WILD SWIMMING IN THE SOUTH HAMS

Anna Turns

A far cry from swimming countless lengths in a pool, swimming outdoors offers the chance to become part of your environment by literally immersing yourself in it. Every swim is a new experience: spot sand eels in the shallows, watch moon jellies drifting by, or swim over a shoal of seabass. It's easy to lose track of time and distance when the view above and below the surface constantly changes. Wild swimming is all about the journey, whatever the distance. It can be a social occasion too, whether it's a gentle swim with friendly chatter or a mass participation event with a real buzz.

Tempted to dip more than just a toe in the ocean? There are so many wild and watery places to explore along Devon's rivers, estuaries and coastline. As a keen outdoor swimmer based in the South Hams, I've spent the last year discovering a diversity of wild swims. Here are my favourites:

- A great novice swim is from South Milton Sands at high tide to Thurlestone Rock, under the arch and back again. The diversity of seaweeds in such a small patch of seashore is amazing – go back on a low spring tide and carefully walk through the arch to admire the marine life from a different perspective.
- Swimming up the Avon River against the tide is the wet equivalent of a treadmill. Park at Bantham (at the estuary mouth just north of Thurlestone), then walk anticlockwise around the 'ham' and take the first path to the pink thatched boat-house and slipway. Stick to the outside edge of the bend (the river runs fastest mid-stream) and swim upstream on a dropping tide for a real workout, then it's a quick drift back.
- Build up your stamina by swimming 200-yard widths at North Sands, Salcombe. The water is crystal clear and you're never far out of your depth; just avoid the boat lane in summer.

South Devon's Area of Outstanding National Beauty lists and describes some good walks: ⌐ www.southdevonaonb.org.uk.

THE SLAPTON AREA

First impressions are not that exciting: a long stretch of coarse sand/fine shingle and slate on one side and a lagoon on the other. But the interest here is what it is rather than what it seems, for not only is **Slapton Ley** one of Devon's most prized nature reserves, but **Slapton Sands** played a pivotal role in World War II (see box, pages 108–09).

- Swimming across Salcombe estuary is dangerous, but once a year safety measures are in place for the Salcombe Regatta Harbour Swim from Small's Cove to Bakerswell every August.
- For the more adventurous, persuade a friend with a boat to escort you from Starehole Bay to North Sands (just south of Salcombe) on an incoming tide. Alternatively, cross by ferry from Salcombe to East Portlemouth and walk south to the Hipples, a magical part of the sand bar exposed at low spring tides, then swim up past Mill Bay, back to East Portlemouth.
- The jewel in the crown of Devon's sea swims has to be Burgh Island. With two annual events around the island, you can choose the official 'Round the Island' race in August or the more relaxed Chestnut Appeal Burgh Island Swim in autumn – a chance to savour the spectacular 360° views.

Top tips
- Never swim alone – swim with a buddy or have someone close by watching you.
- Check tide times and ask lifeguards about rip tides. Swim within your limits.
- Wear a brightly coloured silicone swim hat to increase your visibility.
- For extra protection from rocks and the cold, wear wetsuit boots and gloves.
- Wetsuits are not essential but if you prefer the extra layer, invest in a triathlon wetsuit – more flexible and less chafing!
- Make sure you have a flask of hot drink and plenty of cake to hand.

Follow Anna on Twitter @Annaturns.

John Leland, travelling in the mid 16th century, described Slapton as having 'a very large Poole 2 Miles in length. Ther is but a Barre of Sand betwixt the Se and this Poole; the fresch Water drenith into the Se thorough the Sandy Bank, but the Waite of the Fresch Water and Rage of the Se brekith sumtime this Sandy Bank.' And so it is today. The A379 runs along a narrow spit of land between the 'large Poole' and the sea, and is breached from time to time despite modern engineering providing an outlet for the lake water. In 2001 a severe storm destroyed the road, and isolated the village of Torcross and its neighbours for four months. Now Natural England, which shares responsibility for the area with local councils, says that next time may be the last; it's just too expensive to repair.

1 SLAPTON LEY & SLAPTON

A hundred years or so ago the Ley was of commercial and sporting interest, providing reeds for thatching, and waterfowl and fish for shooting and angling. When it looked as though it was going the way of so much of Devon's coastal landscape, with holiday development taking precedence over scenery and wildlife, it was bought by the conservationist Herbert Whitley, founder of Paignton Zoo, as a wildlife sanctuary. The Ley, the largest freshwater lake in Devon, is now leased to the Field Studies Council by the Whitley Trust.

The nature reserve is well known among bird watchers for its rare species. With luck you could see a bittern or a great crested grebe. There are two bird hides looking out over the reed beds, with information on the species most commonly seen as well as a check list of recent sightings. For those who like to spot their wildlife while on the move, a trail runs through the reserve, sometimes along boardwalks,

"With luck you could see a bittern or great crested grebe."

with a choice of exit points so you can decide on your preferred length. The maximum, if you want to include Slapton, is about three miles. Starting at the car park at Slapton Bridge, the path runs round the northern shore of the lake, then gives you a choice of two short routes to Slapton or a longer one via Deer Bridge. Watch out for the intricately carved handrail on the wooden viewing platform during the early part of the walk. The Field Centre runs a variety of guided walks, courses and events (www.slnnr.org.uk).

You will enjoy Slapton far more if you walk into it, rather than try to drive; the narrow road forms a fearsome bottleneck in the summer. It's an attractive village and both its pubs offer a warm welcome. The Chantry Tower dates back to the religious foundation set up in 1372 by Sir Guy de Brian. He bore the standard of Edward III at the siege of Calais, to encourage six priests, a rector, five fellows and four clerks to pray for him and his family. The foundation was dissolved in the Reformation, and the stone of the associated chapel was used to build the house, also known as The Chantry, in whose garden the tower stands. You can't visit the tower, but can see it from outside the pub. It is home to a noisy congregation of jackdaws and herring gulls.

¶¶ FOOD & DRINK

Kings Arms Strete ☎ 01803 770377 ⌂ www.kingsarmsstrete.co.uk. Strete is northeast along the coast from Slapton. The pub has a beer garden, and the views over Start Bay alone justify a visit here.

The Laughing Monk Strete ☎ 01803 770639 ⌂ www.thelaughingmonkdevon.co.uk. An upmarket restaurant. Not cheap, but arrive before 19.00 when the splendid three-course meal comes at a bargain price.

Queen's Arms Slapton ☎ 01548 580800 ⌂ www.queensarmsslapton.co.uk. Good, honest pub food, and fish and chips on Friday. It has an intimate walled garden, plus the ultimate prize in Slapton, a car park.

Tower Inn Slapton ☎ 01548 580216 ⌂ www.thetowerinn.com. Has a garden overlooked by the Chantry Tower and a rooftop view of Slapton. The 14th-century flower-bedecked building has low beamed rooms and flagstones, and the food is excellent. Parking is awkward.

Start Bay Inn Torcross ☎ 01548 580553. A 14th-century beachside tavern serving outstanding fish and chips.

Torcross Boathouse Torcross ☎ 01548 580747. Family-friendly dining in stylish nautical surroundings. A local resident told me 'Forget fine dining – my favourite dinner in Devon is nipping to Torcross Boathouse on a summer's evening, getting takeaway fish and chips or the yummiest beanburger I have ever tasted, and sitting on the beach watching the boats sail past and the sun set'.

2 SLAPTON SANDS

The 'sands' are not that inviting, being fine shingle so not the sort of stuff you can build sandcastles from. Swimming is 'bloody cold' according to a resident, because the shore shelves steeply so you are quickly out of your depth and the sun has little effect (however, these two aspects make swimming here particularly attractive to keen 'wild swimmers'). The northern part of the Sands is popular with naturists. For families it's perfect browsing territory for beach pebbles, with plenty of flat stones good for skimming.

Near the middle car park is a monument presented to the people of South Hams by the US army as a thank-you to the 3,000 villagers who vacated their homes to allow for the military exercises that led up to D-Day (see box below).The Sherman tank at the **Torcross** end is a memorial to the American troops killed during Exercise Tiger; it

EXERCISE TIGER

In November 1943 the inhabitants of nine villages in the Torcross area were ordered to leave their homes for an indeterminate period. Slapton Sands was similar to a beach in Normandy, codenamed Utah Beach, which would be used for the D-Day landings, and the American troops needed to practise. The locals, however, were told only that the area was needed for 'military purposes'. Just imagine what was being asked of these 3,000 villagers: Torcross, Slapton, Stokenham, Chillington, Frogmore, Sherford, Blackawton, East Allington, and Strete were farming communities, their winter and spring crops had been planted, winter fodder was stored in the barns, and their ration of coal in the shed. They had to decide what to do with their cattle or sheep, and how to move heavy farm machinery. Then there were the churches to worry about. The little village church has always been at the heart of the rural English community, and in those days most villagers will have been churchgoers. Church valuables, including the carved wooden screens, were dismantled and removed to a place of safety, those that couldn't be removed were sandbagged, and in each church was pinned the following notice:

To our Allies of the USA. This church has stood here for several hundred years. Around it has grown a community, which has lived in these houses and tilled these fields ever since there was a church. This church, this churchyard in which their loved ones lie at rest, these homes, these fields are as dear to those who have left them as are the homes and graves and fields which you, our Allies, have left behind you. They hope to return one day, as you hope to return to yours, to find them waiting to welcome them home. They entrust them to your care meanwhile and pray that God's blessing may rest upon us all.
Charles, Bishop of Exeter.

was retrieved from the sea in 1984 through the tireless efforts of Ken Small, a local hotelier.

3 FROM TORCROSS TO BEESANDS VIA THE CLIFF PATH

This short but varied and scenic walk takes you over the cliffs with good views of Start Point lighthouse, through some woods, and on to the long shingle beach at Beesands. The beach is beloved of mackerel fishers, families seeking seclusion, and also foodies, for the wonderful fresh fish at the unassuming Britannia café.

Various exercises were held from March to April, all involving heavy bombardment of the beach area. To replicate as closely as possible the Normandy landings, live ammunition was used. Exercise Tiger took place between 26 and 29 April 1944, as a full rehearsal for Operation Overlord planned for June. The first exercise went without a hitch, but during a routine patrol of the English Channel German E-boats discovered the vessels preparing for the second assault and fired on two ships with torpedoes, setting fire to one with the loss of at least 749 lives. The radio message that could have summoned help in time to save some of them was delayed because a typing error gave the wrong frequency. Accounts suggest that a thousand or so Americans were killed during the months of exercises, some through 'friendly fire'.

Everyone involved in Exercise Tiger was sworn to secrecy; Operation Overlord was imminent and proved to be the beginning of the end of the war. The villagers started to trickle back to their damaged and rat-infested homes a few months later. Some never returned.

Further reading

The American Forces at Salcombe and Slapton during World War Two by Muriel March (Orchard Publications).

Exercise Tiger: the D-Day Practice Landings Tragedies Uncovered by Richard T Bass (Tommies Guides).

The Forgotten Dead by Ken Small (Bloomsbury).

The Invasion before Normandy: Secret Battle of Slapton Sands by Edwin P Hoyt (Scarborough House).

The Land Changed its Face: the Evacuation of the South Hams 1943–44 by Grace Bradbeer (Harbour Books).

Charles Harper, writing at the beginning of the 20th century, described the villagers keeping chickens in upturned decaying boats. 'They are the most trustful cocks and hens in the world, and follow the fishermen into the inn and cottages like dogs.' He goes on to describe the Newfoundland dogs of Beesands, and neighbouring Hall Sands, which were trained to swim out through the surf to meet the incoming fishing boats. The dogs would grab the end of the rope and bring it to the beach so the boats could be hauled on shore.

Beesands (TQ7 2EN) is accessible via a network of narrow lanes and has a large car park.

¶¶ FOOD & DRINK

Beesands has a very good pub, the **Cricket Inn** (✆ 01548 580215), but it is the **Britannia** (✆ 0845 055 0711 ⌂ www.britanniashellfish.co.uk) that has fish enthusiasts jostling for a table. Run by fisherman Nick Hutchings and his wife Anita, this is better described as a shack than a restaurant. It is mainly a fresh-fish outlet, but its tiny canvas-sided eating area provides a freshly caught selection of seafood dishes. There are only a few tables so reservations are essential if you want to be sure of a place.

DEVON'S FAR SOUTH

With the towns of **Kingsbridge** and **Salcombe** dominating, this most southerly part of Devon is the honeypot of the South Hams. It has all the attractions that holidaymakers need: sandy beaches, boats, fishing, walking, and the mildest climate in Devon. There is also the small pocket of little-known South Hams, north of Kingsbridge, where the village of **Goveton**, with its thatched cottages, and Buckland Tout Saints, lie tucked into folds of the hills.

4 HALLSANDS TO START POINT

For cliff-path walkers, the first place for a rest stop along this stretch after Beesands is **Hallsands**. Harper describes the village which, when he visited (probably 1905), was beginning the process of falling into the sea. Half of the only inn had already gone 'while the landlady was making tea' and it was only a matter of time before the rest of the village met the same fate. This entirely preventable disaster was caused by the commercial dredging of shingle for the construction industry (Plymouth breakwater), with the result that the beach was about 12 feet lower by the time they stopped in 1902. Without their natural defences, the cottages were exposed to every storm and by 1917 they had almost all gone. You can see what's left of them below the cliff path, but a Hallsands resident reports that two fishermen's cottages remain standing and privately owned: 'No electricity, only kerosene lamps and an outside shower. Water pouring down the chimney on rough days!'

Continuing along the coast path you'll reach **Start Point**, about four miles from Torcross. The name comes from the Saxon 'steort' which means tail, as for example in redstart. There is no public transport in this area, so you'll need either to continue to Salcombe Harbour or to take the easy option and leave your car at Start Point's car park and make a circular walk to the point and back.

5 EAST PRAWLE

This is the southernmost village in Devon, far from anywhere and approached by miles of narrow lanes. Prawle Point is a significant corner on the coast where there is a daily watch on shipping (which visitors can often join – there is a small museum here, and sometimes access to the main lookout room). The village is perched some 370 feet above sea level, and six paths radiate like spokes to different parts of the coast offering a great selection of short or long circular walks. Within a short range you can explore soaring cliffs, ragged rocky headlands, secluded coves and picture-perfect small sandy beaches, conveniently facing south. As a taster try Gammon Head with adjacent Maceley Cove (low tide best) or walk further to other beaches.

"You can explore soaring cliffs, ragged rocky headlands, secluded coves and picture-perfect sandy beaches."

East Prawle village also offers useful facilities: the quirky Pig's Nose pub famous for it's live music, an excellent shop/café, parking, toilets and basic camping. There is the charm of old buildings and a slow-changing history with a real sense of community. However, before making the pilgrimage be warned that amenities tend to the simple end of the spectrum – many are caught out with the frugal opening hours – and the magnificent views are only achieved by walking. It's rarely level and of course the rain often lashes in from the ocean. Authentic Devon, in other words.

6 BUCKLAND TOUT SAINTS

The linguistically odd name of this hamlet apparently comes from the Toutsaint family who owned the land in 1238. It seems that it had nothing to do with saints but rather with health: *sain* as in the French 'sain' meaning healthy, so something like 'all-healthy'. **St Peter's Church**, its chunky little silhouette on a hilltop easily visible as you approach from Kingsbridge or Goveton, was rebuilt on its present site in 1778 to serve the family and staff of Buckland Manor House as well as the villagers of Goveton and Ledstone. Its predecessor, a chapel of ease built earlier for Buckland House, had fallen into disrepair and by the early 18th century was a ruin. Substantially renovated in 1889, St Peter's is now a grade 2 listed building. Although it has no single feature of particular historic interest, this is a much-loved and tranquil little church. A fine tapestry kneeler in front of the altar portrays the life of the parish, and there is a wild-flower area in the churchyard. Visitors are welcome to Sunday services, whose times are shown on the notice board.

The 17th-century **Buckland Manor** was substantially remodelled in the late 19th century and is now an extremely comfortable luxury hotel – see page 24. The striking interior has many historical links: for example some panelling and decorative Jacobean pew-ends are said to have come from Carfax Church in Oxford, which was demolished in 1889. Even if you're not staying there you could call in to sample one of its delicious cream teas, whether by a cosy log fire in the lounge or out on the terrace with wide views across the countryside.

7 KINGSBRIDGE

These days the only shipping that calls here is the *Rivermaid* which plies the estuary between Kingsbridge and Salcombe, but in the early 20th century a 'market packet' steamer ran between Kingsbridge and Plymouth, calling at Salcombe on the way. Limestone was brought by ship from Plymouth, and its by-product, quicklime, produced in the limekilns that are still to be found between Kingsbridge and the sea.

Kingsbridge retains a lot of charm, its steep Fore Street the very antithesis of Clone Britain with varied and interesting shops. There's also a museum, a cinema, and regular happenings throughout the year. I found the tourist information centre at The Quay exceptionally helpful, and they publish a comprehensive (free) guide to the area which lists all

THE BIRD-MAN OF KINGSBRIDGE

George Montagu (1753–1815) is sometimes called the 'founder of British ornithology', because of his *Ornithological Dictionary* (published in 1802, and referred to by Charles Darwin in his writings) and his contribution to the knowledge and understanding of British birds. You may spot a blue plaque outside Knowle House in Fore Street, commemorating him. Among other findings he showed that several 'new' species had been wrongly recorded as such because males of the same species differed in appearance from females, or because a species had different summer and winter plumage. The Montagu's harrier is named after him, and following his death his bird collection was bought by the British Museum. He was also the first naturalist to describe the Lesser Horseshoe Bat.

Birds weren't his only interest; he was fascinated by marine biology and in 1803 published a history of British marine, land and freshwater shells, describing 470 species of mollusc, of which 100 were new to the British list. He wrote numerous papers on the birds and shells of southern England and recorded some species of fish previously unknown in British waters, hence the naming of the Montagu's blenny and the Montagu's snapper. Some of his shell collections are now in Exeter Museum.

He felt constricted by marriage, wishing he could travel more freely in pursuit of his interests. In 1798 he left his wife of 25 years and moved to live in Kingsbridge with his mistress, Eliza Dorville, who did many of the drawings that appear in his books. He called her his 'friend of science' – but the friendship was apparently rather warm, as by 1805 they had four children. Montagu died of lockjaw in 1815 after treading on a rusty nail: a sadly prosaic end for someone who contributed so much to our knowledge of natural history. He is buried in Kingsbridge.

the major events and attractions. **The Crabshell Inn** (see page 114) on Embankment Road is more than just an eatery. Learn paddleboarding and hear live music at this dynamic place.

The **Cookworthy Museum** is a restored 17th-century grammar school, still in use in the early 1900s, which gives insights into what life was like in Kingsbridge and area over the centuries. It's named after William Cookworthy, who discovered china clay in Cornwall and went on to develop porcelain manufacturing in England.

Harbour House on the Promenade (☎ 01548 854708 ⌂ www. harbourhouse.org.uk) is well worth a visit; in its attractive **art gallery** the exhibitions by local artists change monthly, and there are courses in yoga, meditation, pilates, tai chi, psychology, kung fu – and more; see page 114 for its café.

If you'd like to create art rather than look at it, the **Art Café Ceramic Studio** in Fore Street (☎ 01548 852802 🖰 www.theartcafe.biz) allows you to do just that. You can choose a piece of unfired pottery (mug, bowl, plate etc) and paint it with your own design; it will then be fired and ready for collection a few days later or can be posted to your home. It's surprisingly absorbing. To feed your inspiration there's a range of hot and cold drinks, toasted sandwiches, toasted teacakes, cream teas etc. It's best to check in advance that they're not expecting a big group when you plan to go.

¶¶ FOOD & DRINK

A farmers' market is held on The Quay on the first and third Saturday of the month.

Crabshell Inn Embankment Rd ☎ 01548 852345. For the best views overlooking the creek, go at high tide. Learn to paddleboard and enjoy great music events too.

Harbour House Café Harbour House, Promenade ☎ 01548 855666 🖰 www. harbourhousecafe.com. The tasty range of lunches and snacks here features free-range eggs, organic milk, and (wherever possible) natural, seasonal, organic and allotment-grown ingredients. Don't worry, there are cream teas and calorific cakes on the menu too – but teatime needs to be early because it's open only 10.00–15.30 (Mon–Sat).

8 MALBOROUGH

This must be one of the most frequently misspelled village names in Devon. It's an attractive village with a good number of thatched cottages, including one painted an eye-popping blue, and at least two pubs. The large church, with its spire, dominates the view from miles around and makes a handy landmark for walkers. I found it too austere for my taste, but there are some nice touches inside such as the informative map of the village drawn by a member of the WI and a floor-stone in memory of William Clark with a misspelling and some letters seemingly inserted as an afterthought.

Malborough's post office sells OS maps and a leaflet *Footpaths in Malborough* Parish which details all the car parks in the area as well as a selection of footpaths connecting to the most glorious section of the South West Coast Path between Bolt Head and Bolt Tail. Thus car drivers can avoid the hassle of parking in Salcombe.

9 SALCOMBE

Salcombe *is* boats. The town has always looked seawards, building its prosperity from fishing and maritime trade and, in recent times, from hobby sailors. Most people who come here regularly love messing about

SOME LIKE IT HOT

If you use your satnav to take you from Exeter to Kingsbridge or Salcombe, you'll follow increasingly narrow lanes until you reach the village of Loddiswell. Shortly before the village a sign on the left announces 'South Devon Chilli Farm'. Stop and take a look – it's a great place. And unique.

Jason Nickels and Steve Waters started the chilli farm in 2003. Realising there was a gap in the market, they started by renting some land and planted a few chillies. 'We both liked gardening, but neither of us had any horticultural training. But chillies are easy, they grow fast and don't need any special care.' Except, I noted, from snails. 'Snails can't taste the hotness in a chilli' was the explanation, 'and they go for the fruit rather than the leaves. Apparently there's calcium in the centre of the chillies which they need for their shells.'

Jason left the business in 2011, and Steve has been joined by three other directors: his wife Heather; his friend from their Plymouth school days, Martin Phillips and Martin's partner Kaz Lobendhan.

The farm has around 140 varieties of chilli, with perhaps 20,000 plants growing in greenhouses and poly tunnels. Visitors are welcome to visit the show tunnel and see the different varieties. The farm shop sells plants and a huge range of chilli products including chilli chocolate, made on the premises, which is addictive after the initial shock.

There is an onsite café serving food for all tastes with indoor and outdoor seating offering fine views over the South Hams countryside, and in 2013 they added a plant nursery for customers to browse through. They also have a chilli-themed play area for children (including a chilli tractor).

'We like to think we offer a first-rate mail order service, especially in seeds, and this year we have added seedlings and plants to the products available by post.' The plants in the chilli collection (140 varieties) are labelled in detail: where they come from, what they look like when mature (so the decorative side) and – most important – the degree of hotness. The very hottest is Bhut Jolokia from India, and there are plenty of mild ones with the encouragement 'a good plant for inquisitive children'.

South Devon Chilli Farm Wigford Cross, Loddiswell TQ7 4DX ✆ 01548 550782 🖰 www. sdcf.co.uk. The shop and café, selling a huge range of chilli products from sauces and chutneys to jellies and soft drinks – and of course the famous chocolate – is open year-round except for weekends in January and early February. The best months to visit are July to October, when the chillies are ripening.

in boats, and just about everyone will take an estuary cruise or at least one of the ferries, to either Kingsbridge, East Portlemouth or South Sands. Do-it-yourself sailors can hire a sailing boat, a self-drive motor boat, or a kayak. As befits this book, there is a speed limit in the estuary, so forget about hiring a speed boat. And it's actually not a real estuary since there's no river; it's a flooded valley, or 'ria'.

You can also learn to sail here. The Island Cruising Club runs courses for all ages, either living aboard the old Mersey Ferry, *Egremont*, or ashore, going out daily for tuition on a variety of dinghies. Typically the courses run for a week but can be adjusted to need.

Estuary cruises are good for wildlife spotting. You might be lucky enough to see Dave the dolphin, who prefers the autumn when it's quieter, and Sammy the grey seal. Neither showed up when I was there, but I was happy to look at herons, egrets and shags, and the smartly dressed shelducks which, surprisingly, nest in old rabbit burrows. And to learn what lay under the water – huge fan mussels, for instance, and even sea horses. Their relatives, the pipe fish, are sometimes found in rock pools, along with cushion stars, brittle stars and anemones. The town itself is a maze of little streets, alleys and tourist shops, and has a good **Maritime Museum** (open summer only). This and the Overbeck's Museum (see page 118) have photos of the old sailing ships, built in the 19th century, both in Kingsbridge and Salcombe. Many of these are of the schooners, designed for speed, which carried pineapples from the Bahamas and oranges and lemons from the Azores, for the markets in London. However, ships had been built in the estuary, on any convenient foreshore, for centuries.

East Portlemouth & Mill Bay

Across the water, at **East Portlemouth**, are some particularly inviting sandy coves. Most of the sand is covered at high tide so a tide table is handy if you want to spend time here with the family building sand castles. An easy and scenic walk of five miles 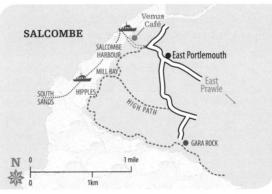 or so can be done by following the coast path to Gara Rock, where the sumptuous Gara Rock restaurant (and self catering cottages – see page

241) provides the ultimate in indulgence and views (✆ 01548 844810 ⏀ www.gararock.com).

You can return via the less scenic 'high path'. I did this walk on Boxing Day, revelling in the lack of crowds and clear views. A variation, possible only at low spring tides in the early afternoon, is to walk along the foreshore all the way to a sand bar called Hipples at the harbour's entrance. It is only exposed for a couple of hours. If the tide is not quite low enough there is access from the cliff path.

On the way you will cross **Mill Bay**, where the Americans were based during World War II, bringing a sparkle to the eyes of local girls. They had a workshop there, and the remains of the big concrete slipway are still on the beach. During the preparations for D-Day, in 1944, the estuary was full of American ships, with landing craft concealed under the trees along the shores of the estuary. Over in Salcombe, Normandy Way and the Normandy Pontoon are named to commemorate their embarkation.

"As you go through the five-barred gate, look to your left and enjoy one of the most spectacular views the region has to offer."

Back at the ferry, a cannonball was recently discovered in the foundations of a wall. It is now proudly on display in the Village Hall.

When arriving by ferry, pause at the **Venus Café** for some energy-boosting calories before climbing the 138 steps to the village. As you go through the five-barred gate at the top of the path, look to your left and enjoy one of the most spectacular views the region has to offer. The estuary lies below you, right up to Kingsbridge. On a fine day the southern fringe of Dartmoor can be clearly seen. Pass the cottages on your right and, at the top of the hill, you will find the 12th-century **Church of St Winwaloe** (St Guénolé), whose followers came over from the Abbey at Landévennec in Brittany. He is also patron saint of at least six churches in Cornwall. The medieval screen, with its panels of saints and fine carving, was restored in the 1930s.

There is no shop in East Portlemouth, but pubs can be found at **East Prawle** (see page 111) and South Pool, both within walking distance.

ᵀᵎ FOOD & DRINK

Blue House Crab Company Salcombe Rd, Malborough TQ7 3BX ✆ 07801 281048 ⏀ www.bluehousecrabcompany.co.uk. Order local fish boxes, Salcombe hand-picked crab or dressed lobster from chef Tom Bunn.

Burger Belles Salcombe 📞 07773 370556 🖥 www.burgerbelles.co.uk. Look out for the 1972 gourmet burger van serving delicious burgers handmade by Jess and Lynne.

Dick and Wills Fore St 📞 01548 843408 🖥 www.dickandwills.co.uk. A favourite with discriminating locals, this waterside brasserie 'serves great food, with a New England style feel inside'. Go here for a special treat.

Millbrook Inn South Pool TQ7 2RW 📞 01548 531581 🖥 www.millbrookinnsouthpool.co.uk. Contributor Anna Turns says that this pub in South Pool, at the end of the southeast prong of the estuary, is accessible at high tide by boat. 'It's always magic on a summer's evening, and the lanes there are perfect for seeing glow worms and bats in late evening in July/August.' If you haven't a boat it can also be reached by road.

Sailor V, Ice cream parlour and café Fore St 📞 01548 843555. Indulgent sweet and savoury sundaes – a real treat for all ages.

Salcombe Harbour Hotel Cliff Rd 📞 01548 844444 🖥 www.salcombe-harbour-hotel.co.uk. This has the Jetty Restaurant and the Crustacean Bar for fresh seafood. Join head chef Alex Aitken aboard a local fishing boat for the 'Catch it, cook it, eat it!' experience.

Salcombe Yawl Sandwich Shop Off Fore St 📞 01548 842143. Good crab sandwiches and excellent homemade deli treats for a beach picnic.

The Winking Prawn, North Sands TQ8 8LD 📞 01548 842326 🖥 www.winkingprawn.co.uk. This beachside café at the cove just south of Salcombe is fun, relaxed and open all year round – a welcome pitstop for coast path walkers.

BOAT HIRE IN SALCOMBE & KINGSBRIDGE

Island Cruising Club 📞 01548 531176 🖥 www.icc-salcombe.co.uk. Sailing holidays and instruction from the age of five upwards.

Salcombe Dinghy Sailing Whitestrand Quay 📞 01548 511548 🖥 www.salcombedinghysailing.co.uk. Dinghy hire for experienced sailors or tuition for beginners. Canoeing and kayaking tuition.

Sea Kayak & SUP The Old Lifeboat House, South Sands Quay 📞 01548 843451 🖥 www.southsandssailing.co.uk. Stand up paddle-boarding, coastal kayak tours and sea kayaking. Also Bo's Beach Café.

Singing Paddles Kingsbridge 📞 07754 426633 🖥 www.singingpaddles.co.uk. **Whitestrand Boat Hire** Whitestrand Quay 📞 01548 843818 🖥 www.whitestrandboathire.co.uk. Self-drive boat hire, plus mackerel fishing trips.

10 OVERBECK'S MUSEUM

Sharpitor TW8 8LW 📞 01548 842893; National Trust. Open mid-Feb to Nov.

Otto Overbeck was an eccentric chemist of Dutch ancestry, and an insatiable collector. His former house is full of objects collected during his travels, a maritime room with model ships, and a mini natural-history museum with cases of mounted butterflies, beetles, stuffed animals including an armadillo, and a monitor lizard's foot. And there are cases and cases of birds' eggs. In 2006 the museum received a mysterious parcel. It contained a little bustard's egg, stolen by a teenager in 1963 and returned by the remorseful adult who had rediscovered it when clearing his late parents' home.

"I requested the 'Hallelujah Chorus' and considering it's all done by mechanically plucking metal struts it sounded pretty impressive."

Pride of place is given to the Overbeck Rejuvenator, a rather alarming collection of cables, combs and cylinders which passed an electric current from the head to the affected part of the body. It could cure most ills, Overbeck claimed, and its rejuvenation qualities were proved by photographs of the young-looking inventor: 'My age is 64 years, but I feel more like a man of 30'. His book, *Overbeck's Electronic Theory of Life*, was published in 1931.

One room is dominated by a polython, a sort of giant music box, and the predecessor to the gramophone. I requested the 'Hallelujah Chorus' and considering it's all done by mechanically plucking metal struts it sounded pretty impressive.

The sub-tropical gardens are exceptional, dropping down the hillside in a series of terraces, each with its own character and plants, and with views over the Salcombe estuary.

The easiest means of getting here is by the ferry to South Sands.

RIVER AVON, BIGBURY-ON-SEA & BURGH ISLAND

It's confusing, to say the least, that this small river that rises in Dartmoor has the same name as the much larger one that flows through Bath and Bristol. A few hundred years ago it was called the Awne or Aume, and local people still pronounce it Awne. When and why it changed its name is open to conjecture.

The river is very scenic, with sandy shores, gnarled oak trees overhanging the eroded banks, plenty of birdlife, and quite a few boats. There's a marked Avon Estuary Walk which, however, mostly follows paths high above the river. It is clearly marked on the Croydecycle map of Bigbury.

Bus-assisted walk: Inner Hope to Salcombe

✳ OS Explorer map OL20; start from Inner Hope, grid reference SX675398.

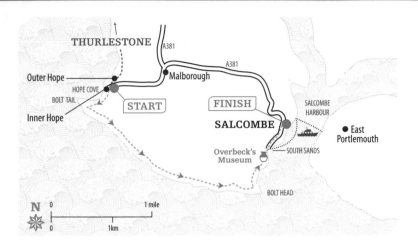

THURLESTONE
A381

A381

Outer Hope
HOPE COVE
BOLT TAIL
Inner Hope

Malborough

START

FINISH

SALCOMBE

SALCOMBE
HARBOUR

● East
Portlemouth

SOUTH SANDS

Overbeck's
Museum

BOLT HEAD

N

0   1 mile

0   1km

This walk is around seven miles and takes you along some of the most dramatic coastal scenery in South Devon, much of it owned by the National Trust. The bus trip, on the glorious 162 route operated by Tallyho, is as scenic and interesting as the walk.

Park at Kingsbridge or Malborough and take the 162 bus to Inner Hope. The early morning departure goes straight from Kingsbridge to Malborough before passing through Galmpton to Hope, but one at noon takes the little lanes through the villages of Thurlestone (see *Bus-assisted*

To do justice to this area you need a tide table, both to enjoy the tidal road at Aveton Gifford and know whether you will walk to Burgh Island or take the sea tractor. The only bus into Bigbury-on-Sea is on Fridays, and the timing doesn't work out for a bus-assisted walk. So all walks need to take circular route.

11 AVETON GIFFORD

The pleasant village of Aveton Gifford (pronounced Awton Jifford), with its Fisherman's Rest pub (✆ 01548 550284), is a convenient starting point for riverside walks including the 7½-mile Avon Estuary walk described (along with lots of other walks in the area) on ⌨ www.southdevonaonb.org.uk, which uses paths along both banks and the *walk* on page 123) and South Milton before Malborough. It was full of locals when I took it, chatting happily with the driver whom they obviously knew well. He paid scant regard to bus stops, dropping them off at their homes, or in one case the pub.

Of the two Hopes, Inner Hope is the pretty one, and the view from the bus terminus overlooking the bay will make your spirits soar. There are thatched cottages hugging the curve in the road, a steep hill down to the family-friendly **Hope Cove**, the **Sun Bay Hotel** (see page 241) in case you decide just to potter in the area, and a forested cliff where the trees have been forced into retreat by the wind, creating a natural amphitheatre. Then it's simply a case of abandoning Hope (sorry) and following the coastal path to Salcombe, via Bolt Tail where you can admire the view towards Burgh Island. Bolt Head is six miles away past splendid scenery.

Around Bolt Head and Sharpitor the landscape really surpasses itself, with craggy rocks high above you and poking out from the sea below. Sailing boats indicate that that you are nearing Salcombe and soon you'll have a spectacular view of the harbour surrounded by wooded hills. Look out for signs to **Overbeck's Museum and garden**, a National Trust property, which offers a well-earned break in its tea room (and a free cup of tea if you arrive without a car) as well as an eclectic collection and a beautiful garden (see page 118).

From Overbeck's you descend steeply to the South Sands beach from where there is a ferry to Salcombe, with **Bo's Café** by the quay. Or you can walk into town along the road.

Buses back to Kingsbridge via Malborough run hourly until the early evening or, if the tides are right, you could get the ferry to Kingsbridge.

ferry across the river mouth. If it's low tide you can walk along the tidal road from Aveton Gifford which brings you eye to eye with swans, and is slippery with seaweed. There's a sign at the far end: 'Caution: these fish are lesser spotted Amazonian piranha. Do not feed by hand.' Yes, the water covers the road at high tide and piranhas abound. If you are

"The water covers the road at high tide and piranhas abound."

beginning the walk here and continuing down the west side of the estuary to Bigbury-on-Sea, keep a keen eye out for a turning where the path leaves the shore and turns right up some concrete steps. We went straight on into ever-deepening mud, as had a fair number of other people judging by the footprints.

12 THURLESTONE & SOUTH MILTON

The name **Thurlestone** comes from its rock (thurled being another word for pierced). This spot close to the South West Coast Path is justifiably popular with families, having sandy beaches (**Thurlestone Sands** and **South Milton Sands**) and plenty of accommodation. Its 13th-century church has some fine carvings, a Norman font and an appealing 17th-century wall monument of a couple and their six children, all dressed in blue except the baby in its red christening robes.

Also at South Milton is the innovative **Sea School** (✆ 07811 349966 ⌖ www.learntosea.co.uk) where children can learn about the coastal environment through rockpool rambles and other beach activities with marine ecologist Maya Plass.

¶¶ FOOD & DRINK

Beach House South Milton Sands ✆ 01548 561144 ⌖ www.beachhousedevon.com. A seafood café and takeaway offering the likes of moules marinière or ice cream.

13 AYRMER COVE & RINGMORE

Ayrmer Cove is nicely secluded, with enticing tide pools and flanked by craggy silvery-grey cliffs. It's owned by the National Trust so utterly unspoiled and is also only accessible on foot which keeps the crowds away. The cove can be visited using the car park at Ringmore, making a short but steep circular walk. Descend to the beach down Smugglers Lane, and return along a section of the coastal path towards Bigbury-on-Sea before heading back to Ringmore via a footpath; or you can park in Bigbury and make a day of it.

In either case, take the opportunity to visit one of the region's prettiest villages, **Ringmore**, and its Journey's End Inn. This is a classic Devon village with lots of thatch and tall, crooked chimneys. The church has a funny little spire plonked in the middle of the tower like an afterthought. If the name of the pub sounds familiar to theatre-goers it's not surprising: the playwright R C Sherriff wrote his play in the 1920s while staying there, and the pub was named after it. In its colourful past the inn was thick with smugglers and they say there was a false wall behind which their booty was stashed.

More innocently, the pub hit the headlines by nurturing a piglet called Incredible. Born prematurely just after the war, Incredible's dad was a champion, and the pub's owner was not prepared to let him die like his

Bus-assisted walk: Aveton Gifford to Thurlestone
✸ OS Explorer map OL20; start from Aveton Gifford, grid reference SX694475.

This four- to five-mile walk takes you down the well-marked Avon Estuary Walk, following the eastern bank of the river to the pretty village of **Bantham** (lots of thatched cottages) and then to **Thurlestone** along the coastal path.

Park in Kingsbridge and take bus 93 to Aveton Gifford; there's a regular summer service from around 9am, though not on Sunday. Walk down to the main roundabout (where you can park if you prefer this free car park to Kingsbridge) and follow the main road in the direction of Kingsbridge. Just after the bridge there's a small road to the right which leads to the signed Avon Estuary Walk. After that it's quite straightforward until you reach Bantham. At Bantham, where the **Sloop Inn** (✆ 01548 560489) can provide a welcome pub break, you have a choice: either follow the South West Coast Path, hugging the coast until you see Thurlestone's famous pierced sea rock, then head up to the village, or take a short cut across the golf course along a signed public footpath. Your choice probably depends on how much time you have to catch the 162 bus back to Kingsbridge; it stops outside the village shop and there's a pub nearby. The last bus leaves late afternoon and takes a scenic hour (nearly) to reach Kingsbridge, while others take a mere 15 minutes.

siblings. During his infancy he consumed three bottles of brandy mixed with glucose and milk, and was kept snug by the Journey's End stove. He flourished but there was, for a while, a downside: he was addicted to alcohol and refused his unfortified feed.

If coming from Bigbury-on-Sea, take the coastal path through the Challaborough Holiday Park and keep walking along the coastal path to the blessed seclusion of Ayrmer Cove, then up Smugglers Lane to Ringmore. From there you could extend the walk to Bigbury (and its pub), visit the church (see below) and then pick up the Avon Estuary Walk back to Bigbury-on-Sea. Or take the shorter route from Ringmore to Bigbury-on-Sea. Either way you will be walking along a section of road leading down to the bay which gets busy in the summer.

14 BIGBURY-ON-SEA & BURGH ISLAND
The names Bigbury and Burgh both derive from the original name of the island, Borough. This seems to have been in use at least until the early 20th century, perhaps later. Almost as old is the general disapproval of Bigbury-

on-Sea by visitors looking for 'unspoilt Devon'. Writing in 1907 the author of *The South Devon Coast*, Charles Harper, describes the estuary thus:

> Wide stretch the sands at ebb, but they are not so wide but that the prints of footsteps have disfigured them pretty thoroughly; for where the land slopes down to the shore in grassy fields, the Plymouth people have built bungalows, and are building more. Burr, or Borough, Island is tethered to the mainland at ebb by this nexus of sand. It is in these circumstances a kind of St Michael's Mount, and like it again in that it once owned a chapel dedicated to St Michael. The chapel disappeared in the lang syne, and when the solitary public-house ceased business, civilisation and Borough Island wholly parted company.

Let me state straight away that I don't share the disapproval of **Bigbury-on-Sea**. When I was there on a sunny(ish) July day the broad sands were full of children playing and their parents relaxing. Across the water at **Bantham** there were black specks of surfers on the waves. Everyone was having a thoroughly good time, and that's what a car-accessible beach is all about. It also has secluded bays within walking distance for those of a more solitary nature. There is a nice café, the Venus, which is open all day. If you decide this is the time to learn how to surf, check out the South Devon Discovery Surf School (✆ 07813 63962 🖰 www.discoverysurf.com).

The comment that 'Borough Island' has 'wholly parted company with civilisation' is particularly ironic given that Devon's most exclusive hotel is here, along with the once-closed pub which now does a thriving business serving the numerous visitors who stroll across the sand to the island or take the historic sea tractor there.

Burgh Island

A hotel that can cost as much as £650 per night (all inclusive) seems, at first acquaintance, to be the antithesis of Slow. So much so that I was in two minds as to whether to include it. But I thought I ought to see it for myself, and I absolutely loved it. And it is as true to the spirit of this book as anywhere listed because to stay at the Burgh Island Hotel you must step back in time, to the 1930s, when life was indeed much slower (see page 241).

First, some history. **The Pilchard Inn** has been serving ale to visitors, on and off, since 1395. In its smuggling heyday there was supposedly a tunnel running from a cave on the beach where Tom Crocker, the king of smugglers, hauled his booty to the pub where it could be safely stored. Apart from a few fishermen's cottages, the first accommodation on the island was a wooden summer house built by a famous music-hall artist, George Chirgwin, who bought the island in the late 19th century as a retreat from his adoring fans. Known in those non-PC times

"What is so special about the hotel these days is not just the place itself in the 1930s style, but that everything about it is in period."

as 'The white-eyed Kaffir' he performed in black greasepaint with a white diamond around one eye. The summer house is still there in the grounds of the hotel, and is now used as a staff house.

The **hotel** was built in 1929 by Archibald Nettlefold, who bought the island in 1896 and commissioned the architect Matthew Dawson to design him a 'Great White Palace'. Less was known in those days about the effects of severe weather on a steel and concrete building – corrosion of the steel has brought many problems to subsequent owners. But that was to be in the future. Until the war, the luxurious hotel drew the rich and famous from all over Britain. Among its visitors were Amy Johnson, Agatha Christie (who wrote *And Then There Were None* here), Noël Coward, Winston Churchill, and royalty: the Mountbattens stayed here, as did the Prince of Wales with Wallis Simpson. The hotel closed in 1955 but continued as self-catering accommodation. New owners from 1985 to 2001 ran it again as a hotel, but with little investment, so when Deborah Clark and Tony Orchard bought it in 2001 it took years gradually to restore it to its full Art-Deco-style glory, and make Burgh Island a visitor-friendly place.

What is so special about the hotel these days is not just that the place itself is in the 1930s style, but that everything about it is in period. So, for instance, there are no TVs in the bedrooms (although one has been allowed into the lounge) and the library only has books, mainly Penguin paperbacks with the classic orange and maroon covers, dating from that era. The background music is, of course, 1930s, and guests dress for dinner as they would in its heyday. That means black tie. 'You should never worry that you might be overdressed, as this is simply impossible' states the information leaflet. If your budget doesn't run to staying here, the restaurant is open to non-residents for Sunday lunch, and in the evenings providing the dress code is observed.

Much of the island is open to non-guests, so the walk across the causeway – or more fun, crossing by sea tractor at high tide – is recommended. The view from the top of the island is stunning; even the cliffs around Ayrmer Cove seem to be in the Art Deco style.

¶¶ FOOD & DRINK

The Oyster Shack Milburn Orchard Farm, Stakes Hill, Bigbury ✆ 01548 810876. Tucked away at the end of the tidal road, slow eating is on the menu. While away the hours with spectacular seafood and good wine.

MODBURY & AREA

15 MODBURY

Modbury became known nationwide for being the first plastic-bag-free town in Britain. They're not banned, but for many years there has been a charge for them so people think before asking for one. You can buy the special Modbury bag in most shops. It's a pleasant town, with a good selection of shops, and an exceptionally helpful Tourist Information Centre.

South of Modbury is a network of steep, narrow lanes ambling down to the coast, then turning around because they're blocked by the unbridged River Erme. This is the attraction for walkers or cyclists. To the east of the river are **Kingston** and **Ringmore** (described earlier), with paths and lanes running down to meet the South West Coast Path. At low tide it's possible to wade across the river using the old ford. Unless it has been raining heavily this should be only knee deep and more of a paddle than a wade.

¶¶ FOOD & DRINK

Bistro 35 35 Church St ✆ 01548 831273. Recommended for intimate dinners.
Lazy Cow Café Poundwell St ✆ 01548 831432. Trendy coffee shop with excellent home-baked cakes.
Valley View Café Rake Farm, near Loddiswell TQ7 4DA ✆ 01548 550413. Part of the butchery and farm shop run by Aune Valley Meat. Terrific breakfasts and snack lunches overlooking the Aune valley.
White Hart Hotel Church St ✆ 01548 831561 🖰 www.whitehart-inn.co.uk. Good for early family dining.

16 HOLBETON CHURCH

This appears in Simon Jenkins' *England's Thousand Best Churches*, so any Jenkins devotee will want to see it, although it's quite a way from the main A379 route to Plymouth and the 94 bus only comes once a day. What makes it remarkable is that it's an example of Victorian restoration that has enhanced a church rather than spoiled it. The restoration was done by J D Sedding in the 1880s and is typical of the Arts and Crafts movement. The elaborate lychgate, porch and doors give you an idea of what is to come, and my impression on entering was that someone had gone wild with a chisel. Every possible surface of stone or wood is carved. The stone pulpit is dense with apostles, vine leaves, and ears of wheat. The bench-ends are a tangle of flora and fauna, and the screen is so intricate that it needs concentration to take it all in. It's admirably done but, to me, lacks the surprises and primitive appeal found in older churches; realism is everywhere, with creatures and plants correct in every detail so leaving little to speculation.

"The elaborate lychgate, porch and doors give you an idea of what is to come ... my impression was that someone had gone wild with a chisel."

The knight propped up uncomfortably on his elbow had more appeal because of the large number of children he appears to have fathered. In fact three generations of the Hele family are here, all called Thomas. Even so, 22 offspring was not bad going, in between fighting wars and the like. The earliest Thomas died in 1613 and his grandson in 1670. All but the armoured Sir Thomas are kneeling devoutly in prayer.

The church is perched on a hillside overlooking the village, its 120-foot steeple heralding its presence as you descend the suicidally steep hill. The views from the graveyard down to the Erme valley towards Mothercombe are splendid and all in all it's worth the diversion.

UPDATES WEBSITE

You can post your comments and recommendations, and read the latest feedback and updates from other readers, online at www.bradtupdates.com/southdevonanddartmoor.

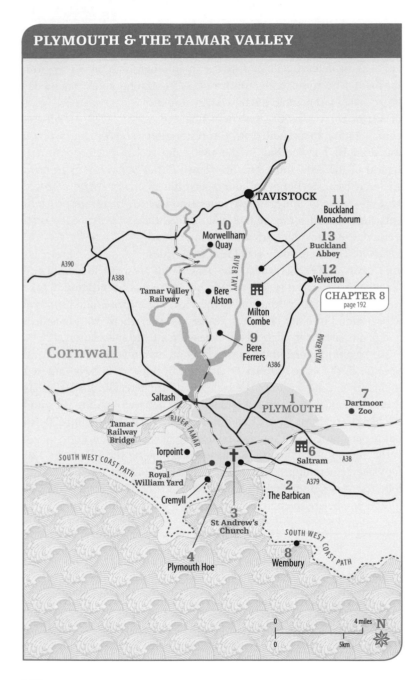

TAVISTOCK

11
Buckland
Monachorum

10
Morwellham
Quay

13
Buckland
Abbey

A390

A388

RIVER TAVY

12
Yelverton

CHAPTER 8
page 192

Tamar Valley
Railway

Bere
Alston

Milton
Combe

RIVER PLYM

Cornwall

9
Bere
Ferrers

A386

Saltash

1
PLYMOUTH

7
Dartmoor
Zoo

Tamar
Railway
Bridge

RIVER TAMAR

6
Saltram

A38

SOUTH WEST COAST PATH

Torpoint

5
Royal
William Yard

2
The Barbican

A379

Cremyll

3
St Andrew's
Church

4
Plymouth Hoe

8
Wembury

SOUTH WEST COAST PATH

0   4 miles

N

0   5km

5
PLYMOUTH &
THE TAMAR VALLEY

Plymouth in the last century was a poor village inhabited by
fishermen. It is now so increased in buildings and population,
that it may be reckoned among the best cities of England...
This great advantage it derives from the capaciousness and
convenience of a large bay, which, extending itself inland
between two promontories, not only admits ships to a
tranquil and secure sheltering place, but conveys them with
the tide, which is here very powerful, into two other bays
still further inland, being the spacious channels of two rivers.
Cosmo III, Grand Duke of Tuscany 1669, as recorded by Count L Magalotti.

More than 400 years before the Duke's appreciation of Plymouth, one of
the 'spacious channels' he mentions, the River Tamar, was carrying tin,
lead and silver ores seaward from the mines on and around Dartmoor.
Then copper was discovered and, by the 19th century, the Tamar valley
was Europe's largest source of copper ore. Visiting it today, it's hard to
believe that for a short while Morwellham Quay was England's busiest
port. Plymouth, on the other hand, has 'increased in buildings and
population' still more, and the Elizabethan seafarers who once knew
every nook and cranny would have a hard time finding their way around.

GETTING THERE & AROUND
BY CAR & PUBLIC TRANSPORT
The **A38** links Plymouth and the surrounding area to both Cornwall
and Exeter. Plymouth has **rail** connections from most parts of Britain,
and regular direct daytime services from London. From Exeter, sit on
the left-hand side for an exceptionally scenic stretch along the shores of
the Exe and Teign estuaries. Locally, the Tamar Valley line covers the

15 miles between Plymouth and Gunnislake. Countrywide **buses** and long-distance National Express **coaches** serve Plymouth, often with a change at Exeter, and there's a good network of local buses. Try to avoid lingering at Plymouth's Bretonside bus station; it's deeply unappealing.

CYCLING

The Tamar valley offers great **cycling** possibilities, from moorland on Dartmoor's fringes to the deep lanes near the river. The largely traffic-free **Plym Valley Cycle Trail** has now been linked with **Drake's Trail** (and the whole route is now more commonly known as Drake's Trail) to provide a scenic cycling route between Plymouth and Tavistock (21 miles). It can be justifiably claimed to be one of the best cycle routes in the county; see ⌁ www.drakestrail.co.uk. Part of the Devon coast-to-coast route, the original Plym Valley section runs for seven miles along an old railway line from Plymouth to Clearbrook near Yelverton. The ride begins at Laira Bridge or Marsh Mills, where the Plym Valley Railway is being restored. It follows the Plym estuary past Saltram House and through bat-hung tunnels, ferny railway cuttings and shady woodland, then on to Bickleigh Vale and Clearbrook. From there you're ideally placed to explore the Tamar valley and Bere peninsula. Continuing on to Tavistock, the trail mostly follows a disused railway line, with some spectacular views from the new viaduct (Glen Bridge) and then down to this ancient town.

Bikes can be hired from **Plymouth Cycle Scene** (✆ 01752 257701 ⌁ plymouthcyclescene.co.uk).

WALKING

The most rewarding named walking trail in the area is the **Tamar Valley Discovery Trail**, a 35-mile route from Tamerton Foliot, on the outskirts of Plymouth, ending up at Launceston in Cornwall (leaving Devon as it crosses the River Tamar to Calstock); the first part can be walked only between February and September since it uses some permissive paths which are closed in winter. If you're starting from Tamerton, check the tide table beforehand: you'll be crossing the Tavy at Lopwell Dam by a causeway, and it's above water only for two hours each side of low tide. Some people prefer to start at the Lopwell Nature Reserve where there is plenty of parking space. Once on the Bere peninsula you can follow the trail (its apple logo reminds us of the fruit grown in this area) as it skirts the east bank of the Tamar, or choose any of the little lanes that confound car drivers entering this cul-de-sac. And since you're right on the Cornish border, it's highly tempting to stray out of Devon by taking the foot passenger ferry across the estuary from Plymouth to **Cremyll** in Cornwall: from there the peninsula offers wonderful walking, along the coast path to the remarkably unspoilt conjoined villages of Kingsand and Cawsand, and on to Rame Head; or wander at will through **Mount Edgcumbe Country Park** (where there's free access).

1   PLYMOUTH

Cities aren't generally 'Slow', but big bustling Plymouth does have its gentler side. It also has probably the most spectacular location of any British coastal city: at dusk, looking seaward from the historic Hoe, it's easy to imagine great high-masted ships turning gently at anchor in the bay, their sails curving to some ancient evening breeze. Sir Francis Drake sailed from here, along with Raleigh, Grenville, Hawkins and so many other Elizabethan seafarers; the Pilgrim Fathers finally set off for their 'promised land' from here, and England's

"At dusk, it's easy to imagine great high-masted ships turning gently at anchor in the bay, their sails curving to some ancient evening breeze."

battle-fleet of galleons sailed from the harbour to defeat the Spanish Armada. Captain James Cook began his voyage around the world here, in 1772, as did Sir Francis Chichester in 1966.

Today's cosmopolitan city originated as the 'littel fishe towne' of Sutton, owned by the monks of Plympton Priory until the 15th century.

---

i   **TOURIST INFORMATION**

Plymouth Tourist Information Centre 3–5 The Barbican (opposite Mayflower Steps) ✆ 01752 306330 ◌ www.visitplymouth.co.uk. Open daily Apr–Oct, Mon–Sat Nov–Mar. Also see ◌ www.goplymouth.co.uk.

Its deep harbour (still known as Sutton Harbour) offered safe anchorage to the English fleet during the Hundred Years' War. In 1439 it became the first town in England to receive its charter by Act of Parliament, and it was a prosperous naval and trading centre in Elizabethan times. The Royal Naval Dockyard at next-door Devonport was completed in 1698 and brought further prosperity to the town. Stroll around Plymouth and you're strolling through history.

Severe bombing during World War II destroyed some 20,000 buildings, including 100 pubs, 42 churches and 24 schools, so massive post-war reconstruction took place. This introduced some characterless architecture but also reduced congestion; enough old buildings remain or have been restored, and Plymouth has more listed post-war buildings than any British city except London. The centre feels spacious: wide, traffic-free Armada Way stretches from near the railway station down to the Hoe, studded with gardens, benches, pavement cafés and small shops, while the historic Barbican area retains strong echoes of its Elizabethan past. You might not want to spend a night here, but it shouldn't be neglected.

GETTING AROUND THE CITY

Plymouth has several **car parks** but they do get busy. Three **Park and Ride** bus services run from the outskirts (Coypool near Marsh Mills roundabout off the A38, the George Junction near Derriford in Tavistock Road, and Milehouse by Plymouth Argyle Football Club) to the city centre, linking with the very convenient network of **Citybuses** (✆ www.plymouthbus.co.uk). Bus maps are available from the Tourist Information Centre and bus station. In terms of bus routes, 'city centre' generally means Royal Parade.

For a quick chuff on a **heritage steam train** – possibly pulled by a little red engine named Albert – check out the Plym Valley Railway (Marsh Mills Station, Coypool Rd, PL7 4NW ✆ www.plymrail.co.uk), which runs on the rebuilt 1½-mile stretch of line between Marsh Mills (opposite the Coypool Park and Ride) and Plym Bridge. Passenger trains operate on selected dates.

You might well not choose to **cycle** around Plymouth, although the Plymouth City Council encourages it and has produced a leaflet *Enjoy Plymouth by Bicycle*. Maps and information are available on ✆ www.plymouth.gov.uk; click on *walking and cycling* under *transport and roads* and follow the links.

Various designated **walks** cover the main points of interest; leaflets are available from the Tourist Information Centre. The interesting places are pretty much all within walking distance of each other and the steepest hill you'll need to climb is up from the Barbican to either the Hoe or the centre.

2 THE BARBICAN

The surviving cobbled streets and quaysides of the Barbican were the heart of ancient Plymouth, stamping ground of sea captains, sailors, merchants and even pirates. Now speciality shops, workshops and restaurants jostle together among the old port buildings and alleyways. Pause at a café, and you could be sipping your coffee on the spot where Elizabethan explorers planned their next voyage over a glass or three of fine French brandy.

Secondhand bookshops are bursting at the seams with literary temptations; the Tudor House in New Street, built in 1599, sells Liberty prints; while the Parade Antiques and Curios Museum (also in New Street) has a mass of improbable memorabilia. There's a button emporium, a Tuck Box with old-fashioned sweeties, baby clothes, jewellery, competing varieties of Devon and Cornwall ice cream, various galleries displaying local art and crafts, a huge branch of the Edinburgh Woollen Mill – and lots more.

At 60 Southside Street is the **Black Friars Distillery**, the working home of Plymouth Gin since 1793 and before that a private home and even a debtors' prison. Tours will take you through the gin-making process and you can sample it in the striking refectory bar, said to be where the Pilgrim Fathers spent their last night before embarking on the *Mayflower*. The Barbican Kitchen Brasserie is here: see page 137.

The **Mayflower Steps** are reputedly close to the spot where the Pilgrim Fathers started their voyage, and the **Mayflower Exhibition** in the Tourist Information Centre building opposite tells the story of the ship, the harbour, and the people who have lived and worked there down the ages. Most fascinating are facsimile pages from William Bradford's original handwritten journal, *Of Plimoth Plantation*, written between 1630 and 1647; the history of the first 30 years of the colony, it's the single most complete authority for the Pilgrims' story and the original was a great treasure. And if, on the quay nearby, you should spot a giant prawn clinging to the top of a pillar – it's actually supposed to be a sea monster, representing the Barbican's rich maritime history. On the base of the pillar are descriptions of other sea creatures.

The **National Marine Aquarium** (✆ 08448 937938 ⊕ www.national-aquarium.co.uk; open year-round), across a small footbridge from the Barbican, is the UK's largest and the first to be set up solely for purposes of education, conservation and research. It acted as an adviser to the

BBC's 'Blue Planet' TV series, among other productions. The realistic habitats on view start with the sea life of Plymouth Sound (there's more than you'd think, including sharks and octopus) and then the British Isles; move on (in the deepest aquarium tank in the UK) to the Atlantic Ocean; and finish with the Blue Planet, introducing the most eye-catching marine animals from around the world. The number 25 bus stops nearby. If you've come by bus or train (it's a 20-minute walk from the station), show your ticket and you'll get 10% off the entrance fee. By car, follow the brown signs or key PL4 0DX into your Satnav.

AROUND THE CITY

Of other historic attractions, the **Merchant's House** just up from the Barbican area is Plymouth's largest and finest 16th-century home. It was 'modernised' in the early 17th century by seafaring adventurer William Parker, who later became Mayor of Plymouth; he'd raided the Spanish treasure fleet in the Caribbean in the 1590s, which no doubt helped to pay for the work. The seven rooms each have a specific period theme – for example one is a pre-war chemist's shop, another a Victorian schoolroom. **The Elizabethan House**, with its low ceilings and creaky sloping floors, was the home of some Elizabethan sea captain or merchant; the rooms have been atmospherically restored to recreate the conditions of the time. Nearer to the railway and bus stations, the impressive **City Museum and Art Gallery** (✆ 01752 304774 ⌂ www.plymouthmuseum.gov.uk; open Tue–Sat) in Drake Circus has 11 galleries ranging from Maritime Plymouth (of course!) through porcelain, sculpture, silverware, natural history and 'Artists of St Ives and the South West' (including Dame Barbara Hepworth). There's a small tribute wall to Beryl Cook, one of Plymouth's best-loved artists.

For market fans, **Plymouth City Market** at Frankfurt Gate (closed Sundays) has a mass of family-run stalls selling everything from Devon lamb, fresh vegetables, pasties and locally caught fish to household goods, clothes, crafts and toys. Many of the food stalls have the label 'own grown'. A **farmers' market** with yet more fresh local produce is held in Armada Way's Piazza, on the second and fourth Saturdays of the month.

3 ST ANDREW'S CHURCH

This minster church dates in its present form from the 15th century, although there's evidence of a Christian community there since the 8th century and the first vicar, Ealphage, was named in 1087. Elizabethan seafarers including Drake, Grenville and Hawkins worshipped there, as did Catherine of Aragon and (it is said) both Charles I and Charles II. War is no respecter of history, however, and two nights of heavy bombing in 1941 left it a burnt-out shell. The next morning, a local schoolmistress placed a wooden board over the north door with the inscription *RESURGAM*, meaning *I will rise again*. For some years it remained a roofless 'garden church' with services held in the open air, but then was indeed rebuilt, with stained-glass windows in gloriously rich colours designed by John Piper. On the feast-day of St Andrew in 1957 a moving service of reconsecration was held, attended by around 2,000 people. Imagine the singing, echoing up into the new roof!

"Elizabethan seafarers including Drake, Grenville and Hawkins worshipped there, as did Catherine of Aragon."

St Andrew's is peaceful and lovingly cared for, its size is impressive, and it has good displays illustrating its past. No historically interesting architecture remains, but some of the surviving (or restored) old monuments have enjoyable inscriptions. Look out for the 1665 one to Mrs Mary Sparke, starting 'Life's but a Sparke...'

Behind St Andrew's is the **Prysten House**, dating from 1498; it was built by Thomas Yogg or Yogge, a wealthy merchant involved in the French wine trade. 'Prysten' (priest's) seems to have been a misnomer attributed to the house in the 19th century. At the time of writing it's not regularly open; ask in the church about seeing inside. Next to the church in Royal Parade, the impressive **Guildhall** with its tall, landmark tower is a relative newcomer: completed in 1874 and then restored after bomb damage sustained in World War II. If you like neo-gothic carvings, it has them aplenty.

4 PLYMOUTH HOE

Plymouth's must-visit attraction is of course the historic **Hoe** (the name comes from a Saxon word meaning *high place*), where Sir Francis Drake is said to have been playing bowls when told of the approach of the Spanish Armada. When I was there on a sunny autumn day, people were strolling, walking their dogs, flying kites, picnicking on the grass, and gazing out across Plymouth Sound from helpfully placed benches. The large island in the bay is now known as Drake's Island; it isn't open to the public, but the various harbour cruises (see page 140) will take you past and tell you about its history.

The **Citadel** at the Hoe's eastern end, with massive 70-foot walls, was built in 1665 by Charles II and remained England's most important coastal defence for around 100 years. Today it's used by the military but tours are available from March to September. **Smeaton's Tower**, 72 feet high, was built in 1759 as the Eddystone lighthouse, but was moved (apart from its base) from the Eddystone rock to the Hoe in the 1880s because of sea erosion. Its interior has been restored and is open to visitors (Tue–Sat, year-round). From 1937 until decimalisation, its image appeared behind Britannia on the English penny coin.

The Hoe has various **war memorials**: the large naval memorial, in Portland stone, contains dozens of plain, neatly lettered bronze panels recording the names of the 22,443 (yes, that many) men and women of the Commonwealth navies who lost their lives at sea during both World Wars.

At the seaward end of the Hoe thrusting out into Plymouth Sound is the huge Art Deco lido, the **Tinside Pool** (✆ 01752 261915 🖱 www.plymouth.gov.uk/tinsidelido; open May–Sep), a wonderful place to swim, in natural salt water with the wide harbour views all around you. To its east, between the Hoe and the Barbican, is a small, shingly beach, as well as the possibility of swimming off the rocks.

5 ROYAL WILLIAM YARD

This is a fascinating area, towards the western end of the waterfront; formerly the old Royal Naval victualling yard, built to supply the Navy with everything from gunpowder to rum and ship's biscuits, it has been opened for development and the majestic old buildings in their waterfront surroundings are now accessible. It would have been named the Royal George Yard, but George IV died of dropsy and cirrhosis in 1830 five years before its completion and was succeeded by his brother William IV. In olden times it was a strictly secret area, its storehouses and manufacturing areas closed to the public eye. Then, up to 100 bullocks could be killed in a day at the slaughterhouse to provide the naval rations of salt beef; the Mills Bakery with its 12 giant ovens and heavy millstones could produce 20,000 loaves of bread daily and the brewhouse (in fact used to store rum) 137,000 litres of beer.

Barrels used to store the mass of food and drink on board ship were made there in the Cooperage – which over the next year or so will be transformed into Ocean Studios, with space for 100 artists, in a £3.2-million makeover. It's an exciting project for Plymouth and for art in the South West. Cafés, galleries, boutiques, offices and other enterprises are already opening in the imposing buildings, and diners spill out colourfully on to the once silent quaysides. In summer there's an **open-air food market** on The Green on the first Sunday of the month, with 30-odd local producers participating.

Royal William Yard is about a 20-minute walk from Royal Parade, it's served by Citybus 34, and there's a central parking area.

ANNUAL EVENTS

These include a half-marathon and Lord Mayor's Day in May, the spectacular British Firework Championships in August and 'Meet the Navy' days in September. The recently refurbished **Theatre Royal** (✆ 01752 267222 ⁂ www.theatreroyal.com) hosts shows from (among others) the National Theatre, Chichester Festival Theatre and Glyndebourne. Main national sporting events (including Wimbledon tennis) are shown on the big screen in the Piazza.

🍴 FOOD & DRINK

England's 17th-largest city – as Plymouth proclaims itself to be – is well stocked with bars, cafés and restaurants. The Barbican, for example, has plenty: just browse, wherever you are.

The two restaurants run by celebrity chefs James and Chris Tanner (of BBC TV's *Saturday Kitchen* and *Ready Steady Cook*, Good Food Channel's *Great Food Live*) have consistently good food focused on local ingredients, some collected for them by their forager. They are the **Barbican Kitchen Brasserie** (✆ 01752 604448 ⁂ www.barbicankitchen.com; open daily) in the Barbican's Black Friars Distillery, and the slightly more pricey **Tanners Restaurant** (✆ 01752 252001 ⁂ www.tannersrestaurant.com; open Tue–Sat, booking recommended) in the Prysten House near St Andrew's Church. Very different in style is **Platters** in the Barbican (✆ 01752 227262), a deservedly popular, unpretentious restaurant known for its good, very fresh seafood. The chips are good too, and look for the 'catch of the day' specials straight from the bay. Tables can get crowded at peak times.

A new leisure and eating area emerging in Plymouth is at the historic **Royal William Yard**, where new shops, galleries, offices and other enterprises are mushrooming fast. It's *the* place to go. It has a central parking area, and is served by Citybus 34 from Royal Parade. There will be more fooderies open by the time you read this; meanwhile **Prezzo** (✆ 01752 261120) and the **Seco Lounge** (✆ 01752 229375) in the old Mills Bakery are both lively places where you can sit either inside or out on the quayside, although the staff initially seemed a bit overwhelmed by their popularity. The **Royal William Bakery** (✆ 01752 265448) has wonderfully fresh bread – the smell draws you in – plus self-service breakfasts and main meals which you eat at long wooden tables. The **River Cottage Canteen** (✆ 01752 252702 ⏱ www.rivercottage.net/canteens/plymouth), on the quayside in the old Brewhouse building (what better place for a restaurant?), is a brilliant extension of Hugh Fearnley-Whittingstall's original River Cottage Canteen in Axminster. The dining area feels brighter and more spacious than Axminster's, while the shop and deli have all manner of local foods, drinks, books, ceramics and so forth. If you don't want a full meal, you could just enjoy a coffee and some home baking on the large outdoor terrace, looking across the Sound to Cornwall. Hugh's commitment to good,

SIR FRANCIS DRAKE

Born around 1540 in a small leasehold farmstead near Tavistock, the young Francis Drake first 'went to sea' some ten years later when his parents travelled by boat from Plymouth to Kent, and found lodging in one of the old hulks moored in the Medway estuary near Chatham. The youngster was now surrounded by maritime life, from small fishing and cargo vessels to the towering men-o'-war in the naval dockyard. In his teens he was apprenticed to the captain of a small merchant boat trading across the channel, and inherited her some years later when her owner died. His cousin, the wealthy Plymouth ship-owner John Hawkins, had set up lucrative trading links with the New World; seizing the opportunity, Drake sold his boat and enlisted in his cousin's fleet.

In 1569 Drake married his first wife, Mary Newman, in Devonport's St Budeaux Church. She came from nearby Saltash in Cornwall, where her restored 15th-century cottage can be visited.

Drake's father Edmund, a farmer, was an ardent Protestant lay preacher in turbulent religious times, so the young Francis probably acquired strong anti-Catholic attitudes. He encountered (Catholic) Spaniards on a voyage to the West Indies and the contact wasn't friendly; dislike turned to hatred after a Spanish attack in 1568 in which three English ships were lost. From then on, he sought revenge against Spain.

With the Queen's blessing, he became a thoroughly successful pirate, capturing Spanish vessels and bringing home rich spoils. In 1577 he embarked on his famous circumnavigation of the globe (pausing to raid the Spanish harbours in Cuba and Peru on the way); he then claimed California for England, arranged a treaty with the sultan of the Moluccas for the trading of spices, sailed home with a glittering amount of treasure – and was knighted. He also became Mayor of Plymouth and bought himself Buckland Abbey, as well as other manors and businesses. Never reticent about his abilities, he entered parliament, as MP for Bossiney in Cornwall.

In 1585 the Queen sent him off – to his delight – to raid Spanish settlements in the Caribbean. The Spaniards prepared to counter-attack, but in 1587 Drake sailed into Sir Francis Drake Cadiz harbour sustainable food is already well known: vegetables from within 50 miles of Plymouth, meat organically reared, seafood from the local daily catch and other nearby ethical sources. All dishes are prepared on the spot by the River Cottage team of chefs, and the names of favourite local suppliers are chalked up on a board. More than that, it all tastes good! Last time I was there the menu (which changes daily) included grilled local sardines, Portland crab, duck leg, pan-roasted pollock and slow-cooked pork. In fact it's a perfect 'marriage': a spacious and eye-catching location for the Canteen, and quality dining for Plymouth. Booking is recommended.

and did immense damage, 'singeing the King of Spain's beard'. Spain retaliated the following year with its Armada, a massive fighting force of 151 warships and almost 30,000 men. The high-born Lord Thomas Howard was appointed Admiral of the English fleet, the lowlier but more flamboyant Drake a Vice-Admiral. For almost a week fierce battles raged along the English Channel. In a nutshell, England outmanoeuvred the Spaniards, 'drummed 'em up the channel' and routed them, to huge popular acclaim.

Drake was lauded in prose and poetry, and souvenir-makers had a field day. However, his star was waning and his final voyage was a failure. He had set off from England to Panama in August 1595, with a fleet of 26 ships, hoping to take Panama city for the Queen; but the Spanish force proved too strong. While retreating, Drake contracted dysentery and died; he was buried at sea, off Panama. It was a sadly inglorious end for a sailor and adventurer who had made a lasting contribution to the England of his day.

To the public Drake was a hero; to his peers less so. An arrogant, flamboyant, self-made man of relatively lowly birth, he was looked down on by some sectors of the aristocracy.

He was a favourite of the Queen and revelled in his glittering social status, yet one of his main land-based undertakings was the very practical construction of a leat (channel) to bring fresh water to Plymouth from the River Meavy. An old legend tells that he rode off to Dartmoor and searched until he found a suitable spring, then turned his horse about, spoke some magic words to the spring, and galloped back to Plymouth with it bubbling along obediently behind him. Such was his popular image.

Queen Elizabeth called him 'my pirate', a Spanish ambassador called him 'the master-thief of the unknown world', and the Elizabethan historian John Stow wrote 'He was more skilful in all points of navigation than any'. Tristram Risdon, writing 20 years or so after Drake's death, went even further: 'Could my pen as ably describe his worth as my heart prompteth to it, I would make this day-star appear at noon day as doth the full moon at midnight.' And reputedly he also played a mean game of bowls.

PLYMOUTH FROM THE WATER

Various boat trips and ferries enable you to experience Plymouth from the sea, and it's a very pleasant way of spending an hour or more. The Torpoint Ferry is the only ferry that carries cars.

CRUISES

Plymouth Boat Trips Commercial Wharf ✆ 01752 253153 or 07971 208381 ⌂ www.plymouthboattrips.co.uk. Using boats of various sizes, this company offers short and longer fishing trips, also harbour, wildlife and eco cruises including to Mount Edgcumbe Country Park. After the longer fishing trips you can have your catch cooked and eat it at the Boathouse Café on Commercial Wharf (⌂ www.theboathousecafe.co.uk). The scenic Calstock Cruise (see box, opposite) takes you past the Dockyard and Brunel's rail bridge, and up through the leafy Tamar valley to visit Calstock. Dockyard and Warship Cruises show you Plymouth Sound (including Drake's Island) as well as Devonport Naval Dockyard. In summer there are occasional trips up the River Yealm and to Morwellham Quay.

FERRIES

Cawsand Ferry ✆ 01752 253153 and 07971 208381 ⌂ www.cawsandferry.com. Run by Plymouth Boat Trips (above), this service carries people, prams, bicycles and dogs between the Barbican and the beach beside the strikingly unspoilt Cornish village of Cawsand on the Rame peninsula.

Cremyll Ferry ✆ 07746 199508 ⌂ www.cremyll-ferry.co.uk. An eight-minute trip between Admiral's Hard in Plymouth and Mount Edgcumbe in Cornwall, carrying passengers, bicycles, small packages – and walkers on the South West Coast Path. There's thought to have been a ferry here since 1204. Admiral's Hard is near the Royal William Yard, reached via Citybus 34 from Royal Parade.

Royal William Yard Ferry ✆ 07979 152008 ⌂ royalwilliamyardharbour.co.uk. Runs daily between the Barbican (near the Tourist Information Centre) and Royal William Yard, with good views of Plymouth's waterfront.

Tamar Passenger Ferry ✆ 01822 833331. This small seasonal passenger ferry (Apr to late Sep) links the attractive riverside village of Calstock with the National Trust's historic Cotehele Quay in Cornwall. It's useful for walkers on the Tamar Valley Discovery Trail. Check beforehand if and when it's running.

Torpoint Ferry ✆ 01752 812233 ⌂ www.plymouth.gov.uk/torpointferry. This large car ferry, running across the Tamar between Plymouth and Torpoint in Cornwall, also takes buses and lorries. It's a regular, 24-hour, daily, all-year service, with ferries only ten minutes apart at peak times.

THE TAMAR ESTUARY: A GUIDE FOR BIRDERS

Tony Soper

Sailing from Phoenix Wharf on the four-hour Calstock Cruise offered by Plymouth Boat Trips will reveal the astonishing variety of scenery and birdlife on the Tamar estuary. These are general-interest cruises, so if you're a birder don't forget your field guide and, whatever your interest, binoculars are highly desirable.

As you pass the imposing Citadel and see the grassy expanse of the Hoe, the sheltered anchorage of Plymouth Sound opens on your port hand. Maybe you'll spot a fleet of racing dinghies or yachts; certainly there will be some naval warships or auxiliaries, for you are about to enter the Hamoaze, the deepwater anchorage that serves the Naval Base. Check the upper rigging of any laid-up vessels, for cormorants delight in colonising ships that sit here for more than a season or two. This part of the trip showcases the marine industrial history of the city, from its 18th-century slips and dry-docks to the nuclear facility.

The twin suspension bridges mark the beginning of the wildlife-rich middle section of the estuary. As you work up on the rising tide there will be exposed mudflats on either side. Shorebirds with short legs probe the soft mud for lugworms and assorted invertebrates, those with long legs wade in the shallows and pounce or sweep for shrimps. It's along these wet mudscapes that the elegant avocets show up in early winter.

In early summer parties of young shelducks hoover their way across the mud, finding sustenance in the uncountable numbers of tiny Hydrobia snails. Herons, jealously guarding the riparian rights to their allotted stretch of foreshore, stand knee-deep in water and wait patiently for the fish to come to them. Cormorants jack-knife to chase an eel or a flatfish on the muddy bottom. As the tide rises and covers the mud, the birds find a safe roosting place ashore until the ebb reveals their hunting grounds again. The herons, solitary fishermen, now enjoy some sociable company. Check the waterside trees as you sail higher into the narrower reaches to find a communal cormorant roost. And at each end of the summer comes the time when an osprey, passing by on migration, may stop for a week or two to plunge for a takeaway mullet.

The upper reaches of the tidal Tamar offer fine reed beds, alive in summer with the chatter of warblers. There will be otters here as well, but you'll be lucky to see one. Devonians call them 'dim articles', a reference to their invisibility not their intelligence. And around the Cotehele bend at last you reach the waterside village of Calstock. There's time to stretch your legs ashore and go for a cream tea before your return down a high-water scene, totally transformed from that of the upward journey.

Incidentally, if you want to be a proper Devonian please say Tamar as 'tamer'!

AROUND PLYMOUTH

6 SALTRAM

Plympton, near Plymouth PL7 1UH ☎ 01752 333500; National Trust; house opening hours are very limited; grounds open seasonally.

The park around Saltram, perched high above the River Plym on the outskirts of Plymouth, is one of the city's valuable 'green spaces'. Citybus 22 from Plymouth will drop you at Merafield Road half a mile away; cycle path NCN27 and the West Devon Way run along the bank of the Plym (in the park) from Plymouth's Laira Bridge. There's a spacious car park.

The magnificent Georgian **house** – it played the part of the Dashwoods' home, Norland Park, in the film of *Sense and Sensibility* – has exquisite Robert Adam interiors, original furnishings and fascinating collections of art and memorabilia. It has been the home of the Parker family for 300 years and one-time owner Lord Boringdon was a close friend of Sir Joshua Reynolds, so naturally the latter's paintings are featured.

The striking landscaped **gardens** attached to the house are dotted with follies and a fine array of shrubs and trees, but the real delight is the surrounding **park**: open daily from dawn to dusk and offering a range of walks, cycle rides and gentle strolls, whether inland or along the river. Maps are available from reception or you can follow your nose and the signs. Dogs are allowed in the woods and parkland.

The **Chapel Gallery** has local arts and crafts, and the **Park Restaurant** serves a good choice of local and seasonal food.

7 DARTMOOR ZOO

PL7 5DG ☎ 01753 837645 ◌ www.dartmoorzoo.org. Bus Target 59 from Plymouth's Royal Parade, but not all that frequently; check times with Target Travel ☎ 01752 242000 ◌ www.targettravel.co.uk.

Only five miles from Plymouth near the village of Sparkwell, via a turning off the A38, this small zoo was the subject of the book *We Bought a Zoo* by Benjamin Mee, subsequently turned into a Hollywood film of the same name starring Matt Damon and Scarlett Johansson. It's a pleasantly laid-back place, and the helpful staff are happy to talk to visitors about the animals – which seem relaxed and well-cared-for.

Quite a bit of walking is involved as the enclosures have plenty of space between them; also it's a stiffish uphill walk from the car park, although the compensation is a good view of a family group of capybaras when you're halfway up. There's disabled parking at the top. As well as the smaller animals (including meerkats and several reptiles and amphibians) there are big cats, bears, lynx, wolves, tapirs, reindeer and ostriches. Regular events are held each day (feeding time, talks, close encounters and so on) and are listed on a board at the entrance. There's generally plenty for children to enjoy; and the education department also works with schools, spreading the message of conservation. The Jaguar Restaurant serves hot and cold meals and snacks.

8 WEMBURY

Wembury's **beach** is the perfect seaside escape. With shale/shingle at high tide and a wide expanse of sand at low tide, it offers safe, clean bathing and paddling as well as surfing. Views are stunning, of sea and cliffs. Rock-pool browsing may reveal sea anemones, starfish, crabs, shrimps, limpets, tiny fish, variously coloured seaweed and more; beach-combing should yield several varieties of shells, including cowries and blue-rayed limpets. By the beach are a café, a small Marine Conservation Centre and a shop selling basic beachy things. From Plymouth, bus 48 goes to Wembury village, a short walk from the beach, or you can follow the South West Coast Path from Bovisand in the west or (via a summer ferry) Newton Ferrers and Noss Mayo in the east. For drivers, there are car parks outside St Werburgh's Church and near the café. The National Trust owns the whole area; Wembury Beach and its surrounding coast and sea are designated a Special Area of Conservation and a Voluntary Marine Conservation Area.

"Rock-pool browsing may reveal sea anemones, starfish, crabs, limpets, variously coloured seaweed and more."

It's a short stroll from the beach out to Wembury Point with spectacular views across the bay and coastline to the historic Mewstone, a tiny triangular island that is now a bird sanctuary but in times gone by was a haunt of local smugglers and a prison.

The **Marine Conservation Centre** (Church Rd ☎ 01752 862538 ⌨ www.wemburymarinecentre.org) nearby is open from roughly Easter to October, with good, family-friendly explanations of flora and fauna, illustrations of local sea life, hands-on exhibits, quizzes and leaflets about nearby attractions. Regular rock-pool rambles are held in the summer; other events and talks are listed on the user-friendly website.

St Werburgh's Church has stood on the cliffside above Wembury for many centuries, looking across the bay towards the Eddystone lighthouse. It's believed there was a Saxon church on the site in the 9th century, but the present one is described as 14th century on a Norman foundation.

The oldest item is the Norman stoup (12th century) inside the north door; there is also a great deal of carved oak, probably from the 16th century. Among interesting memorials, one chattily commemorates 'a most vertuous Pious Charitable Religious Sweet & lovinge Lady Mightily afflicted with a cough & Bigge with child'.

FOOD & DRINK

Lemon Tree Café & Bistro 2 Haye Rd South, Elburton PL9 8HJ ✆ 01752 481117 ⌂ www. lemontreecafe.co.uk. On your way to or from Plymouth, whether by bus or by car, you could stop off at this friendly little place, featured in several successive editions of the *Good Food Guide*. Cooking is loosely Mediterranean-style, using fresh local produce; there's a blackboard listing daily 'specials'. Open Tue–Sat 10.00–12.00 for coffee, 11.30–14.30 for lunch.

Old Mill Café Wembury beach ✆ 01752 863280. In a centuries-old stone mill-house by the beach, with large grindstones as outdoor table-tops and fabulous seaward views. It's open roughly March to October (and some winter weekends) for hot and cold snacks, good home baking and the usual range of drinks.

THE TAMAR VALLEY

For the fruit markets, cherries, pears, and walnuts are raised in great abundance; especially in the township of Beer Ferrers; which is said to send out of it a thousand pounds worth of fruit (including strawberries) annually.

The Rural Economy of the West of England by William Marshall, 1796.

Bere means spit of land, and this peninsula, locked between the Tamar and the Tavy, is less accessible today than it was two hundred or so years ago when ships regularly carried cargoes of fruit down the river to Plymouth. The railway provides the only direct connection between Bere Ferrers, the village near the apex of the triangle, and Plymouth; for car drivers it's a cul-de-sac and they must make a wide detour to Denham Bridge, near Buckland Monachorum, to reach the city, a journey of about twenty miles. This enforced peacefulness means that the walker or cyclist can stroll or pedal the lanes with little danger from cars. It's deservedly one of Devon's Areas of Outstanding Natural Beauty (www.tamarvalley.org.uk).

The Bere peninsula is still a major fruit producer, and walkers will see apple orchards galore, as well as the ever-present river views with clusters of sailing boats. A few centuries back this land between the rivers became valuable for its silver mines; when the silver ran out, lead was discovered. Then, in 1890, the railway arrived and visitors poured in. It is probably quieter now than at any time in its history.

Bere Ferrers has an exceptionally interesting church, a 'Heritage' railway station with displays of memorabilia, and a friendly pub with a beer garden overlooking the Tavy. **Bere Alston** is larger and less picturesque, but has shops where you can buy provisions, and a good pub.

Continuing north, the Tamar remains unbridged, save for the railway, until Gunnislake in Cornwall. The Tavy's first bridge, Denham, opens up the western fringe of Dartmoor and the picturesque village with the grand name, **Buckland Monachorum**. To its south is **Buckland Abbey**.

THE TAMAR VALLEY LINE

This delightful railway, from Plymouth to Gunnislake, is a commuter service with its roots firmly in yesteryear. On its flower-bedecked and old-fashioned stations you must hail the oncoming train by raising your hand; yet it rescues the residents of Bere Ferrers and its surroundings from a long detour by road to reach workplaces in the city.

The Tamar Valley Line is only 15 miles long, but the changing scenery from viaduct to fruit orchards to rivers is always diverting. The summer service is two-hourly, and the Dartmoor Sunday Rover (see page 199) is valid here.

9 BERE FERRERS

The Ferrers were a leading family at the time of the Norman Conquest and Henry de Ferrers was chairman of the Domesday Commission. When he received the Bere estate from Henry II it will have been prime land, situated so close to the river and Plymouth harbour.

The **Church of St Andrew** was built – or rather rebuilt since the tower is earlier – by Sir William de Ferrers, who died in 1280. His monument is one of its treasures. He lies, with his wife Isolda de Cardinham, next to the altar, dressed in chainmail, his bare legs crossed and a shield at his side. Both hands are on his sword, ready to draw. His wife wears a simple robe and on one shoulder is a small, disembodied hand, said to be that of a child although it's hard to see where the arm or body could have been. And the fingers are too long for a child; a mystery.

"This gentleman lies with his body half-turned, his shield over his hands, poised to draw his sword."

The memorial to his father, Sir Reginald, who died in 1194, seems to have been carved by the same sculptor. This gentleman lies with his body half-turned, his shield over his hands which are also poised to draw his sword. His knee raised, he seems ready to leap from his tomb and defend his honour. Sadly both lower legs are missing, as is the lion on which his feet rested, although the paws and curly tail remain.

Another notable feature of the church is the stained glass in the east window, claimed – rightly or wrongly – to be the oldest in the county apart from some in Exeter Cathedral. The window was a gift of William de Ferrers, and one of the lights shows him – or one of his family – holding a model of the church.

Elsewhere St Andrew's has Tudor carved bench ends, the design echoing the shape of the windows, and lots of granite reflecting its proximity to Dartmoor. The screen has gone, as have the saints in the panels, scraped off at the time of the Reformation.

In the graveyard is a sad little tombstone with no name, just 'Cholera 1849'.

¶ FOOD & DRINK

Olde Plough Inn ☎ 01822 840358 🖰 www.oldeploughinn.co.uk. A nicely sited pub next to the church, with a pleasant beer garden. They served us delicious treacle tart at 11.00 in the morning, out of season. Log fires in winter, local guest ales, and occasional live music in the evenings.

THE BERE FERRERS RAIL ACCIDENT

In 1917 ten servicemen from New Zealand were mown down by an express train at Bere Ferrers. The boys – mostly teenagers – had disembarked from their troopship in Plymouth and were *en route* to Salisbury Plain for training. They had been told that when the train made its first stop, at Exeter, two men from each carriage should alight and go to the back of the train to distribute rations. When the train made an unscheduled stop at Bere Ferrers they jumped onto the line and were struck by the Waterloo–Plymouth express. They are commemorated in a little rose garden by the station.

Walking the Tamar Valley Discovery Trail from Bere Ferrers

❄ OS Explorer map 108; start from Bere Ferrers, grid reference SX453635.

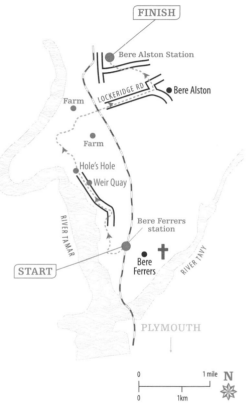

Taking the train to Bere Ferrers and walking to Bere Alston gives you a good overview of the region, with the bonus of a pub at each end. A section of this long-distance trail runs west of Bere Ferrers, across some meadows, and skirts the Tamar (the view of which is often obscured by hedges). You have a choice of path at Liphill Quay; if it has been raining the lower one to the left is very muddy: take the higher. Along a quiet lane you'll pass the intriguingly named Hole's Hole, from where minerals from the Dartmoor mines were shipped, then it's back to the path past orchards and farms to Bere Alston.

The walk takes two to three hours, depending how often you stop. It's not the most beautiful walk in Devon, but pleasant and a handy link between the two villages.

The station is about half a mile north of the town. If you want to continue on the Discovery Trail to Calstock in Cornwall, there's a summer-only pedestrian ferry (✆ 01822 833331) across the Tamar at Ferry Farm a further mile away. You can follow the route on the OS Explorer map 108; also, according to a notice near Bere Ferrers station, details of the area's walks are available from 'outlets in the village'.

10 MORWELLHAM QUAY

Morwellham Quay Tavistock PL19 8JL 📞 01822 832766 🖰 www.morwellham-quay.co.uk.

Morwellham Quay is on the River Tamar, four miles west of Tavistock. When Queen Victoria visited in 1856 she had a dreadful journey; having moored the Royal Yacht at Plymouth she continued up-river in a paddle steamer named *Daisy* – which, by Cotehele, started leaking, so the Queen, Albert and all their children had to switch to another vessel which she described as a 'dirty little thing'. Three carriages were waiting (amid considerable crowds) at Morwellham to take the royal party several miles along small lanes to Endsleigh, to have lunch with the Duke of Bedford. Back at Morwellham after lunch the tide was going out, so small boats (which will have been pretty wet after a massive rainstorm) had to transfer them back to the *Daisy*.

"Looking at the beauty of Morwellham Quay today, it's hard to believe it was known as 'the richest copper port in the Queen's Empire'."

By the time they reached Plymouth the queen had had enough of water; abandoning the Royal Yacht she continued to Southampton by train and thence to Osborne House on the Isle of Wight. Things are somewhat easier now. Morwellham's nearest rail stations are Gunnislake (only three miles) and Calstock. In summer there are buses from Tavistock and Gunnislake. It's a peaceful boat trip up-river from Plymouth, with good views (see page 141); some smaller operators plan eventually to start seasonal river trips so phone Morwellham for latest news of these. By car it's just off the A390 between Tavistock and Gunnislake, and there's masses of free parking space. Or you can cycle.

Looking at the beauty and tranquillity of Morwellham Quay today, it's hard to believe that at the time of Queen Victoria's visit it was known as 'the richest copper port in the Queen's Empire'. Originally built in the 10th to 11th century by the Cistercian monks of Tavistock Abbey, as a means to transport goods and themselves to and from Plymouth, it quickly developed; by the late 12th century ships came to load up with locally mined tin, lead and silver ores. Later, the Industrial Revolution caused a huge demand for metals of all kinds; the hills of west Devon and east Cornwall were rich in tin, lead, copper, arsenic and manganese, and these were shipped via Morwellham to north Wales, with its substantial coal supplies, for smelting. It was said that Morwellham's quayside sometimes held enough arsenic to poison the entire world! A canal was laboriously dug from Tavistock, to facilitate transport.

In 1844 Europe's largest known copper lode was discovered just four miles from the quay, and Morwellham became a busier port than even Liverpool. Vessels from Europe and further afield came to collect their loads of gleaming ore. But – then the copper began to run out. Eventually the company running the mine was forced to close, with huge loss of employment. The Great Western Railway's arrival at Tavistock superseded river transport; the great quays gradually fell silent, machinery rusted and the waterways silted up. After 1,000 years of activity, Morwellham Quay slept. In 1933 the canal was bought by the West Devon Electric Supply Company, and the hydro-electric plant they built there still provides power to the National Grid.

Restoration began in 1970 and UNESCO designated the quay a World Heritage Site in 2006. Nowadays, costumed staff man the quay's exhibits and help to recreate its 19th-century heyday. A riverside tramway carries visitors deep into the heart of the old George and Charlotte copper mine; children can dress up in period costume and join in with period activities such as maypole dancing and rope making; various traditional crafts are demonstrated and the old cottages have been reopened, showing the furnishings of earlier times. The old Assayer's Workshop is there, and the Cooper's Workshop, and the Victorian village school. The 100-year-old ketch *Garlandstone*, built on the Tamar, is moored at the quayside. Echoes of the past are everywhere and staff work hard to bring it alive for visitors. Despite all the displays and demonstrations, it's hard to imagine the hectic buzz and clatter of earlier days when the great machines were turning; there's an enveloping sleepiness about the place. But it's still one of Devon's most unusual, atmospheric and historic sites.

EAST OF THE TAVY

Here we are back on the western edge of Dartmoor, with heather and spacious views only a mile or so away. However, it's still an area of woodland and deep valleys, impregnated with the name of Drake.

11 BUCKLAND MONACHORUM & AREA

The village street is so narrow that you proceed at your peril, but it broadens out at the church and the grand Lady Modyford's School, which she endowed in 1702 with an annual allowance for the schoolmaster of £7.10s.

The church of St Andrew is, at first glance, plain inside with a simple barrel roof, but then you notice the angels. They hang on the horizontal beams, wings half open, merrily playing a range of musical instruments.

"Then you notice the angels. They hang on the horizontal beams, wings half open, merrily playing a range of instruments."

There's a Saxon font, looking like a cottage loaf, and the rather alarming Drake Chapel (not Sir Francis, but descendants of his brother Thomas) to the south of the nave. The huge Gibraltar Memorial to General Elliot, who successfully defended The Rock against Spain in 1779–83, is thickly planted with dead bodies and heroic words. There's no question which side God was on. The general married into the Drake family.

Close to Buckland Monachorum is **The Garden House** (☎ 01822 854769 🖱 www.thegardenhouse.org.uk), a gorgeous mixture of formal and informal gardens. It has a wildflower meadow, an area of South African plants, a glade of acers which blaze red in the autumn, and much more.

Before visiting Buckland Abbey, follow the lane south to the almost inaccessible little village of **Milton Combe**, about two miles from Buckland Monachorum, folded into a ravine like a pressed flower. The white cottages find a footing where they can, a stream runs through it, and the pub stands in the square ready to reward your efforts to get here. It's called the Who'd Have Thought It.

12 YELVERTON

You're likely to drive or cycle through this busy little village or to change buses here. It's thoroughly geared for passing traffic, with its petrol station, supermarket, pub, deli, post office and public toilets. The paperweight museum signposted from the centre is currently closed.

Close by, as you take the main turning towards Buckland Abbey from the A386, you pass the old **RAF Harrowbeer Airfield** (🖱 www. rafharrowbeer.co.uk), now grassed over and scenic with some chunky, Dartmoor-style outcrops of rock. Harrowbeer became operational in 1941 and was an important wartime RAF base; shops in Yelverton's main street had to have their upper storeys removed because of low-flying aircraft. Commemorative events are held annually, and there's an explanatory board at the site. In 1960 there was talk of it becoming Plymouth's airport, but there was strong local opposition and it was eventually demolished.

13 BUCKLAND ABBEY

Yelverton PL20 6EY ☎ 01822 853607; National Trust. Opening times vary seasonally.

'The outside looks like a church but the inside feels like a home' says one of the introductory displays at this peaceful place, and a home is indeed what it became in the hands of Sir Richard Grenville of *Revenge* fame (see pages 152–3). His grandfather (also Richard) had bought the 270-year-old abbey, together with 570 acres of land, from Henry VIII in 1541, but did little to it. Eventually the estate passed to the young Richard, when his father drowned in the sinking of the *Mary Rose*. In the 1570s he began developing it, and decided to make his home in the church itself. He demolished cloisters and monastic buildings on its north side, inserted fireplaces and added a new kitchen wing, as well as dividing the interior into three floors and creating the well-proportioned rooms. The great hall, with its fine plasterwork ceiling and decoration, was completed around 1576. Then in 1581 his money ran out and he sold the whole property – reluctantly, by all accounts – to Sir Francis Drake, who paid for it with some of the spoils from his capture of the Spanish galleon *Nuestra Señora de la Concepcion* off Ecuador in 1579. Drake also owned around 40 other properties and, although he did live there on and off for some 14 years, he made no particular mark on it; but it remained in the Drake family (although with periods of disuse) until 1940 when it was presented to the National Trust. More changes were made by subsequent owners, particularly in the 1770s, although none so dramatic as Grenville's.

"'Great' is inadequate: it's truly massive, with an amazing beamed roof and a huge cider press at one end."

On the way to the house you pass the Great Barn, a relic of the original Cistercian monastery that was founded here in 1278. 'Great' is inadequate: it's truly massive, with an amazing beamed roof and a huge cider press at one end. The spirit of the old monastery is evoked more strongly in this building than elsewhere; cowled monks could well be padding on soft sandalled feet through the shadows, their robes swishing in the dust.

Inside the house, memorabilia and objets d'art are attractively displayed. There are paintings, documents, fine furniture, maps, weapons, ornaments – and of course Drake's drum, which, according to legend, will summon the old swashbuckler back to fight for England if his country ever needs his help. The rooms themselves are attractive too, some with original Tudor panelling and views over the gardens.

SIR RICHARD GRENVILLE (1542–91) & THE *REVENGE*

Historian A L Rowse, in his authoritative biography *Sir Richard Grenville of the 'Revenge'* (Jonathan Cape, 1937), lamented the lack of personal records. The Grenvilles seem to have been careless about such things. Over the years family documents were burned, lost, discarded or destroyed, so that Rowse had to ferret out details at second or third hand.

In 1545 when Grenville was three years old, his father Roger, captain of the *Mary Rose*, was drowned in her dramatic sinking, leaving the toddler as sole heir to his estate. Richard studied at London's Inner Temple, then (aged 24) joined a brief 'crusade' against the Turks who had invaded Hungary. Next he bought land in Ireland and became involved in organising settlements there. He comes across as a somewhat severe character, obstinate and domineering; but a loyal and courageous leader, respected by his peers, although lacking Drake's charm and easy popularity.

Unlike his cousins Humphrey Gilbert and Walter Raleigh, he was not (apart from his father) from a particularly seafaring family, but he hankered after adventure, and in 1574 sought the Queen's permission to seek new lands and treasure south of the equator. For various military and political reasons, it was not granted. He owned ships and financed voyages but spent little time at sea, until in 1585 he was offered command of a voyage carrying 100 settlers to today's North Carolina, newly acquired for the crown by Raleigh. He embraced this new maritime career, for 'the pleasure of God on the seas', but it proved short-lived, as other commitments then kept him at home for several years. He was still involved in Ireland, and was a commissioner for the coastal defences of Devon and Cornwall.

One of the paintings shows the surrender of the *Nuestra Señora del Rosario* (see pages 54–6). The cavernous old kitchen gives some idea of the scale of the feasting, with space enough for cooks to handle whole carcases of meat. The Refectory Restaurant/Tearoom in the grounds uses somewhat more modern equipment! Outside there are also craft workshops, a secondhand book store and even a Letterboxing Trail.

There's a full, year-round programme of events, including several for children, from bluebell and woodland walks to charcoal making, weaving, storytelling, concerts and historical re-enactments – and of course presentations of Sir Francis Drake in all his aspects. Poor old Grenville is much less remembered.

Finally, in 1591, came his finest hour. Captaining the *Revenge*, he was second in command (under Lord Thomas Howard) of a small squadron sent to tackle Spanish treasure ships off the Azores. The superior Spanish fleet caught them by surprise when they were at anchor; Howard ordered his ships to flee to safety but Grenville lagged behind to pick up crew who were ashore ('waiting to recover the men that were upon the Island that had otherwise bene lost', wrote Raleigh later in his *Report of the Trueth of the fight about the Isles of the Açores*). He then tried to run the *Revenge* forward through the 15 advancing Spaniards but the great ships blocked his way and his wind. Still he could have escaped by turning tail but 'Sir Richard utterly refused to turne from the enemie, alleaging that hee would rather choose to die, than to dishonour himselfe, his countrey, and her Majesties shippe'. An astonishing 15-hour battle then raged, the little *Revenge* firing fiercely into the Spanish galleons and fighting their men hand-to-hand when they swarmed aboard. By dawn next day she had no resources left: her masts and rigging had been shot away and she was badly holed. Sir Richard, grievously wounded, called on his gunner to sink her rather than let her fall into Spanish hands; but his seamen struck a bargain with the Spaniards, deserted their captain and surrendered. Sir Richard was taken to the Spanish flagship *San Pablo*, where he later died.

As the *Revenge* – a considerable prize – was being towed back to Spain, 'the water began to heave and the weather to moan' and a fearful storm arose. The *Revenge* was smashed on to rocks and broke apart, and many Spanish ships and men were also lost. Confrontation had turned to tragedy: there was no prize for the King of Spain, painful loss for the Spaniards, and Sir Richard Grenville passed into heroic history.

With its variety of attractions, Buckland Abbey is a place for all seasons – and for all weathers too, since you'll be well sheltered inside the house on a rainy day.

If you don't want to visit the house itself, for a reduced entrance fee you can just park and stroll around the grounds: meadows, orchards, and four woodland walks along the River Tavy. Visitors with restricted mobility can arrange to hire Trampers, neat little off-road mobility scooters, to help them get around the grounds. From Plymouth there's a **bus**, the 48, on Sunday only; on weekdays you'll need the 55 from Yelverton, which you can reach from Plymouth either by train or by buses 83, 84 and 86. For drivers there's ample parking.

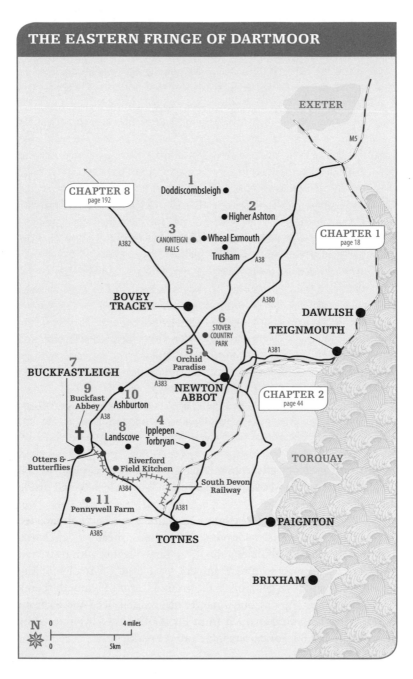

EXETER

M5

CHAPTER 8
page 192

1
Doddiscombsleigh ●

2
● Higher Ashton

3
CANONTEIGN ● ● Wheal Exmouth
FALLS
Trusham ●

A382

A38

CHAPTER 1
page 18

**BOVEY
TRACEY** ●

6
● STOVER
COUNTRY
PARK

A380

DAWLISH ●

TEIGNMOUTH

A381

5
● Orchid
Paradise

**NEWTON
ABBOT**

CHAPTER 2
page 44

7
BUCKFASTLEIGH

A383

9
Buckfast
Abbey

10
● Ashburton

A38

8
● Landscove

4
Ipplepen ●
Torbryan

† Otters &
Butterflies

Riverford
Field Kitchen

South Devon
Railway

TORQUAY

A384

11
● Pennywell Farm

A381

PAIGNTON ●

A385

TOTNES ●

BRIXHAM ●

N
0   4 miles
0   5km

6

THE EASTERN FRINGE OF DARTMOOR

The River Teign turns south at Dunsford, and gives map-makers the eastern border of Dartmoor National Park before its final journey to Kingsteignton and Teignmouth. Although technically some of the towns and villages in this section lie within Dartmoor National Park, their gentler, leafier character fits better here. Along the river are some of the prettiest wooded areas of Dartmoor, splashed by waterfalls, and networked by footpaths and narrow lanes. Not surprisingly, the Teign river gives its name to many places around here, with England's highest waterfall, **Canonteign Falls**, just one of them.

"Along the river are some of the prettiest wooded areas of Dartmoor, splashed by waterfalls, and networked by footpaths and narrow lanes."

The surprising aspect of this area is how remote some of the villages feel despite their proximity to Exeter and Newton Abbot. Try to find your way to **Doddiscombsleigh**, even with a good map, and you'll see what I mean. Within the **Newton Abbot triangle**, formed by the major roads of the area, lies a village lost in time, **Torbryan**, as well as Stover Park with its inspirational **Ted Hughes Trail**. Then there's Buckfastleigh, which draws large numbers of tourists to its various attractions which include the **steam train**, **Buckfast Abbey** and the enchanting miniature pigs at **Pennywell Farm**.

GETTING THERE & AROUND

Drivers will find this one of the most easily accessible regions, with all the places described lying near the A38 from Exeter. It's once you leave that dual carriageway to track down the little villages that you're in trouble without a satnav.

The **bus** service down the A38 is frequent and fast, so it's easy to get from Exeter to Buckfastleigh, and there's a local bus to Doddiscombsleigh, but that's all, unless you plan to supplement bus services with a fair amount of walking. The *Teignbridge* bus timetable covers the area. The cream of the getting-there options is the **steam train** which runs between Totnes and Buckfastleigh. See below.

SOUTH DEVON RAILWAY

This is one of those lovely dollops of nostalgia that Devon is good at. The scenic branch line of the Great Western Railway which runs along the River Dart was axed by Dr Beeching in 1958, but only 11 years later it was reopened – ironically by Dr Beeching himself – and is now run by a charitable trust and operated by volunteers (0843 357 14200 www.southdevonrailway.co.uk).

The line between Totnes and Buckfastleigh is one of the prettiest in the county, following the river closely for most of its seven-mile route. Steam locomotives run between four times and nine times a day in summer (April to October) and on Sundays and occasional weekdays during the other months; diesel locos also operate.

CYCLING & WALKING

This region has no off-road **cycle** paths, and its lanes are typically hilly and narrow, but with a bicycle you could see all its major sights in a day.

Compared with many other areas in this book, this isn't great **walking** country, but still some good possibilities can be devised using the *Teignbridge* bus timetable and the Ordnance Survey Explorer map OL110 (for the north of the region) along with Explorer map OL28. Access to Haytor on Dartmoor is achieved via the **Templer Way** (see page 218), which runs through this region, including Stover Country Park.

THE NORTHERN TEIGN VALLEY

Hidden in the hills of the east side of the Teign are two villages with exceptional churches, Doddiscombsleigh and Higher Ashton, while Canonteign Falls and its nearby mine are more closely associated with the river.

1 DODDISCOMBSLEIGH

This little hidden village attracts both pub crawlers and church crawlers. 'Everybody knows the Nobody' they say, and indeed the **Nobody Inn** has been there for centuries, although prior to the mid 18th century it was a cottage. It's speculated that the mining boom brought enough thirsty customers to the village to merit opening a pub (see listing, page 158). The name evolved from The New Inn to The No Body Inn 'with reference to an unfortunate episode concerning a dead landlord'.

St Michael's Church has been providing spiritual refreshment for even longer: it has the finest medieval stained-glass windows in the county, and the original church probably predates the Norman Conquest. It's built from an aesthetically pleasing mixture of local stone of various colours, including granite from nearby Dartmoor. Inside, the famous windows can be observed at eye level since they and the roof are exceptionally low. This makes it easy for the visitor to appreciate their craftsmanship and imagination, and brings a feeling of intimacy. To quote the *Shell Guide*, 'the artist has looked at men without romanticising but with much charity.'

Indeed. I loved the tired face of St Paul, shielding his right eye with one hand. And also St George's cute little horse, which looks more like a sheep. The saint is killing what appears to be a very large dragon indeed, though it's hard to make out whether we are looking at spines or claws. The most complicated window at the far end of the aisle is more difficult to see, but there are photos on the wall showing the detail.

Another interesting feature of the church is the array of stone floor memorials. There's one to three generations of William Babbs, who all

TOURIST INFORMATION

Ashburton North St (behind Town Hall) ✆ 01364 653426 ⌖ www.ashburton.org
Buckfastleigh 80 Fore St ✆ 01364 644522

THE DEVIL'S BITE

Carved at the top of one of the stone capitals in St Michael's Church, Doddiscombsleigh, is a face. It's not a green man, nor a saint or angel. It has funny pointed ears, unusual foliage, and something strange about its mouth. Dr Michael Tisdall is a medical doctor with a passion for the unusual in Devon churches, so he has teased out the (probable) truth here. This carving is at the west end of the church, often called the Devil's End (indeed, some old churches have a little opening through which the devil can escape during services), and he has a hare lip. As a young doctor studying children's diseases, Dr Tisdall came across the expression 'devil's bite' to describe a hare lip. And the foliage isn't the usual rose leaves, it's *Succisa pratensis*, or Devil's bit scabious. So there we have it. A medieval carver portrayed the Devil in an instantly recognisable form – to the villagers of his day – but for us it takes the detective work of a knowledgeable enthusiast to get to the truth.

lived to a fine old age: 90, 84 and 79. As the church leaflet points out, this stone was clearly carved well after the last William Babb, who was 'endowed with few words but many charitable deeds', died in 1667. The lettering is of a high quality and in excellent condition – despite being on the floor – but it is also mostly spelled in the modern way. So who ordered it to be carved and when?

The church is full of helpful explanations and snippets, including an illuminating explanation of the green man at the top of one of the columns, or capitals, and the very intriguing hare-lipped devil which would escape anyone's notice if it hadn't been pointed out by Dr Michael Tisdall (see box above).

Finally, it's touching to see the 1945 *Table of Fees* for burial services posted on the wall. A posh vault in the churchyard cost £7.17s.0d, while there was no charge for the burial of a still-born infant.

Surprisingly, given the remoteness of this little village, the 360 **bus** from Exeter runs here five times a day, so you can view the church and have lunch at the inn without the worry of either finding the place or parking.

¶¶ FOOD & DRINK

Nobody Inn ☎ 01647 252394. The food at this curiously named place (see page 157) is very good, the nicely traditional interior is great for cold days and there's a large beer garden for the summer.

2 HIGHER ASHTON

About 1½ miles south of Doddiscombsleigh is Higher Ashton. The **Church of St John the Baptist** is renowned for its medieval rood screen, intricately carved to set off the 32 panels with their painted saints. You'll easily identify the well-known saints such as St Sebastian with his arrows, and a baby-faced St George killing a tiny, frightened dragon; the more obscure ones include St Apollonia (see box below) looking speculatively at a huge tooth held in the blacksmith's pincers. There is a conspicuous monument to smug Sir George Chudleigh (1657) who fathered nine sons and nine daughters, and a fascinating commemorative stone embedded in the floor, crudely carved, with September and October written as 7ber and 8ber – the first time I have seen this abbreviation.

ST APOLLONIA & ST BARBARA

It's not clear to me why a woman who had all her teeth smashed with giant tongs becomes the patron saint of dentists. However, she appears on so many Devon rood screens that it's worth knowing something about her.

Apollonia lived in Alexandria in the 3rd century AD. She led an exemplary life, preaching the gospel during a time when this held considerable risks. Emperor Philip was none too keen on Christians, especially those like Apollonia who gave succour to his political prisoners. In AD249 she was arrested and, inevitably, tortured to persuade her to renounce her faith. All her teeth were smashed and then pulled out with iron pincers. When this had no effect her torturers piled up firewood, intending to burn her to death, but she leapt into the flames herself thus presenting the church with a dilemma: did she commit suicide (a crime) or was she a true martyr, dying for her faith? They chose the latter and sanctification.

Devon has 14 depictions of St Apollonia holding her torturer's pincers (the kind used by blacksmiths so not really suitable for dentistry). These are usually on painted rood screens or stained glass but one, in Stokeinteignhead, is carved into a stone capital.

If explosives are your thing, then St Barbara is your patron saint. Possessed of exceptional beauty and intelligence, she was kept locked in a tower by her father who had a rich suitor in mind. Here she converted to Christianity and managed to escape, only to fall into the hands of a shepherd. Before he could have his wicked way with her, divine punishment turned his sheep into beetles. Her father then contrived that she should be paraded naked throughout the region, but God supplied her with a robe. Frustrated, Dad then resorted to a variety of tortures before getting fed up and killing her with his sword, whereupon he was struck dead by a thunderbolt. So St Barbara is now the patron saint of artillerymen and their like.

3 CANONTEIGN FALLS & WHEAL EXMOUTH

Canonteign Falls EX6 7RH ✆ 01647 252434 🖰 www.canonteignfalls.co.uk. No buses run here. It is well signposted from the A38, off the B3193.

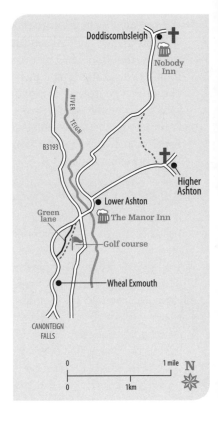

This is one of Devon's superlatives, the highest waterfall in England (220 feet), but it's also man-made which takes the gloss off a bit. Nevertheless it's well worth a visit for the cool, ferny woodland and wildflowers. And for the enterprise of the ten generations of Lords of the Manor who have played their part in creating this tourist attraction. The house is on the site of a monastery owned by the canons of St Mary du Val in Normandy, hence the name Canonteign. After the dissolution of the monasteries it was converted into a manor house which was eventually bought by Admiral Edward Pellew, later Lord Exmouth. His descendants enjoyed a period of prosperity in the 19th century through the nearby lead and silver mines, respectively Frank Mills (named after its owner, a banker) and Wheal Exmouth (see opposite).

In the 1880s the mines fell into decline and the miners found themselves out of a job. But then the third Lady Exmouth stepped in with the idea of putting them to work again by diverting the leat that formerly serviced the mine to create a waterfall tumbling over natural rocks for the enjoyment of family and friends. After World War II there was no money to maintain the waterfall and it, and the nearby paths, became choked with vegetation and virtually disappeared. It was not until 1985 that the tenth Lord Exmouth rediscovered the walk and decided to open it to the public.

In the grounds are a couple of lakes with resident waterfowl, and a gentle path (Grandad's Walk) for those unwilling to tackle the climb up to the falls. The circular walk to Buzzard's View and the top of the falls is well worth the effort, and an Assault Course enables children to work off any excess energy. Helpful labels tell you what you're looking at, and there's a recreation of a Victorian fern garden complete with tree ferns.

To experience the full drama of the next attraction it's best to approach it on foot. Leave your car in the Canonteign car park and turn left at the road. In half a mile you'll come to an astonishing sight: the tall chimneys of the former **Wheal Exmouth** lead mine adjacent to the engine house, now a thoughtfully converted three-storey private home. There are two chimneys, one circular with finely worked corbels, and the other octagonal, topless, and with trees billowing out of its ragged opening instead of smoke. The whole complex is both scenic and historic, spanning the commercial history of the area from mining to 'grand design' conversion.

¶¶ FOOD & DRINK

For a walk ending at a pub, you might like to take the green lane beyond Canonteign Manor, next to the golf course, to the **Manor Inn** at Lower Ashton, set by the river. The walk takes around 20 minutes. For variety when returning to your car there's a footpath that runs parallel to the golf course (left at Byteign Lodge) through woods full of flowers and birdsong. **Cridford Inn** Trusham TQ13 0NR ☎ 01626 853694 ⏁ www.vanillapod-cridfordinn.com. The village (just south of Lower and Upper Ashton) has some thatched cottages and this charming pub (also thatched, and containing what is thought to be Britain's oldest domestic

A WILY PARSON

Parson Harris, who served the parish of Hennock, was known not only for his kindliness and fairness but also for his occasional recourse to a little white magic for the benefit of his flock. One day three fine fat geese were stolen from a farmer named Tuckett; and the following Sunday Parson Harris announced this from the pulpit, declaring also that he had cast a spell on the feathers of the birds so that three of them would stick to the nose of the thief. Immediately he spotted a member of the congregation raise his hand and anxiously touch his nose – so was able confidently to denounce him as the culprit! Other 'spells' that he cast tended to have similarly unmagical outcomes, but still served to impress his parishioners.

window), whose Vanilla Pod restaurant serves seriously good food, if the fishcakes I had are anything to go by. Worth a detour.

The Old Church House Inn Torbryan ✆ 01803 812372 ⊕ www.oldchurchhouseinn.co.uk. The meat served here comes from nearby farms, the fish from Brixham and the vegetables from local growers. This fine old inn is deservedly popular.

THE NEWTON ABBOT TRIANGLE

The A38, A380 and A385 trunk roads form a triangle with **Newton Abbot** roughly in the centre. Although the busy town itself is best avoided unless you have shopping to do (it has a big outdoor market on Wednesdays), there are places here that merit a Slow visit. If you do find yourself in Newton Abbot, perhaps with time to spare in between buses, you could check out its little **museum** in St Paul's Road (✆ 01626 201121 ⊕ www.devonmuseums.net). Open Monday to Saturday from March to late October, it has exhibits relating to (among many others) Isambard Kingdom Brunel, railways and the wreck-salvage pioneer John Lethbridge.

4 IPPLEPEN & TORBRYAN

Ipplepen is a surprisingly dreary village for this appealing area, but if you're nearby is worth visiting for its church: it's huge and has a particularly magnificent rood screen, with inset saints and fan vaulting, and a 15th-century carved and painted pulpit resting on an old millstone. In the graveyard is the tomb of a coachman who took Sir Arthur Conan Doyle around Dartmoor to gain inspiration for a book. The man's name was Baskerville.

The tiny hamlet of **Torbryan** was described by Hoskins in 1954 as having 'perhaps the most uniformly attractive village church in Devon'. What makes Holy Trinity exceptional is that there has been no architectural messing around with its interior since it was built in the 15th century. It has the lime-washed exterior characteristic of Devon, and clear glass windows that let in plenty of light to set off the carved, polychromed screen, said to have been among the best-preserved medieval rood screens in the country. However, tragedy struck in 2013: two painted panels from the oak screen were hacked out roughly by thieves, leaving a gaping hole, and a third was damaged. So far they haven't been traced nor any perpetrator caught. They represented St

Victor of Marseilles and St Margaret of Antioch. Together with many other panel paintings of saints in Devon churches they are reproduced in *A Cloud of Witnesses* by Diane Wilks (see page 10).

Holy Trinity Church has been declared redundant now, and is cared for by the Churches Conservation Trust (the key-holder lives at the farm behind the church); but the outraged reaction of the villagers to the theft shows that they still feel it very much their own. The old church house, dating from the 14th century, has become an inn.

5 ORCHID PARADISE

Forches Cross TQ126PZ   01626 352233   www.orchids.uk.com.

Anyone who loves the variety and beauty of orchids might enjoy a visit to Burnham Nurseries, to which is attached the permanent display that is Orchid Paradise. The 'growing area', housing plants that are for sale, is much larger, with a series of interconnecting greenhouses. One of the great pluses of this small attraction is that it is open seven days a week, all year, and is comfortably warm on a cold day. And dry on a wet day. Also, so I've heard, cool on a hot day, although I haven't had the chance to test that.

6 STOVER COUNTRY PARK

TQ12 6QG   01626 835236   www.devon.gov.uk/stover_country_park.

Whoever thought up the idea of linking poetry with nature in this country park deserves an award. Stover is one of those agreeable places which has 'nothing to see' yet everything to observe. Within its 114 acres it brings you over heathland thick with gorse and heather, through deciduous trees and coniferous forests, along the banks of a river, adjacent to a tumbling stream and around a lake where herons stand sentinel among the reeds. A 100-yard, wheelchair-accessible aerial walkway looks over ponds and woodland. The interpretation boards are informative and the place is child-friendly in the right way.

"Stover is one of those agreeable places which has 'nothing to see' yet everything to observe."

No coloured plastic, just an attention-grabbing introduction to the wonders of nature. The reason I came here, above all the similar country parks in Devon, was for the **Ted Hughes Poetry Trail**. Now I never thought that I particularly liked Ted Hughes. Too gloomy. But at the end of the two hours and 16 poems that it takes to complete the trail,

I was a convert. This was evocative, accessible poetry, fitting perfectly to the location, about birds, fish and animals and the natural world in general. And not a crow in sight. Sadly, because of copyright problems, the centre has not been able to publish a booklet with all the poems, so take your time to enjoy them *in situ*.

The park is 300 yards south of the Drumbridges roundabout on the A382; it's linked by cycle routes to Bovey Tracey and Newton Abbot, and bus 39 (Exeter to Newton Abbot) passes by.

BUCKFASTLEIGH & AREA

7 BUCKFASTLEIGH

Buckfastleigh is a tourist hub which deserves its popularity. It is the terminus/start of the steam train that runs between this town and Totnes, and has otters and butterflies, an abbey, and a restaurant with a difference.

The town's Tourist Information Centre is in Fore Street next to **The Valiant Soldier**, the town's best-known attraction. They call it 'The pub where time was never called'. When the brewery withdrew their licence in 1965 it seems that the landlords simply said 'sod this', locked up, and walked away. Mr and Mrs Roberts continued to live upstairs but, perhaps understandably, since they'd run the pub for 27 years, left their memories intact in the untouched pub area. It was only after the widow Alice Roberts sold the property in the mid 1990s that anyone realised what had happened, and Teignbridge council stepped in and bought the premises. It now offers the older generation a burst of nostalgia, with everything just as it was, including the jumbled attic which has been recreated on a lower, safer floor. The only nostalgia you can't indulge in is an actual pint of bitter.

"The only nostalgia you can't indulge in is an actual pint of bitter."

The South Devon Railway

☎ 0843 3571420 🖰 www.southdevonrailway.co.uk.

Talking of nostalgia, the South Devon Railway has it in dollops. Just a peep through the carriage windows at the compartments brings back a flood of memories to oldies, as does the acrid smell of the steam, and the breathy toot of the whistle. A perfect day out is to leave your car at Buckfastleigh's free car park by the station, and buy a 'triple ticket'. This gives you the 30-minute train ride to Totnes via Staverton plus a visit to Otters & Butterflies and/or the Railway Museum in Buckfastleigh and the Totnes Rare Breeds Farm (see pages 70 and 165). Both animal places are small and owner-run. It doesn't work as well in reverse: in Totnes parking is limited, expensive and some way from the station.

The recently refurbished **Railway Museum** (✆ 0843 3571420; open all year) has all sorts of displays, including Ashley, a steam engine, which shows children – and adults – how a steam train works. One exhibit focuses on Isambard Kingdom Brunel, who decreed that this railway should be broad gauge. The line was later converted to standard gauge, but the only surviving broad-gauge locomotive, Tiny, is here. There is also a description of Brunel's 'atmospheric' railway from Exeter to Newton Abbot: literally atmospheric, since it used air pressure to drive the train (see page 3).

Dartmoor Otters & Buckfast Butterflies (Otters & Butterflies)

Just off A38, about 1 mile from Buckfastleigh; TQ11 0DZ (satnav may take you past the station turn-off so watch out for the signs) ✆ 01364 642916 ⌂ www.ottersandbutterflies. co.uk. Open Apr to end Oct, and some winter weekends.

The butterfly centre was founded in 1984 by David and Sue Field, who added the otter part in 1988 because of the proximity of the river Dart. 'It seemed an obvious thing to use this in some way. Originally we wanted to divert a stream to run through the grounds to create otter pools but this wasn't permitted, so the water is pumped out and in each day so they are swimming in river water.'

Even on a gloomy autumn day there were plenty of eye-catching butterflies in evidence, including my favourite, the brilliant blue Amazonian *morpho*, but Sue told me that they are far more active on bright, warm days. More easily studied are the rows of chrysalises attached to bamboos, showing the range of colours and sizes of these pre-butterflies.

Otters, on the other hand, are completely protected from the elements by their thick, waterproof fur, and are particularly active before feeding times: 11.30, 14.00 and 16.00. There are three species here, North American, Asian short-clawed and British, all displaying different characteristics. The large North American river otters, for instance, are particularly adept at balancing upright, meerkat style. 'That's Toronto,' said Tim, the keeper. 'He's nicknamed Kenwood because he's such an efficient food processor and never gets full.'

Buckfastleigh Caves
William Pengelly Cave Studies Trust Russets Lane, Buckfastleigh TQ11 0DY ☎ 01752 700293
🖰 www.pengellytrust.org.

A visit to the little-known Pengelly Centre is a serious, but highly rewarding, undertaking. Unlike Kents Cavern in Torquay there is no attempt here to provide entertainment – the newly-refurbished museum with its informative displays and the 1½ to 2-hour tour are aimed at adults and bright children who want to know about local history, geology and palaeontology.

Most of the work here is scientific, and volunteers from the William Pengelly Cave Studies Trust are only available to give tours a few times a week, normally Wednesday and Thursday in the summer, so check their website or phone before making plans. Bear in mind too that there is quite a bit of walking along sometimes muddy tracks.

The caves were discovered by local boys exploring the disused quarries in the 1930s. On the floor of one cave they found some bones and took them to the museum in Torquay. 'Nothing of importance – just pigs and cows' they were told. Not satisfied by this explanation, they sent them to the Natural History Museum in Kensington. This time the reaction was quite different, and the area was cordoned off until the experts, who had correctly identified the fossilised bones of elephant, hippopotamus and hyena, could take a look.

These huge animals, all larger than present-day species, thrived in Devon during the warm period that preceded the last ice age – around 130,000 years ago – when the vast continent that contained Britain was in the southern hemisphere.

The tour starts up a nearby green lane with a look at the local history, geology and natural history including a description of the greater horseshoe bats which roost in one of the caves (see box opposite). The nub of the tour is a visit to Joint Mitnor Cave, now easily accessible via a system of boardwalks, where the most exciting finds were made – over 3,000 bones, dug out of the cave floor and walls. Some 120,000 years ago an earthquake opened a hole in the roof of the cavern, and animals fell in.

GREATER HORSESHOE BATS

In Britain, this bat is found only in the southwest of England and in Wales. The colony at the Buckfastleigh Caves is the largest in the UK, and particularly important since this species is in decline. It's a strange-looking animal with its large mobile ears and fleshy 'noseleaf' (looking like a horseshoe, hence its name) which amplifies the bat's calls; it makes these through its nose with its mouth closed, so that it can judge the distance of its prey. These bats have small eyes, but the expression 'blind as a bat' has little truth as bats can see fairly well, although only in black and white. However, in complete darkness they have to rely mainly on their echolocation 'sonar'.

Greater horseshoe bats are among the largest European species of bats, and can live for 30 years. They mate during the autumn but delay fertilisation until they have emerged from hibernation in the spring. Their impressive wingspan is about 16 inches and, as with all bats, their wings are versatile.

Apart from enabling them to fly – bats are the only mammals that have evolved this way – the wings act as a cooling system in flight, since they contain innumerable blood vessels, and are a means of finding underground sites by detecting temperature changes from draughts emerging from entrances. Dozing bats wrap their wings right round their bodies. And when it comes to birth, the wings are more like an open umbrella, allowing the newborn baby to drop from its upside-down mother into safety. At times the baby hangs from a false nipple, positioned at the lower end of the abdomen, while the real nipples are near the armpit (or wingpit). The mother can fly with her infant thus attached, though she also parks it in the roost, hanging upside down, while she goes hunting. The young can fly and catch insects from about three weeks.

Bats emerge from their roosts about half an hour after sunset. Sit quietly and watch them, but do not disturb this protected species.

My thanks to Geoff Billington of Greena Ecological Consultancy for information.

Herbivores such as bison were followed by their predators, hyenas. These two species provided the majority of bones found, but there were also wild boar, hippopotamus, bear and rhinoceros, as well as four straight-tusked elephants – two adults and two babies. The adults, in fact, were too large to fall through the hole but probably became wedged and unable to escape. These elephants were far larger than present-day African elephants, the adults standing at around 15 to 20 feet high. Together with these monsters were found the bones of brown bears and animals familiar in the British countryside today: foxes, voles, badgers, red deer and fallow deer. Quite a few bones have been left in the cave to add interest to what is already a fascinating visit.

There's a milk tooth of a baby elephant – but still an impressive size – and a leg bone gnawed by a hyena, as well as fossilised hyena droppings (the excavators could afford to leave some – they found five buckets full).

Eventually the cave filled up with animal remains and debris and was no longer a death trap. The last ice age, around 80,000 years ago, probably covered it completely until the quarry men opened it up in the mid 20th century.

¶¶ FOOD & DRINK

Riverford Field Kitchen Wash Barn, Buckfastleigh TQ11 0JU ✆ 01803 762074 ⌂ www. riverford.co.uk. Emphatically more than just a restaurant, this is part of the pioneering organic farm that first introduced the concept of Veg Boxes, where seasonal vegetables are delivered to local homes as well as hotels and restaurants. A tour of the farm is part of the 'field to plate' experience. Lunch or dinner consists of a fixed menu of five vegetable dishes and one meat dish, and diners sit together at a large table so a desire to be convivial should accompany a good appetite (you help yourself from the communal dishes). Dining here is a unique experience and gastronomically very rewarding. Advance booking is mandatory. If you feel like a DIY Riverford taster, there are recipe suggestions on the website. The **Riverford farm shop** nearby (✆ 01803 762059) has a good stock of seasonal organic vegetables, fruit, meat and poultry, milk, eggs, cheeses, baking and more. Mail order is available to most parts of the country.

8 LANDSCOVE

This small village is home to **Hill House Nursery** (TQ13 7LY ✆ 01803 762273 ⌂ www.hillhousenursery.com), which has been described as being 'awash with treasures and temptations'. It also has pleasant gardens – you may spot a magnolia that came from Dame Agatha Christie's garden at Greenway (see page 87) – and a good tea room (summer only). It's tucked away behind the village church of St Matthew; in fact Hill House (which is not open to the public) used to be the church's vicarage. A friend told us: 'We happened upon it by chance, and it was enchanting. Completely uncommercial and the homemade lunch we had in the tea room was excellent.' It's only a few miles from both Buckfastleigh and Ashburton but the narrow lanes can be a bit of a tangle: from Buckfastleigh take the A384 towards Totnes, then about quarter of a mile after the Dartbridge Inn take the first turning left signposted Landscove and Hill House.

9 BUCKFAST ABBEY

TQ11 0EE ✆ 01364 645500 ⌂ www.buckfast.org.uk.

This is an extraordinary place. The brochure says that Buckfast Abbey, founded in the 11th century and demolished in the 16th following the Dissolution of the Monasteries, is now 'home to a community of Benedictine monks who lead a life of prayer, work and study'. I don't doubt it, but somehow they have created a thriving commercial enterprise teeming with visitors willing to pay high prices at the Monastic Produce Shop, and who fill the modern abbey in numbers exceeding those to our great cathedrals.

"There's a wonderfully relaxed feeling about the place, with people strolling contentedly, quietly enjoying all it has to offer."

It's utterly commendable in the sense that the profits from tourism undoubtedly sustain the life of prayer. Nevertheless, something about it leaves me feeling a little uncomfortable.

That said, it's a peaceful setting and there's a wonderfully relaxed feeling about the place, with people strolling contentedly, quietly enjoying all it has to offer without any laid-on entertainment. There's also the extraordinary achievement of the rebuilding of the Abbey church by just a handful of the monks themselves, starting around a hundred years ago. By hand they cut the great stones to shape, lashed wooden scaffolding together, hauled the stones up on rudimentary pulleys . . . it took them 32 years, and the imposing **St Mary's Church** that you see today is the result.

Beekeeping here is also an interesting story, and Brother Adam, who worked with the Abbey's bees for over 70 years, is world famous for breeding a new strain which was a high honey producer, relatively gentle, and resistant to disease. During four decades he travelled some 100,000 miles to isolated areas of Europe, Asia and North Africa, persuading local beekeepers to give him queens from their indigenous strains; these he posted back to Buckfast. The result is known as the Buckfast bee, and its products are sold in the Monastic Shop – along with the famous Buckfast Tonic Wine, which made headlines a few years ago because of its apparent and rather incongruous popularity among young and anti-social drinkers. In Scotland it's affectionately known as Buckie. Beekeeping courses are held, for both beginners and improvers as well as for those deciding whether or not to start.

Bees are contented visitors to the **lavender garden**, which has around 150 species of lavender (when it's in flower, the perfume is wonderful), and there are also sensory and physic gardens. **Retreats** of various lengths are available in the monks' guest accommodation.

Buses serve Buckfast from Newton Abbot, Ashburton and Buckfastleigh; and a tourist leaflet on the Abbey can be downloaded from ⊕ www.tourismleafletsonline.com.

¶¶ FOOD & DRINK

The recently refurbished **Grange Restaurant and Tearoom**, which incorporates the 12th-century arch of the old north gate, provides a good range of food (lunches, teas, snacks, very fresh baking) in pleasant surroundings.

10 ASHBURTON

One of Devon's four 14th-century stannary towns (see page 196), along with Tavistock, Chagford and Plympton, Ashburton manages to combine its historic past with some energetic modern bustle. It's 'Slow' only if you're trying to ease your car through its busy streets – but there are some attractive old buildings, a good scattering of unusual independent shops and a warm

ALE TASTERS, SCAVENGERS & PIG DROVERS

Ashburton is one of only a handful of towns in Britain to have retained the old Saxon office of Portreeve, dating back to 820 AD and meaning the 'reeve' or supervisory official of a 'port' or trading centre. In those days the Portreeve was often the only person in the community who could read and write, and his chief duty was to represent the king in legal transactions. Today Ashburton's Portreeve may have rather less need to represent Her Majesty but is still elected annually, in November, along with his bailiff, bread weighers, ale tasters and other lesser officers such as Viewers of the Market, Viewers of Water Courses, Tree Inspector, Searcher and Sealer of Leather, Scavengers and Pig Drovers. You'll understand how vital these are for the smooth running of any 21st-century town.

Before Magna Carta there was no official check on the quality of ale or bread, and the first Ale Connors were appointed in London in 1276. Soon afterwards, there are records of brewers in Ashburton being fined for selling substandard ale. The tradition is renewed annually with a bread-weighing and ale-tasting ceremony in July, followed by a colourful medieval fair. One woman told me: 'As soon as there's a celebration of any kind, everyone pitches in and we have a right knees-up.'

For more on this, see ⊕ www.ashburton.org.

sense of community. The small **Ashburton Museum** (part-time summer opening only), housed in a former brush factory in the centre of town, has a collection of miscellaneous local memorabilia and – rather surprisingly – North American artefacts. **The Chapel of St Lawrence** in St Lawrence Lane, one of Ashburton's oldest buildings, started life as the private chapel of the Bishop of Exeter, but in 1314 he gave it to the town stipulating that it should be used as a school; so for more than 600 years it was the town's Grammar School. It's now a **heritage centre**, irregularly open to visitors and for talks and concerts (⌂ www.stlawrencechapel.org.uk).

The mixture of shops includes just about everything, with good local produce (meat, vegetables) and fresh baking. I commented to someone that the quality of the clothing and household goods suggested a reasonable level of wealth; she replied that in times gone by the richer section of the population had traditionally lived in Ashburton while their poorer neighbours stayed down the road in Buckfastleigh. I couldn't possibly comment… Among the small shops I was surprised to spot one, **Gnash** (9a West St ℡ 01394 653835 ⌂ www.gnashcomics. co.uk), selling just graphic novels and comics – they were so smartly and artistically displayed that at first I'd thought it was a gallery. The owner told me that she had started slowly a couple of years before but that business had built well, with plenty of local interest, so clearly Ashburton shoppers are less conservative than I might have imagined. Another welcome surprise was a small gallery with work by sculptor **Heather Jansch** (see page 8), who creates (among other art) amazing life-sized horse sculptures from driftwood. Items in the shop (12 East St ℡ 07775 840513 ⌂ www.heatherjansch.com; open Fri and Sat) are more manageably sized and include books, cards and prints.

‖ FOOD & DRINK

The Ashburton Cookery School in Old Exeter Road (℡ 01364 652784 ⌂ www. ashburtoncookeryschool.co.uk) runs a variety of cookery courses, lasting from one day or a weekend to three weeks and more; B&B accommodation is available too, and the receptionist told me that some couples split their holidays so that one partner cooks by day while the other – the cookery widow or widower – follows some alternative pursuit or goes off to explore the area. Courses cover a huge range: Indian, Italian, Mediterranean, Thai, modern British, vegetarian, fish and seafood, pastry and puddings, patisserie, sauces, bread-making, taste of the West Country, dinner parties, Christmas dinner and more. And participants get to eat the food that they have learned to cook.

As befits a town with a cookery school, Ashburton takes food seriously, and the culinary scene is developing. New restaurants will have opened by the time you read this, so follow your nose, study menus and shop around. There are plenty of small tea rooms and cafés – my ham and cheese toastie at the **Lazy Daisy** near the central car park was brimming with very good ham – and the 12th-century **Exeter Inn** in West Street, where Sir Walter Raleigh was arrested in 1603 before being dispatched to the Tower, has real ale, fine wines and traditional pub food.

PENNYWELL FARM

TQ11 0LT ☎ 01364 642023 🖱 www.pennywellfarm.co.uk. Closed Nov–Feb.

Forget conservation and endangered species, this hands-on animal place is just that – its aim is to bring humans and animals as close together as possible and as such it offers one of Devon's most rewarding experiences for children. Just look at the expression of a little girl gently stroking a tiny dozing piglet, and you'll see how well it works. Or sometimes doesn't: the squeals of disgruntled piglets can be heard from far off, but whenever a baby cries there are nursemaids – or nursemen – on hand to take it back for a soothing word or two.

Pennywell has been selectively breeding miniature pigs since 1992 (see box below), with the result that a piglet weighs just eight ounces at birth and grows to about the size of a springer spaniel. It's not just

PENNYWELL'S MINIATURE PIGS

I talked to the ebullient Chris Murray about his miniature pigs. 'I've always loved pigs. I studied agriculture at Seale-Hayne in Exeter and got interested in breeding pigs then. They're ideal animals for selective breeding because they have two litters a year and up to 18 piglets per litter. Of course in those days we were breeding for improved meat, and we wanted our pigs to grow fast. Now it's the opposite – we want small, slow-growing pigs. All sorts of traditional breeds have been used in our breeding programme: Iron Age wild boar, Gloucester old spot and Tamworth for colour, Berkshire, middle white because they're small with smiley faces, kune-kune which have a nice temperament, and English lop, which are docile. We aimed for other small details too – for instance we wanted prick ears rather than lop. But not too small because tiny ears look mean. And we wanted a short snout, because it's more appealing, and the right mouth. It took us 16 years to breed the smile!

Yes, we sell them. As pets, of course. We have some lovely customers here. One lady has a pig that sits on the sofa and watches television with her and there's a man who takes his pig on bike rides.'

A TASTE OF DEVON'S DAIRIES

Apart from its wonderfully varied local meats and seafood, Devon has local dairies that offer many smaller gastronomic pleasures. Top of my list is its **clotted cream**, thick, velvety and yellow, tasting quite unlike the thinner creams found elsewhere in Britain. The very best comes from Devon and Cornwall; there's no specific difference between the two counties, but the taste can vary according to the breed of cow and the preparation (milk is heated very slowly and then cooled, so that the cream rises to the top and can be skimmed off). A recent transatlantic visitor expected her 'Devon cream tea' to be a cup of tea with cream in it, but of course it's a far more sumptuous meal: freshly baked scones spread thickly with clotted cream and jam, accompanied by a pot of tea. In Devon, the jam usually goes on top of the cream, in Cornwall underneath. Various places sell clotted cream by mail order, for example the Dartmouth Dairy (01803 832801 www.dartmouthdairy.co.uk),

Langage Farm, Plympton (01752 337723 www.langagefarm.com) and Roddas (01209 823300 www.roddas.co.uk). Then there are the **cheeses**, ranging from hard and nutty to soft and squashy, enriched with all manner of local herbs and flavours. Different dairies have their own specialities. To pick just a few: Ticklemore's Devon Blue from Friesians has a rounded, buttery taste (www.ticklemorecheese.co.uk); Sharpham's plain rustic made from Jersey milk is creamy and lemony when young, nuttier as it matures (www.sharpham.com); Quickes traditional mature cheddar is satisfyingly as it sounds, from land farmed by the same family for over 450 years (www.quickes.co.uk); and Curworthy Farm near Okehampton produces traditional Curworthy cheese from a 17th-century recipe and the popular creamy-textured and cheddary Devon Oke (www.curworthycheese.co.uk). The cheese used to make the Blueberry Brothers' blueberry cheese (see page 216) also comes from Curworthy Farm.

the miniature piglets you can hug. Although I would challenge the statement that 'Pennywell animals love to be cuddled' (very few animals really enjoy being held), the rabbits and older piglets are remarkably tolerant of human attention, and selected ones are held in pens where visitors can join them for a stroke. As a pig enthusiast I was just as thrilled as the little kids around me when a piglet collapsed on its side in ecstasy as I scratched it under the chin.

Every half hour there is something different happening, such as ferret racing, pig racing (14.30 daily, in season), bottle feeding or a falconry display, and there are plenty of non-animal activities for children too; much of it is under cover.

N

4 miles

5km

0

0

Dartmoor Railway

Sticklepath 1

South Tawton 2

South Zeal 3

A30

Sampford Courtenay 6

Belstone 4

Nine Maidens Stone Circle

Jacobstowe

A386

OKEHAMPTON 5

MELDON RESERVOIR

Meldon

Sourton

A30

A386

Lewtrenchard 7

Lydford 8

LYDFORD GORGE

North Brentor 9

BRENT TOR

Coombe Trenchard

CHAPTER 8
page 192

7

THE NORTHWESTERN FRINGE OF DARTMOOR

This is an area where the ancient underlies the merely old. Medieval thatched cottages, centuries-old inns and much-loved little village churches occupy land where prehistoric monoliths, hut circles and burial cairns once stood, and the footprints of early people stretch back a long, long way. Sheep and red Devon cattle graze in the fields, and crops ripen through deepening shades of green to dusty gold. Between gaps in the trees, the hills and tors of Dartmoor appear as a distant backdrop.

Parts lie away from the tourist routes, allowing the occasional hamlet to be unselfconsciously unadorned. In one tourist information centre the assistant told me: 'The cottages down there are lovely because they haven't been titillated,' leaving me to wonder just what a titillated cottage could possibly get up to. Others are in their full thatched and whitewashed finery, with competitive gardens and cats dozing on windowsills.

GETTING THERE & AROUND

PUBLIC TRANSPORT

Although none of the county's heritage steam **trains** runs in this area, the next best thing is a diesel train service operated by Dartmoor Railway from Okehampton. This normally uses a heritage 'Hampshire' diesel unit, lovingly restored by volunteers from the Dartmoor Railway Supporters Association to provide a tourist service to Meldon Quarry which has no public road access. They run it at weekends in the high season; check times and availability first by phone (✆ 01837 55164) or on the website

WET-WEATHER ACTIVITIES

Okehampton Museum (page 181)

🖱 www.dartmoor-railway-sa.org. One of those volunteers, Dave Clegg, describes the short trip: 'The journey to Meldon Quarry may take only ten minutes but there is plenty to see. You have an unbeatable view of Okehampton Castle, with its leaning eastern wall, down below in the valley, alongside the West Okement river. The castle was the seat of the Sheriff of Devon and was built soon after the Norman Conquest. The train then passes through a wooded area – carpeted with bluebells each May – before tunnelling underneath the A30 and immediately into the Dartmoor National Park and Meldon Quarry.'

Meldon Quarry station is currently the end of the line, but the track continues as the Granite Way cycle path to Lydford. And the good news is that a guard's van on the train can carry up to 20 bicycles as well as pushchairs. Walkers can return to Okehampton by train or on foot (downhill!) along the Granite Way, or continue, perhaps to Sourton to lunch at the extraordinary Highwayman Inn (see box, page 187). But even if you are not a walker, you shouldn't miss the two-minute stroll from the train to the Meldon Viaduct (now a scheduled Ancient Monument) which straddles the West Okement Valley. The views as you walk across the viaduct are magnificent. On Sundays in the high season, the national rail operator (currently First Great Western) runs five trains a day from Exeter to Okehampton calling at Crediton and Sampford Courtenay stations in connection with Devon County Council's 'Sunday Rover' initiative. Sampford Courtenay is another pleasant walking area – and historically interesting (see page 183).

The appropriate **bus** timetable for the area is *West Devon*. Okehampton is covered by buses X9, 510 and 599 from Exeter, 118 from Tavistock to Barnstaple and 178 from Newton Abbot. The 178 also goes to the 'beacon villages' apart from Belstone, which has the 670 from Okehampton but only on Thursdays. Sampford Courtenay is served by the 168 from Okehampton as well as – on summer Sundays – by the Dartmoor Railway. **The Sunday Rover** gives access to both rail and bus services on Sundays from May to September (see page 199); a leaflet showing all its routes and timetables is available from TICs.

CYCLING & WALKING

Roads are good throughout the area and it's not excessively hilly. The **Granite Way** is an 11-mile walk/cycle route from Okehampton to Lydford, mostly following the course of the old Southern Region railway

i **TOURIST INFORMATION**

Okehampton Tourist Information Centre Museum Courtyard, off West St ✆ 01837
53020 🖰 www.okehamptondevon.co.uk. It's possible that this helpful little centre may
close in 2014 for lack of funding. If so, the Museum next door (see below) should have some
information and the website is likely to be kept up to date.

line so gradients are gentle; it's part of the National Cycle Network
(NCN) route number 27 'Devon Coast to Coast' between Ilfracombe
and Plymouth, and much of it lies within Dartmoor National Park.
It's relatively easy going, entirely off-road for six miles between
Okehampton and Lake Viaduct, and ideal for families and those whose
cycling is rusty. Devon County Council has produced comprehensive
details; the leaflet is in TICs or can be downloaded from 🖰 www.devon.
gov.uk/cycling-leismaps-graniteway.pdf. There are numerous smaller
walks, some on lanes and some on footpaths. The relevant OS maps
are Landranger 191 and Explorer OL 28 (Dartmoor). Cycle hire is
available from Adventure Okehampton in Klondyke Road (✆ 01837
53916 🖰 adventureokehampton.com) or **Devon Cycle Hire**, Bridestowe,
Okehampton (✆ 01837 861141 🖰 www.devoncyclehire.co.uk) at the
start of The Granite Way.

For walkers, the 24-mile **Two Castles Trail** links the Norman castles
of Okehampton and Launceston, which was the ancient capital of
Cornwall. It never strays far from bus or train routes so you can easily
break it into sections. Again Devon County Council has produced a
very comprehensive guide: it's available in TICs or you can download
the pdf from 🖰 www.devon.gov.uk/two-castles-trail-booklet.pdf.

THE BEACON VILLAGES

The four Beacon Villages – Sticklepath, South Tawton, South Zeal and
Belstone – are so named because they're all located at the base of **Cosdon
Beacon**, a broad 1,804ft hill where signal fires were lit in medieval times;
it was thought to be the highest point on Dartmoor. There are tracks to
the summit from South Zeal. Extensive prehistoric remains, including
hut circles and cairns, have been found scattered on its slopes; during
the 19th century, many were robbed of their stones by villagers seeking
free building materials. Roads leading from one beacon village to the

other are a bit labyrinthine but the signposting is reasonably clear. Driving or walking between them you'll be playing hide-and-seek with the outline of Dartmoor – now it's there as a backdrop and the next minute it's hidden. Sharp, blurred, misty, grey, calm, menacing: it's never the same two days running.

1 STICKLEPATH

Sticklepath has some fine thatched cottages, but its main point of interest is that it houses the **Finch Foundry** (✆ 01837 840046; National Trust; café and gift shop) which in fact isn't a foundry at all but the last working water-powered forge in the country, now managed by the National Trust. In its heyday it was making around 400 tools a day (sickles, scythes, shovels and more) for local farmers and miners. Regular demonstrations are given of the machinery in action, and the precision of the great hand-made wheels, cogs and other parts is amazing. Tucked away behind the forge is a peaceful little Quaker graveyard, probably dating from soon after 1700. The small, recently restored thatched arbour there was built by a certain Thomas Pearse (yes, that's the one, and presumably he had a grey mare) who was himself buried in the graveyard, in 1875, aged 81.

2 SOUTH TAWTON

This village is notable for its surprisingly large church and medieval church hall. South Tawton was a royal manor at the time of the Domesday survey and its fertile land made for successful farming; wealth from the wool trade expanded a smaller, probably 11th-century chapel into the mainly 15th-century granite **Church of St Andrew**, a listed building that towers above the village today.

"The picturesque thatched Church House was where all parishioners could gather to enjoy 'Church Ales'. "

Beside the church the picturesque thatched Church House (✆ 01837 840418 🖥 www.thechurchhouse.org.uk; open to the public on Wed and/or Sun in summer, phone or check the website for details) was built soon after 1490 as a parish centre where all parishioners could gather to enjoy 'Church Ales', which were parties organised to fundraise for the church's upkeep and to help the poor – in much the same way that churches hold fundraising coffee mornings today. On the ground floor was the kitchen where ale was brewed and food was cooked in the great fireplace; the feasting hall upstairs with massive roof trusses and a large window could have housed a great deal of medieval jollity. In the 17th century the hall was used as a school, and from 1804 through Victorian times as a poorhouse. During World War II, soldiers were billeted there after Dunkirk. It received a grant from the National Lottery in 2005, for restoration; when it's open, coffees and cream teas are available.

3 SOUTH ZEAL

In the mid 13th century, the de Tony family who held the manor of South Tawton requested and were granted royal permission to form a borough – a 'new town' – straddling the main route between Exeter and Cornwall: that town became South Zeal. In 1298 it was granted a charter for two annual fairs and a weekly market. The 'strip' layout at right angles to the single broad main street, still visible today, allowed householders street access in front, with a narrow strip of land continuing behind the house where gardens, workshops etc could be sited. South Zeal also has a number of medieval through-passage and Tudor houses, and the history of the town has been carefully researched; the South Tawton and District Local History Group has produced a booklet *South Zeal: a glimpse at the village's past*, on sale together with some good local produce and fresh baking in the **Village Store and Tearoom** (itself a through-passage house, with a splendidly large fireplace). There's a **14th-century market cross** and the appealing little **St Mary's Chapel** with its unusual 15th-century bell turret, as well as two pubs.

¶¶ FOOD & DRINK

King's Arms ℡ 01837 840300. This is a cheery place, dating back to the 16th century but very involved in today's village activities: you may find local folk groups playing here, or seasonal themed evenings. There's hearty pub food available with an emphasis on seafood (for example lemon sole, beer-battered cod, steamed mussels in lemon and coconut broth).
Oxenham Arms ℡ 01837 840244 ⌂ www.theoxenhamarms.com. An imposing listed building looking more monastery than pub, it was possibly built by lay monks in the 12th century. Extraordinarily, set into the wall of one of its inside rooms is a huge prehistoric standing stone, supposedly dating back around 5,000 years; it looks as if the wall was built around it. Another room has a similar menhir supporting the ceiling. The menu is considerably more modern – I've had an excellent meal, well presented – and the two bedrooms available for B&B have been cleverly modernised without losing character. Dickens is said to have stayed here while writing *The Pickwick Papers*.

4 BELSTONE

Belstone appears in the Domesday Book, and many millennia later is a peaceful, charming, leafy village right on the edge of Dartmoor, with some traditional old stone and thatched cottages, grazing ponies, dramatic moorland views, a Norman church and an incised granite ring-cross dated to the 7th–9th centuries, suggesting a much earlier place of worship. Similar crosses have been found and dated in south Wales and early Christian sites in the southwest of Ireland. Unusually for village churches, in the 19th century men and women were separated during services here, with men on the south side of the nave and women on the north.

The old stocks still sit on the village green – slats of wood between two granite pillars – as if awaiting some lingering medieval miscreant, and one house still has its old iron pump outside. Belstone is popular with

THE REVEREND SABINE BARING-GOULD (1834–1924)

Squire, parson, scholar, antiquarian, novelist, hymn-writer, collector of folk songs... and his father had hoped he would be just a mathematician. When he was 34 he married Grace, the 18-year-old daughter of a Yorkshire mill-hand; within the next 21 years they had 15 children and their marriage lasted 48 years. He had carved on her tombstone *Dimidium Animae Meae*, meaning 'half my soul'. In 1872 when he was rector of East Mersea in Essex his father died, and he inherited the Lewtrenchard family estates. The manor house at the time was only one room wide; Sabine extended it, filled it with artistic treasures and created today's stately Lewtrenchard Manor. As squire, he could appoint himself parson of the parish – and did so; he called himself a squarson. He wrote numerous articles and papers, on subjects as diverse as Icelandic folklore and candle-snuffers.

He was also a prolific novelist (some of the novels were quite racy for a clergyman, with a fair bit of bosom-heaving and moustache-twirling), wrote the words of the hymns *Onward Christian Soldiers* and *Now the Day is Over*, and painstakingly tracked down and transcribed old English folk-songs that he feared might otherwise be forgotten. His huge collection, one of the most significant West-country collections of the Victorian era, has now been digitised; for details see www.sbgsongs.org.

He lovingly restored St Peter's Church on the estate, adding art and beauty to it in his own unrestrained style, and is buried in its churchyard; the parishioners installed electricity in his memory. He would be satisfied that St Peter's appears in Todd Gray's *Devon's Fifty Best Churches*, while his own name survives in Okehampton's annual Baring-Gould Folk Weekend (see page 182).

walkers, and no wonder. Nearby, after slaking their thirst at the Tors pub, they can visit a prehistoric stone circle, the somewhat unimaginatively named **Nine Stones** (I counted 21), which is actually a prehistoric cairn: a burial place within a circle of stones. Or, it's a circle of maidens who were turned to stone for dancing on the Sabbath. Your choice. It's easily reached from the village, and is marked on the OS Explorer map 28. Once you're through the gate at the end of the road, follow the track to the end of the stone wall; then head uphill and you'll see it.

OKEHAMPTON & AROUND

5 OKEHAMPTON

This is one of only two market towns mentioned in the 1086 Domesday Survey of Devon, and in medieval times it was a bustling and important centre. Its surprisingly wide main street was once the old London Road to Cornwall and held a third row of buildings, which included an ancient Guildhall and a 17th-century covered market. These were demolished in 1850. The 15th-century St James' Chapel stands out clearly; it's the oldest building and is one of only five in England that is strictly non-denominational. For many centuries its bell was rung in the evening to signal curfew, when fires and lights should be put out, but the tradition lapsed sometime in the 20th century. In olden times pigs were used to hoover up the garbage in the streets and were housed near the chapel; the pig-shaped cycle-stands nearby are a reminder of this.

"In olden times pigs were used to hoover up the garbage in the streets and were housed near the chapel; the pig-shaped cycle-stands nearby are a reminder of this."

The recent collapse of some local industries caused widespread unemployment and some high-street shops have closed or are struggling; but several small independent shops and boutiques are flourishing, particularly those offering fresh local produce: baking, meat, vegetables, fruit etc. There's also good-quality country clothing, and the small shopping arcade that replicates London's Burlington Arcade, but in miniature, is an added treat.

The **Museum of Dartmoor Life** in the town centre is well worth a visit (✆ 01837 52295 🖱 www.museumofdartmoorlife.eclipse.co.uk; open Apr–Nov). It's housed in an old mill (dated 1811) with a restored waterwheel, and its three floors of exhibits cover around 5,000 years from prehistoric times to the present day. You'll find Bronze-age, Roman and Saxon collections, as well as re-creations of historic Dartmoor trades and industries, transport, the military – with quirky personal links bringing history to life, and some intriguing artefacts. The informative staff are happy to talk and explain the items.

Perched on a hillside about a mile from the centre of town is 11th-century **Okehampton Castle** (✆ 01837 52844; English Heritage; open Apr–Nov; good guidebook on sale), an atmospheric and allegedly haunted ruin that is said to have been Devon's largest castle. Originally a motte-and-bailey construction with a stone keep, in the 14th century it was converted into a private residence by the Earl of Devon; in the 16th century, after his descendant fell into dispute with Henry VIII and was beheaded, it was left to decay. The walls are feeling their age now and you can explore the interior only when the site is open; but the view of its ancient stonework silhouetted against the sky is dramatic at any time, and there are attractive woodland and riverside walks nearby. When I approached in February the grass below its walls looked frosty, until I realised that the 'frost' was a mass of snowdrops.

"When I approached in February the grass below its walls looked frosty, until I realised that the 'frost' was a mass of snowdrops."

An unusual and popular annual event in Okehampton is the **Baring-Gould Folk Weekend** (⌂ www.baring-gould.co.uk) in October, inspired by Devon-born Sabine Baring-Gould (see page 180). His was the first systematic attempt to collect the traditional songs of English country folk, particularly in west Devon. An associated **Song School** run by Wren Music (⌂ www.wrenmusic.co.uk) is held after the Weekend.

Okehampton Station & Meldon Viaduct

The future of the Dartmoor Railway is uncertain just now, but it seems likely that **Okehampton Station** (✆ 01837 55164) on the southeastern edge of town may at least continue to open on summer weekends. In that case its loving period refurbishment and displays of railway memorabilia will stir the heart of anyone over a certain age: you're transported straight back to the days of chatty ticket officers, wooden luggage trolleys piled high with trunks and leather suitcases, old railway posters and baskets of flowers. There's a shop crammed with stuff to make any railway enthusiast reach for his wallet, and a café where you might even have your very own brief encounter. The team of volunteers are kept busy, as Dave Clegg (see page 176) explained: 'There are so many aspects to running a railway – train crews, catering, station maintenance, tending flower beds, refurbishing the rolling stock and engines, running tombolas to raise funds, and so on. Volunteers are involved in all of these activities and, speaking as a 'regular', I can say how heart-warming it is when the public give positive feedback about what we are achieving.'

Nearby **Meldon Viaduct**, a scheduled ancient monument with spectacular views, is a dramatic example of Victorian engineering: one of only two examples in Britain of a wrought-iron truss-girder viaduct. Spanning the deep, steep river gorge required a strong but flexible structure; the wrought-iron and cast-iron frame consisted of six 90ft warren trusses on five wrought-iron lattice trestles, riveted together. It was built in 1874 for the main line between Waterloo and Plymouth, then doubled in width (to allow a second track) in 1878 and finally closed to trains in the late 1960s. Now it's a part of the Granite Way (see above and page 176). **Meldon Reservoir**, accessible by road and via a diversion from the Granite Way, is 900 feet above sea level; it was created in 1972 by a dam across the West Okement River, and offers fine views across the moors and to the viaduct.

¶¶ FOOD & DRINK

There's no shortage of cafés in Okehampton, particularly in the arcades. The **Red Lion Bakery** does coffees and wonderfully fresh baking, and the **Panache Coffee Shop** has hot and cold snacks and meals. The **Dovecote Café** in Red Lion Yard has indoor and outdoor seating and seems to specialise in cottage pie; it was full of diners when we checked: always a good sign. The **Victorian Pantry** in Museum Courtyard is apparently such a regular haunt of locals that a couple of them were quite grumpy on finding us sitting at what they considered to be 'their' table – but our lunch there was good. Of the several pubs, the **Plymouth Inn** in West Street is friendly and traditional, with real ales and a beer garden.

6 SAMPFORD COURTENAY

This village five miles or so north of Okehampton is known mainly for its involvement in the Prayer Book Rebellion of 1549 (see page 184). It's also a stop on the Dartmoor Railway's summer Sunday service from Exeter (see page 176) so is accustomed to visitors, and presents itself well. As Arthur Mee wrote 70-odd years ago: 'It is charming, with white cottages and thatched roofs and a lofty pinnacled tower.

"St Andrew's has some fine bosses in its wagon roof, including a sow suckling seven rather elongated piglets, and a descriptive display about the Prayer Book Rebellion."

Old crosses keep watch by the road, and another guards the 15th-century church.' That church, **St Andrew's**, rebuilt from an earlier building in 1450 and mentioned in Simon Jenkins' *England's Thousand Best Churches*, has some fine bosses in its wagon roof, including a sow suckling seven rather elongated piglets, and a permanent descriptive display about the Prayer Book Rebellion. There's also a venerable old oak chest, made from a single block of wood, and a rare walnut pulpit. I bought two jars of local marmalade which were on sale by the door, and it was some of the best I've ever tasted. The Church House nearby which will have been used, like South Tawton's, for communal feasting and 'Church Ales' probably dates to around 1500.

THE PRAYER BOOK REBELLION

As part of the Protestant reforms instigated under Edward VI, the familiar prayer book in Latin was declared illegal and, from Whit Sunday 1549, churches in England were required to adopt the new *Book of Common* Prayer in English and to adapt their traditional rituals. Resistance to this was particularly strong among the villagers of Devon and Cornwall. At Sampford Courtenay they likened the English prayer book to a 'Christmas game', thought to mean something like a Nativity play without true substance; initially their priest obeyed orders, removed his robes and conducted the 'new' Sunday service, but vocal parishioners quickly forced him to revert to the old. Others dissented, a fracas developed, and in the melée a local man was stabbed with a pitchfork on the steps of the Church House and then hacked to death.

Villagers in their thousands, armed with no more than farm implements and staves, rose up together and marched to Exeter, demanding the withdrawal of the English version. Exeter remained under siege for six weeks, but the rebels were no match for the well-armed military force sent to quell them: more than 1,000 died at Crediton, 900 at Clyst St Mary, 300 at Fenny Bridges and 1,300 in a final stand at Sampford Courtenay. The militia continued into Cornwall until, by the time the rebels were crushed, some 4,000 from both counties had died – and to little purpose, as when Edward's half-sister Mary (a devout Catholic) succeeded him in 1553 she re-legalised the Latin version anyway.

Sampford Courtenay is so genuinely attractive – Simon Jenkins describes it as a 'cream-tea village of white cob and thatch', and it has 70-odd listed buildings and monuments – that the house in the centre whose plastering is embossed with scenes from traditional village life seems unnecessarily theatrical.

You can shop for a local treat at the **Sampford Courtenay Cider Company** at Solland Farm (✆ 01837 851638 🖱 www. sampfordcourtenaycider.co.uk). Their cider comes in various strengths and flavours, and they use only apples grown in their own orchard.

A short way from Sampford Courtenay on the Okement River is the small village of **Jacobstowe**, possibly the site of a Saxon settlement. Its 12th-century church of St James, much remodelled in the 15th century, is a listed building. The Reverend Sabine Baring-Gould (see page 180), in his search for traditional folk songs, discovered one – the Jacobstowe Wassail – thought to originate here.

LYDFORD & AROUND

7 THE TRENCHARDS

It's unusual to find two such perfect, traditional country houses, set in extensive and typically English gardens with lawns and terraces, only a ten-minute walk from each other; both have intriguing histories, are accessible to the public and offer luxury accommodation. With sun on their classic stone frontages and flowers splashing their borders with colour, they're an artist's or photographer's delight. The main difference between them is that while Coombe Trenchard was built in 1906, Lewtrenchard is around three centuries older. Although wonderfully secluded they're only a few miles from the A30, also close to the Two Castles Trail (see page 177).

Lewtrenchard Manor

Lewdown, near Okehampton EX20 4PN ✆ 01566 783222 🖱 www.lewtrenchard.co.uk.

The Domesday Book mentions a royal manor here, but the core of the present house seems to have been started around five centuries later. At that time it was a simple oblong building, only the width of a single room; until Sabine Baring-Gould (see page 180) in the 19th century began transforming it into this colourful, imposing and graceful building, now a family-run hotel, looking out across the Devon countryside from its tranquil garden. Inside it's opulent;

Baring-Gould was a great collector, and brought treasures from far and wide: oak and leather, gilt and carvings, knick-knacks and heavy period furniture. It's a delight just to walk from one well-proportioned room to another.

In the gardens, beyond the palm trees and colourful flowerbeds, is little St Peter's Church, originally St Petrock's but dedicated to St Peter when it was rebuilt in 1261. Barely a trace of that old church remains; the present one dates from 1520 and again Baring-Gould brought additions from far and wide to embellish it: a medieval tryptych and 15th-century brass chandelier from Belgium, the lectern from France, the altar painting from Switzerland, the east window from Germany and so on. The richly carved oak pulpit is said to be inspired by the one in Kenton church (see page 26), Some of the many paintings are by his daughter Margaret, others by local or foreign artists. On his tombstone is carved *Paravi Luvernam Christo Mew* or 'I have prepared a lantern for my Christ' – and indeed it burned brightly.

Lewtrenchard Manor has an excellent restaurant, open to non-residents for lunch, afternoon tea and dinner (see *Food & drink* page 188), as well as 13 luxury bedrooms (see page 242).

Coombe Trenchard

Lewdown, nr Okehampton EX20 4PW ✆ 01566 783179 🖰 www.coombetrenchard.co.uk.

This elegant Edwardian Arts-and-Crafts house was built in 1906 by friends of Sabine Baring-Gould, while he was living next door in Lewtrenchard Manor. They had been renting the old rectory on the Lewtrenchard estate for some time; when Sabine invited them to buy that portion of the land they did so, demolished the rectory and began building the current house, using Arts and Crafts architect Walter Sarel and Devon church builders Dart & Francis.

"The interior has an ingenious disappearing wall, thought to be unique, which can be slid down into the basement, rather in the manner of a sash window."

The interior has fine oak panelling, ornate ceilings, gracious rooms and period furnishings – and rather surprisingly an ingenious disappearing wall, thought to be unique, which can be slid down to the basement, rather in the manner of a sash window, to make room for large gatherings. When the current owners bought the property in 2007 the large gardens, originally designed and laid out by Walter Sarel, were so neglected that many features had vanished beneath the overgrowth; now, after a huge amount of work, the forgotten paths, glades, woodland garden, terraces, steps and other structures are back on view.

The **gardens** can be visited through the annual National Gardens Scheme (see page 7), and a Sculpture Trail is open there on summer weekends. Otherwise they are not regularly open to the public but private group visits can be arranged. The **house** is mostly open for cream teas in the afternoons (see *Food & drink*, page 188). Private group visits

THE HIGHWAYMAN INN & COBWEB HALL, SOURTON
Philip Knowling

Putting the lie to the idea that follies are useless is the Highwayman Inn at Sourton, on the bleak west side of Dartmoor. Sourton is the sort of place you could pass through without noticing if it weren't for the hard work, imagination and enthusiasm of the late John 'Buster' Jones, who over a 40-year period transformed two of its key buildings into fabulous, fascinating architectural wonders.

What makes this pub a folly? Well, it's the most lavishly and imaginatively decorated inn you could ever visit. Inside and out there's wit and whimsy, imagination and inspiration – plus a little macabre kitsch. The Highwayman is a fantasy blend of pirate ship, church, museum, junk shop and fairy-tale.

In 1959 Buster Jones moved his family to Devon and took over Sourton's New Inn – a small, run-down pub in a 13th-century building. He and his wife Rita changed the name to the Highwayman Inn and, to promote it, Buster acquired the old Okehampton–Launceston stage coach and set it up as a lobby at the front door of the pub.

He hauled pieces of bog-oak off the moor and used them as bar tops; the dartboard is fixed to a tree-stump set into the wall. There are bits of ship (a carved door from an old whaling ship called *Diana*) and pieces of church (from Plymouth).

One room has a nautical theme – it's below decks on an 18th-century sailing ship cum bric-a-brac shop with bar facilities. Elsewhere, there's an indoor grotto full of stuffed animals (an inventive use of road-kill). Cartwheels and lanterns and sewing-machines also feature.

Buster also turned the former Sourton village hall into a fairytale Gothic *cottage orné* – despite a certain amount of conflict with the planning authorities. Today Cobweb Hall is a holiday let, standing on the edge of rising moorland. It's a novel and intriguing place to stay – and there's a rather special pub just across the road.

The two buildings are now in the good care of Buster's daughter, Sally. The Highwayman is world-renowned – and rightly so. If you visit it, your local will never seem quite the same.

to some of the rooms can be arranged by request. It's also accessible through **Invitation to View** (✆ 01284 827087 🖰 www.invitationtoview. co.uk), a company that organises visits to stately homes. And there are four ultra-comfortable B&B bedrooms (see page 243).

🍴 FOOD & DRINK

The three places mentioned above are all memorable refreshment-stops:

Coombe Trenchard does delectable cream teas, whose array of home-made cakes is a serious test of willpower. I had a hard time choosing between the sticky chocolate and the lemon drizzle. On sunny day, you'll want to linger on the terrace enjoying the view. Check opening hours beforehand.

    Lewtrenchard Manor is open to non-residents daily (15.00–17.00) for sumptuous cream teas; also for lunch and evening meals. The restaurant here is top-class; the chef works closely with local producers, and vegetables mostly come from the hotel's own walled garden. Menus change frequently to make use of whatever is freshly available. It's not particularly cheap; but this is quality dining. For an extra treat, you can arrange a private dinner with the kitchen's activities relayed to you on a large flat TV screen, giving you the opportunity to interact with the head chef and his team. The place is popular locally, and booking is strongly recommended.

    On the A386 only about seven miles from the Trenchards, the **Highwayman Inn** (EX20 4HN ✆ 01837 861243 🖰 www.thehighwaymaninn.net) opens lunchtimes and evenings for a variety of ales, meals and snacks in an Aladdin's cave of eclectic artefacts and curios. Bring your camera. It also holds music and poetry evenings and has quirky accommodation (see page 243). Do check opening hours beforehand, because it's an eccentric place.

8 LYDFORD GORGE & LYDFORD

Hidden away off the A386, this is one of those happy places with plenty to see and a regular bus service. People have always loved waterfalls, and **Lydford Gorge** (🌼 car park: grid reference SX508845) has been enticing visitors to its White Lady Waterfall for around 300 years, although it was the arrival of the railway in 1865 that put it within reach of holidaymakers. Now owned by the National Trust, the 1½-mile stretch of river deserves its popularity – it really does live up to expectations.

The gorge walk is designed as a circular route, and follows a one-way system so you walk west along the southern bank of the river and return the other side. This is a three-mile walk with some steep sections. If you don't want to do the whole thing, I would recommend the Devil's Cauldron circuit accessed from the main entrance. Here the river is forced through a narrow space between rocks, with the path an eyrie overhead, pinned against the steep fern-clad rock face so you look down on the churning white water.

The other end, with the White Lady Waterfall, is drier and less ferny than the eastern section, and the descent to the falls is quite steep – although there is a longer, 'easy' path as an alternative. The waterfall is just that – a waterfall – so unless there has been a lot of rain it is not that spectacular though certainly atmospheric in its wooded environment. The Reverend Stebbing Shaw, who visited Lydford in 1788, was moved to paroxysms of delight.

> *"The river is forced through a narrow space between rocks, pinned against the steep fern-clad rock face so you look down on the churning white water."*

'...you are presented with the finest milky streams imaginable, neither too perpendicular to be one confused heap, nor too much divided to be ungraceful; but one continued silvery chain of 200 feet [actually it's 90 feet]; towards the bottom the rock projects so favourably as to fill the air with aqueous particles, and to imitate the effect of a real fountain, softly falling in a silver shower... This surprising waterfall pleased me altogether more than any in the North of England or Scotland, and being a greater rarity in these parts it is more valuable and striking.' Perhaps I should take another look.

The paths between the two focal points reveal a variety of trees and flowers, including bluebells in May, and a chance to see the different moods of the river, from quiet pools to mini-waterfalls.

Lydford Gorge attracts large crowds so if you have a choice, avoid the busy summer months. Early spring is a perfect time to be there, when the water is high and the woods are touched with green. Autumn, with its yellows and russets, is equally appealing. Some of the trails are closed in winter, but access to the waterfall is open year round.

If you are coming by bus you can halve the walk but still follow the full length of the gorge. The southern section from the main entrance is the most varied, so, if you get off at the War Memorial in the centre of the village and stroll a quarter of a mile down to the gorge, you can walk to the White Lady and emerge to catch the bus outside the Waterfall Entrance; the bus stops are just to the left up the hill.

Lydford is more than just the gorge. The village has the remains of a Norman fort (now visible only as a grassy mound) and a little square

Norman 'castle' that looks as if it were built by a young child out of Lego bricks. This was used as a stannary court and jail, infamous for the harsh judgements meted out in the 17th century. Lydford's position between two ravines gave it a natural defence so the village has prospered since before the Norman Conquest when it had its own mint, producing silver 'Lydford pennies' from 973. Then came the tin boom at the end of the 12th century, when it became a stannary town (see page 196). It was also Dartmoor's biggest parish, necessitating the transport of decaying corpses across Dartmoor, from as far afield as Bellever, to be buried at Lydford. **The Lych Way**, running from Powder Mills (between Postbridge and Two Bridges) to Lydford, is the ancient route that they used to take.

> *"The village has the remains of a Norman fort and a little square Norman 'castle' that looks as if it were built by a young child out of Lego bricks. "*

¶¶ FOOD & DRINK

Castle Inn ✆ 01822 820241 🖱 www.castleinnlydford.co.uk. Lydford's pub in the centre of the village has plenty of unforced charm (it has a darts board and a beer garden) as well as two exceptionally fine stained-glass panels. I wasn't able to find out the history of these, but they may have come from a church since one shows a Green Man, and another the 'tinners' rabbits' or 'three hares' which feature in most stannary town churches (see page 196).

The Dartmoor Inn Lydford EX20 4AY ✆ 01822 820221 🖱 www.dartmoorinn.com. A classy inn with B&B accommodation as well as seriously special meals for non-residents.

9 BRENTOR (BRENT TOR)

The conical hill topped with its proud little church is a landmark throughout western Dartmoor, and the view from the top is, as you'd expect from the highest church in England, magnificent. On a clear day you can see Bodmin Moor and Plymouth Sound. The church is old, some say it was finished in 1130, and stands at an altitude of 1,130 feet, but that sounds a little too neat. There are many legends about why it was built at such a height. One explains that the original intention was to build the church at the base of the tor nearer to the village. However, the devil feared this might encourage the villagers to go regularly to worship, so he sent his imps to move the foundation stones to the top of the hill each night after work had finished. At first the builders rolled the stones back to the bottom again, but soon got fed up with this and

UPDATES WEBSITE

You can post your comments and recommendations, and read the latest feedback and updates from other readers, online at ⌂ www.bradtupdates.com/southdevonanddartmoor.

decided to let the devil have his way. They named the church after St Michael, who is patron saint of grocers, mariners, the police and other emergency services, paratroopers (that must surprise him) and the sick. The saint came to visit his newest church, and took great exception to the fact that the devil had engineered its position outside the village. St Michael then engaged in a fearsome battle with the devil, finally hurling a great boulder at him and knocking him head over heels to the base of the tor. The boulder still lies there today, as a reminder of this saintly victory.

It's only a ten-minute climb to the church for a fit person, up a rough path lined with foxgloves, through cow-grazed pasture, dodging cowpats. The church itself is tiny and utterly simple inside. It's the location that makes it so special; and the fact that it celebrates evensong every Sunday in the summer.

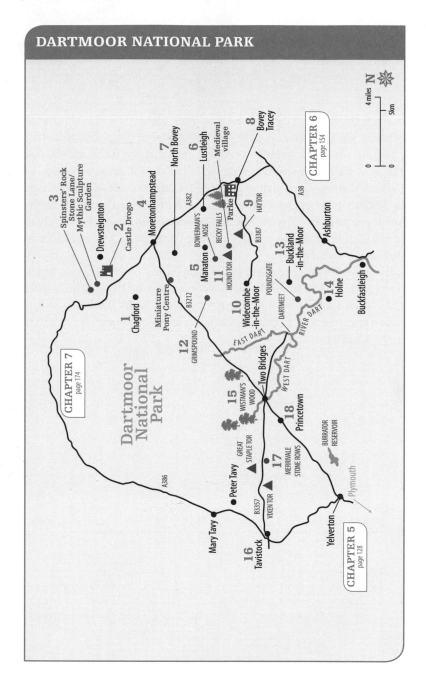

DARTMOOR NATIONAL PARK

N

4 miles

5km

0

0

CHAPTER 6
page 154

3
Spinsters' Rock
Stone Lane/
Mythic Sculpture
Garden

2
Drewsteignton

4
Castle Drogo

Moretonhampstead

7
North Bovey

6
Lustleigh

Medieval
village

8
Bovey
Tracey

A382

A38

BOWERMAN'S
NOSE

Parke

9
HAYTOR

B3387

Ashburton

1
Chagford

Miniature
Pony Centre

5
Manaton

BECKY FALLS

11
HOUNDTOR

13
Buckland
-in-the-Moor

B3212

10
Widecombe
-in-the-Moor

POUNDSGATE

Buckfastleigh

CHAPTER 7
page 174

Dartmoor
National
Park

12
GRIMSPOUND

EAST DART

DARTMEET

RIVER DART

14
Holne

A386

Two Bridges

WEST DART

15
WISTMAN'S
WOOD

18
Princetown

BURRATOR
RESERVOIR

Peter Tavy

GREAT
STAPLE TOR

17
MERRIVALE
STONE ROWS

Plymouth

Mary Tavy

B3357

VIXEN TOR

16
Tavistock

Yelverton

CHAPTER 5
page 128

HOMES OF THE GREAT & THE GOOD

Devon's wealthy families built the county's finest castles, and later the imposing manor houses with their meticulously landscaped gardens. Like the village churches they bring local history to life.

1 Mentioned in the Domesday Book, Lewtrenchard Manor is now a luxury hotel. (LM)
2 Redcliffe Hotel, Paignton, was built in the Indian style in 1856 as a private residence. (S/RE)
3 The castle at Berry Pomeroy, famed for being one of the most haunted in Britain. (SS)
4 The 14th-century Powderham Castle, whose well-kept grounds and majestic interior are well worth a visit. (VB/JH)

INDOORS OR OUT

There's no escaping the fact that it often rains in the West Country, but there are plenty of indoor attractions as well as farms and zoos where you can take temporary shelter.

1 Glass blowing at the House of Marbles, Bovey Tracey. (ss) 2 Kents Cavern, Torquay, home to the oldest fossil of modern man in Britain. (kc) 3 Playful otters at Otters and Butterflies, Buckfastleigh. (oab) 4 Paint your own pottery at The Art Café, Kingsbridge. (tac) 5 Harvesting the hot ones at the South Devon Chilli Farm. (ss) 6 Pennywell Farm's miniature pigs can put on a fair turn of speed. (pf)

classic cottages

The holiday letting specialists.
Over 35 years of finding homes
that make great holidays.

Visit our website at classic.co.uk
Email us at enquiries@classic.co.uk
Talk to us on 01326 555 500

8
DARTMOOR
NATIONAL PARK

Look at any map of Devon and you'll see the largely roadless blob that is Dartmoor. Literature and imagination give it an air of menace: *The Hound of the Baskervilles*, a bleak prison where the surrounding moor is the best security, and craggy tors emerging from heavy, disorientating mists. This national park is high – the highest land in England south of the Pennines – leaving the visitor exposed to raw winds sweeping in from the Atlantic. But there's a softer side to Dartmoor: sheltered, wooded valleys which feel a world away from the typical moor. So if you want Dartmoor bleakness you can find it. Once you cross a cattle-grid the hedges disappear, sheep and ponies raise their heads to watch you pass, and the wind catches your hair as you reach for a sweater. You can walk for hours without seeing a road – or a tree. And everywhere you see granite: rocks as large as cars scattered randomly or piled on top of hills to form the tors that define Dartmoor, quarried and dressed in the walls of the ancient village churches, or rough-hewn and arranged in circles or rows by the first humans to make the moor their home.

The low-lying perimeter is another world, however, networked by deep narrow lanes. Footpaths meander through gentle, flower-filled meadows or dark woodland, or along the banks of rivers. The Tavy, Teign and Dart dominate, but all have tributaries and you are never far from a brook. Hidden in the valleys are small villages, their church towers poking through the trees, and welcoming pubs. But no one visiting here would stay only in the valleys; Dartmoor is the high moor. You may regret venturing up there in mist and rain, but on a sunny day its wildness is alluring. It's aptly called England's last wilderness, and the feeling of space and silence, broken only by the trilling of skylarks and the scrunching of boots on stones, is intoxicating.

WET-WEATHER ACTIVITIES
Castle Drogo (page 208)
Bovey Tracey Devon Guild of Craftsmen and House of Marbles (page 220)
Tavistock Museum and Pannier Market (page 231)
Princetown Dartmoor Prison Museum and High Moorland Visitor Centre (page 234)

Dartmoor also has, uniquely, its visible prehistory in the monuments such as hut circles and stone rows that litter the moor. A newcomer might assume the tors are also the work of prehistoric people. The word comes from the Celtic *twr*, or tower, but these are the work of nature – erosion – not man. And in an area that has blessedly few 'tourist attractions' nature has provided children with some rewarding scrambles and adults with hills to test their stamina, as well as giving Dartmoor its unmistakable horizon.

DARTMOOR: THE HAND OF MAN

There are more prehistoric sites here than anywhere in Europe, and Dartmoor is one of the easiest places in Britain to view the march of history, from Neolithic circles to the Neo-medieval Castle Drogo. In 2009 a ceremonial site, which probably dates from 2000BC, emerged when the Tottoford Reservoir near Bovey Tracey was drained, although some of the flints found there could be 8,000 years old. Most archaeologists believe that the earliest remains on Dartmoor are **Neolithic**, around 4000BC, and that as true settlers these people had the most profound effect on the landscape by domesticating animals and cultivating crops. Then the Beaker people in the early Bronze Age, around 2200BC, built the Grimspound enclosed village (see page 227) and some two thousand other 'hut circles' on the moor. Bronze is an alloy of tin and copper so tin-rich Dartmoor was an obvious place to settle, the metal being easily extracted from rivers and surface deposits. Later, still a few centuries BC, came the **Iron Age**, whose most tangible heritage is the plethora of hill forts that are found in other parts of Devon, but not Dartmoor, and finally the two centuries of Christianity and its enduring symbol, the English country church, its fortunes tied to those of the tinners who continued to extract the valuable metal from Dartmoor until the mid 20th century. Wealthy tin merchants who endowed a church in a stannery ('tin-workers') town were ensured a short cut to heaven.

Visiting Dartmoor today, you may find it puzzling that Neolithic and Bronze-Age people chose to settle in such an inhospitable region. Probably, in an age where finding enough to eat was the main preoccupation, the attraction was the abundance of game in the woodlands that at that time covered low-lying parts of the moor, and the good grazing for both wild and domestic animals in the higher areas. The climate was milder then, and the soil less acid; thousands of years of slash-and-burn agriculture impoverished the land and helped create the moor that we see today. The availability of granite for constructing durable, weather-proof homes and the mysterious stone circles and monoliths will have helped the inhabitants but frustrates archaeologists, since granite cannot be carbon dated. But that is part of the attraction: we just don't know what a lot of these structures were used for, nor even when they were built. We can simply enjoy them for what they are.

"We don't know what a lot of these structures were used for, nor when they were built. We can simply enjoy them for what they are."

It's thrilling to come across the signs of early human habitation on the moor, particularly when we really don't know why these people, living up to 4,000 years ago in a warm, forested place which provided for all their basic needs, went to the trouble of moving huge hunks of granite into geometric patterns. It is also a sobering reminder of the effect of deforestation and climate change on a once green and fertile land. Some of the most striking sites are the chambered tomb known as Spinsters' Rock (see page 211), the easily reached Nine Stones stone circle at Belstone (page 180), the stone rows at Merrivale, the Bronze-Age pound of Grimspound (page 227), and the cluster of prehistoric features on Shovel Down (page 206).

Moving forward to our known history, the **Norman Conquest** in 1066 resulted in tracts of land being set aside for the new King to indulge his enthusiasm for hunting. These areas, rich in game, were called **'forests'** although this did not mean woodland; the moorland of Dartmoor was a royal forest. In those times deer, wolves and wild boar were all plentiful. All have gone now, including the red deer. Penalties for harming animals in the royal forests were severe, and in the 12th century King John gave in to pressure and 'deforested' all of Devon apart from Dartmoor and Exmoor. In 1337 Edward III gave the Forest of Dartmoor to his son, the Prince of Wales and Duke of Cornwall. It remains the property of the Duchy of Cornwall – and the current Prince of Wales – to this day.

Life for farmers on the moor has always been tough, but never more so than today. The 2013 average income for a Dartmoor farm of 40 hectares was £14,000.

DARTMOOR TIN & THE STANNARY TOWNS

Dartmoor, with Cornwall, was the first known source of tin. Some 4,000 years ago, metal workers discovered that by mixing tin (10%) with copper (90%) they created a stronger but easily worked material: bronze. Because tin doesn't rust it is also used to coat other metals. Minerals containing tin are almost always associated with granite, hence tin's abundance on Dartmoor. The ore was originally collected from the streams and rivers, through the simple process of panning or 'streaming'. Once these deposits were exhausted – and streaming continued into the 17th century – the ore was extracted from the ground using pick and shovel, sometimes with the help of leats, or diverted streams, to wash away the debris. Millstones were used to crush the ore and extract the metal which was then smelted. Two smeltings generally took place, one at the site and the second, to produce pure tin, in one of the **stannary towns**. The Latin for tin is *stannum*, hence the term stannary.

Stannary towns in Dartmoor were mining centres where refined tin was collected, weighed and stamped. When sold, the proceeds were passed to the Duchy of Cornwall. In 1305 Edward I established Tavistock,

THE TINNERS' RABBITS

In several places in Dartmoor you can see depictions of three rabbits or hares, so designed that they appear to have two ears each while actually sharing the second ear with their neighbour. No one really knows their significance. Some say they are a symbol of the Holy Trinity, others that they are a secular symbol of the three elements of the tin trade: tin, market, wealth. One thing is certain: they are not unique to Dartmoor, a similar design being found in Iran, Mongolia and along the Silk Route. So this curious emblem has been favoured by Muslims and Buddhists as well as Christians.

My feeling is that artists have always played with clever designs like this, and it may be no more than Escher's tricks with fish and birds gradually reversing their shapes: a creative play with 'now you see it now you don't'.

Ashburton and Chagford as Devon's first stannary towns, with the right to organise their own political affairs through the Stannary Parliament and Stannary Courts. Other stannary towns were established later as mining became more organised. Stannary laws were the first legal code of England, affording the miners considerable power – providing they were honest. Legend has it that any tinner convicted of mixing impurities with his metal was to have three spoonfuls of it poured down his throat in a molten state.

LETTERBOXING ON DARTMOOR

In 1854, a Dartmoor guide named James Perrott placed an empty glass pickle jar by Cranmere Pool. He told hikers and other guides about it, and encouraged them – if they reached it – to put some record of their visit inside. People began to leave postcards and letters, addressed either to themselves or to others, which the next visitor would take and post: the Dartmoor equivalent of throwing a bottle into the sea containing an address. By the early 1900s the Cranmere pickle jar had been replaced by a tin box containing a more formal visitors' book, and in 1937 a granite box was erected there.

Gradually letterboxes were placed in other parts of the moor, each with a notebook and appropriate rubber stamp. Letterboxers now 'collect' these when they find them by marking the stamp into their own notebooks; when their total reaches 100 they can join the '100 Club'. Letterboxes around the moor today range from solid structures to jars and tins to plastic sandwich boxes, generally well concealed. There are strict guidelines about their maintenance, choosing sites considerately and not damaging the landscape; make sure to read them on www.letterboxingondartmoor.co.uk before placing a box of your own.

Remember, too, that a box placed in winter may be hidden by vegetation when you return to check it in the summer. A friend described how the growing bracken swallowed up not only the box but her smallest grandchild who was hunting for it: they found him when a little voice piped up from deep in the fronds 'Granddad, where are you?' Children love the challenge of letterboxing, and another friend told me that her three would be seriously grumpy in the car on the way home if they hadn't managed to find a box.

From Dartmoor, letterboxing has spread to other parts of Britain (including Yorkshire, Isle of Man, Lundy and Scotland). It caught on in the United States in 1998 and also exists in New Zealand and various European countries. A new version called geocaching, using GPS co-ordinates, started in the US in 2000 and now has more than six million geocachers worldwide (www.geocaching.com).

So, if you spot an unexpected container on the moor, you may have taken the first step towards becoming a fully fledged Dartmoor letterboxer!

GETTING THERE & AROUND

Despite my love of public transport, I have to admit that most people will choose to travel by car, especially off-season when the traffic is lighter and public transport to the heart of Dartmoor is less frequent. The national park authorities have been generous with the provision of parking areas, so most walks and places of interest are readily accessible, even in the busy summer months when an attempt to explore the minor single-track roads will result in more mileage done in reverse than forward. On summer weekends in July and August, stick to the wider roads and abandon your car as soon as possible; but please don't just leave it on the roadside, where it may block access for emergency vehicles.

BY BUS

Dartmoor is a destination in itself, and some people will choose to spend their entire holiday there. It's perfectly feasible to do this using public transport, augmented by taxis if necessary.

A SUMMER SUNDAY OUTING AROUND DARTMOOR

This is a terrific circular trip using the Sunday Rover bus and the Dartmoor Railway. It runs anticlockwise round the perimeter of Dartmoor via Lydford Gorge to Tavistock, with time to potter before catching the Transmoor bus back to Exeter.

Start at Exeter railway station (either Central or St David's) with the Dartmoor Railway, run by volunteers; it ambles along to Okehampton with the option of a two-hour break at delightful and historic **Sampford Courtenay** (see page 183). Outside nostalgia-filled **Okehampton** station (page 182) is the stop for the 187 bus to **Lydford**, where you have time to walk the length of the gorge before catching the next bus, two hours later, to **Tavistock**, an inviting town with plenty to explore

including a stroll along the canal. More ambitious walkers can get off at Mary Tavy (page 231) and walk the West Devon Way for a couple of miles. The Transmoor bus (82) back to Exeter leaves Tavistock at 16.15 and is the bus highlight of the day, taking you right across the most open part of the moor via Princetown and Two Bridges. Between Moretonhampstead and Dunsford, the road is as appealing in its lushness as the transmoor route is for wilderness. It runs through the oaks of Bridford Wood, clinging to an almost vertical hillside abutting the Teign and ending at Steps Bridge. You'll arrive at Exeter Bus Station in the early evening having spent only £8 (as at time of writing) on transport for the whole day or – if you have a concessionary bus pass – nothing!

In the summer months just about everywhere is accessible by bus, if only once a week, but initially most car-free people will use **trains** and **taxis** to reach their base. The nearest mainline train station is Ivybridge, a charming little station at the southern end of the national park, where there are at least two local taxi companies: Ivycabs (☏ 01752 895555) and T&C Cabs (☏ 01752 892222). Newton Abbot is a little further from the moor, but convenient for the eastern section; taxis from Station Taxis (☏ 01626 334488). From Exeter station you can catch the hourly X38 express bus to Ashburton (taxis ☏ 01364 652423). Or, if you're basing yourself in the north of Dartmoor, take the 359 bus to Moretonhampstead, which leaves Exeter at two-hourly intervals, and book a taxi from Mr Chard in Chagford (☏ 01647 433219).

One of the most delightful ways of getting an overview of the moor in the summer months is by **local bus**. The **Sunday Rover** gives access to both rail and bus services at low cost on Sundays between May and September, when scenic bus journeys are frequent and 'joined up' (see box opposite for a suggested itinerary). A leaflet showing all the routes and timetables is available from TICs. The service on Saturdays is almost as good, with the delightful **Haytor Hoppa** taking a circular route through some of Dartmoor's most popular eastern places, including Haytor, Widecombe, Hound Tor and Becky Falls. With four departures a day from Newton Abbot (or Bovey Tracey) it provides the perfect means to explore the moor without a car. It runs from Easter to the end of October – and dogs are allowed on board. There are other once-a-week offerings which are equally rewarding. On Wednesdays, for instance, you have the choice of the 671 from Okehampton to Newton Abbot, which stops at some of north Dartmoor's most rewarding villages – Chagford, Manaton and Bovey Tracey – or the 672 between Newton Abbot and Buckland-in-the-Moor via Widecombe – perhaps the prettiest route of all. Both give you ample time for exploration before catching the return bus. And why settle for once a week when you can take the 113 that only runs three or four times a year (see box, page 200)?

The once regular **Transmoor Link** (82) from Exeter to Tavistock is now reduced to one a day, summer weekends only, but it's still worth planning the ride for its dramatic moorland route along the B3212 from Moretonhampstead to Yelverton. Outside the holiday season, however, you will need to get creative with the two relevant bus timetables: *Teignbridge and West Devon* and the interactive map on ☞ www.journeydevon.info.

TAVISTOCK COUNTRY BUSES

When I read about 'Britain's rarest bus' I was intrigued. Who could resist a bus that runs on the fifth Saturday of the month, summer only? So when the 113 made its last journey of the year, having ventured out only twice before, we were aboard. The Tavistock Community Transport Association was founded in 1981 to provide transport to areas not serviced by commercial bus companies. It is run entirely by volunteers, and now I'm able to speak from experience I can say that it's just wonderful.

We picked the 113 for its rarity, and for its enticing route from Tavistock across the moor to Dawlish and back, but there are other equally appealing and more regular services that also cross Dartmoor or venture over the county border into Cornwall. They all return to Tavistock after a break of a few hours to allow for visiting, shopping or sightseeing. We made our way independently to Dawlish having booked our seats in advance (☎ 0758 0260683) – a wise move since the bus was full. There were cheery greetings as our fellow passengers met again after their four-hour break in Dawlish. 'Yes, lovely. Went for a swim!' and 'Thanks, yes, mum's doing fine.' We got a look at Teignmouth, and Ashburton, before plunging into one of Dartmoor's prettiest valleys, bordering the River Dart to Holne. We barely squeezed our way across New Bridge before climbing up to Dartmeet and Two Bridges. On to bleak Princetown and finally Tavistock, arriving dead on time after a journey of two hours. Perfect!

CYCLING

The lanes around the moor are too steep and narrow for all but the most sturdy and courageous cyclists. There are, however, few restrictions to cycling off-road as long as you stick to bridleways and designated cycle tracks. Many of these follow dismantled railway lines with easy gradients but you need a proper mountain bike to cope with the rocks and loose stones. The national park authority has comprehensive cycling information and maps on ⏚ www.dartmoor–npa.gov.uk.

Among the several dedicated cycle paths is The **Dartmoor Way**, a 95-mile circuit around the perimeter of the national park, some of it along abandoned sections of railway. Now clearly signposted, it is strenuous in parts, but always on hard ground so perfectly manageable for an ordinary cyclist. There are plenty of pubs and B&Bs throughout the route so you can do it in two or even three days, using Luggage Transfers (see page 202) or taxis to transport your bags. The Princetown railway track is also a popular route for mountain bikers. Easiest of all is the four-mile circuit round **Burrator Reservoir** in western Dartmoor.

Bikes can be hired at **Devon Cycle Hire**, Bridestowe, Okehampton (✆ 01837 861141) at the start of The Granite Way, at **Tavistock Cycles** (✆ 01822 617630) and **Bikus** (✆ 01626 833555) in Bovey Tracey. **Let's Go Biking** (✆ www.letsgobiking.com) will do a holiday package for you which includes luggage transfer so you can enjoy the Dartmoor Way unencumbered.

If you like cycling but look at Dartmoor's hills in some dismay, consider going on a guided tour with **Dartmoor Electric Cycles** (✆ 07914 184220 ✎ www.highdart.co.uk/electric-bikes) which do the hard work for you.

WALKING & BACKPACKING

Until I came to live in Devon I avoided walking on Dartmoor, imagining waist-deep bogs negotiated in driving rain, and being lost for days in landmark-obscuring mists. So I've been excessively pleased by the reality – strolls along tumbling brooks, walks through bluebell woods, striding out along a disused railway with the knowledge that it won't suddenly take me up an energy-draining hill, and grassy paths up to tors with a 360-degree view.

That said, walkers should take the challenges of Dartmoor seriously. On the moor itself there is no shelter from lashing rain, mist can descend suddenly, leaving you with no idea where you are, and to cap it all there's a Dartmoor speciality, 'featherbeds', which are bogs covered by a firm-looking layer of moss. Step on them and you'll feel as though you're balancing on jelly – until you sink in. So stick to well defined paths and check the weather forecast.

The walks described here are mostly easy, two- or three-hour affairs, but die-hard hikers can get their teeth into the real thing by tackling the 102-mile-long **Two Moors Way** which runs from Ivybridge on the southern edge of Dartmoor (accessible by train), across the roadless area of the southern moor, before revisiting civilisation at New Bridge and continuing north to Exmoor. The first stretch is 18 miles of moorland, so a serious undertaking, but the feeling of being utterly alone in one of the most densely populated countries in the world makes it worth the effort. It also allows you access to **The Dancers**, a group of stones at the head of perhaps the longest prehistoric line of stones anywhere (over two miles), and to an ancient clapper bridge (a somewhat timeless design of all-stone span that appears in various parts of Devon and Cornwall; all Dartmoor's clapper bridges are medieval) that has never seen motor traffic. After Holne the path frequently crosses roads so can be walked as part of a circular route if you are not planning to do the whole thing to Exmoor. When I was last at Ivybridge I met a group of walkers about to set out on the trail. They had arranged taxis to carry their luggage between B&Bs ('much cheaper than a package deal') but **Luggage Transfers** (⌂ www.luggagetransfers.co.uk) will deal with the whole business efficiently.

The **West Devon Way** runs for 37 miles between Okehampton and Plymouth, skirting the western edge of the moor, while the **Templer Way** (see box, page 156), running from Teignmouth to Haytor, is only 18 miles long and accessible in many places by public transport.

Most people will be looking for a variety of **day or half-day walks**. With the help of the OS Explorer map you can safely plan your own route according to energy, weather and interests. Some bus-assisted walks which allow you to walk from A to B without returning to your starting point are described later, but otherwise just spread out a map and get planning. If you have children a route taking in a few tors is ideal since these provide excellent scrambling as well as views for the grown-ups and are perfect picnic spots. They will be less rewarding – or even downright dangerous – on a wet and misty day, however. River valleys are perfect in inclement or warm weather, being protected from driving rain and affording the chance to cool off if it's hot. The disused railway line and quarry tracks make for easy, safe walking even if the weather closes in, and are firm underfoot, and if you check out pub locations on the national park website or in the *Dartmoor Guide* you can build in a well-earned meal or drink.

"River valleys are perfect in inclement or warm weather, being protected from driving rain and affording the chance to cool off if it's hot."

The National Park runs **guided walks** throughout the year, varying in length from two to eight miles and covering every area and aspect of the moor. Led by knowledgeable and enthusiastic guides, these are a great way of getting under the skin of Dartmoor. There is a small fee for the walks, but they are free for those arriving by public transport. Another good reason to take the bus! **Llama walks**, based near Widecombe (✆ 01364 631481 ⌂ www.dartmoorllamawalks.co.uk), offers guided walks where your luggage and picnic are carried by llamas.

Dartmoor is one of the few places in England where true **backpacking** – carrying all your needs for a few days in the wilderness – is both possible and sensible. Camping is permitted almost everywhere, providing you avoid farmland, prehistoric sites and enclosed areas. If you'd prefer not to carry your own tent there are a dozen youth hostels and bunk houses scattered around the moor. However, to my mind once you've experienced the freedom of wild camping, and if you're strong and fit enough to carry a pack, there's no contest between it and dormitory accommodation. See the Dartmoor National Park website (below) for more information on where you can and can't camp.

Walking maps & guides

The OS Explorer map OL28 is the best walker's map – at 1:25,000 scale, double sided, it shows all the national park and all field boundaries. The rights-of-way network on it doesn't initially look that impressive, but once you've worked out that there's free access to much of the open land, and that the little black dashed lines on the map are usually walkable paths, things get a lot easier. If you're driving or cycling, the 1:50,000 Landranger maps 191 and 202 give you just the right level of detail.

Harvey's map of *Dartmoor* at a scale of 1:50,000 is good for planning walks though not really detailed enough to use without the backup of the OS Explorer. It doesn't mark churches.

Even if you're an expert map reader it's well worth buying a **walking guide** so you can get a feeling for what's achievable. The Bossiney guide, *Shortish walks on Dartmoor*, is easy to follow with clear maps, and *Pathfinder Dartmoor: walks* is comprehensive and clear.

Bus-assisted walks

There's something smug-making about combining a bus trip with some walking. You feel complacently green, and there's none of the hassle of parking your car and returning to your starting point. I have given a few ideas in this chapter for bus-assisted walks near Manaton (see page 215) and Merrivale (page 233). Bus timetables change and services are – sadly – being withdrawn, so do check the latest schedules.

RIDING

Climbing the hills on someone else's legs has an obvious attraction, and riders will have an experience far superior to a normal hack along rural bridleways. There are several riding stables on Dartmoor, and all offer a variety of rides ranging from one hour to all day.

I have ridden from most of the stables listed below, and always had an exceptional experience on good horses and enjoying remarkable scenery. Riders need to be honest about their abilities. I was told that

DARTMOOR PONIES

In contrast to Exmoor, where all ponies on the moor are similar in appearance (as you would expect of a distinct breed), Dartmoor's ponies are much more varied. There are few true Dartmoor ponies left now, the result of generations of cross-breeding, there being no rules on which ponies may graze Dartmoor common land as long as the stallions used to breed from do not exceed 12.2 hands (4 feet 1 inch) and are believed by a vet to be fit for surviving the often harsh conditions found on Dartmoor.

Since no pony is truly wild, and many will be sold on at some point, there are commercial considerations. 'Coloured' (piebald or skewbald) ponies attract higher prices than bay or brown, the original Dartmoor pony colour, so they are replacing the less strikingly coloured animals.

Pony drifts, when the animals are rounded up and marked for ownership before being sold on, take place once a year in the autumn. The pony markets are held at Tavistock on the first Friday in October and Chagford the second Thursday in October.

The Dartmoor Pony Heritage Trust (DPHT) was set up to preserve the unregistered Dartmoor pony gene pool, and to maintain the traditional native herds on Dartmoor. It aims to increase the value of the annual foal crop through handling, castrating colts not suitable for breeding and promoting the good temperament and versatility of these moor-bred ponies. Every year the Dartmoor Pony Heritage Trust, supported by Dartmoor Pony Society, assesses the quality and conformation of the foals and awards the cream of the crop Heritage status.

One of the Trust's most successful strategies for highlighting these ponies' exceptional temperament is through its 'Ponies Inspiring People' programmes aimed at young people with physical, emotional, behavioural and learning disabilities. Dru Butterfield, the manager of this charity, explained that through various courses they have been able to help many young people with problems ranging from anger management to attention deficit and autism, along with those with multiple physical disabilities.

The **Trust's visitor and education centre** is in the Parke Estate, near Bovey Tracey, TQ13 9JQ (www.dpht.co.uk 01626 833234; open Sun afternoons Apr to the end of Oct, and during school holidays; it is always best to check in advance if they are open as they are manned by volunteers).

TOURIST INFORMATION

Bovey Tracey Tourist Information Centre ✆ 01626 32047 ⌂ www.boveytracey.gov.uk
Moretonhampstead Tourist Information Centre New St ✆ 01647 440043 ⌂ www.
moretonhampstead.co.uk
Tavistock Tourist Information Centre The Archway, Bedford Square ✆ 01822 612938
⌂ www.tavistockonline.co.uk. Threatened with closure at the time of writing.
Widecombe Tourist Information Centre ⌂ www.widecombe-in-the-moor.com

riders who could count themselves experienced at home, because they rode regularly in an enclosed school, were sometimes unprepared for a hack in such rugged terrain. It's better to underestimate your proficiency. Complete beginners are welcome at most places – the ride will be tailored accordingly and the horses are used to taking care of such people. If you are riding fit, an all-day ride is superb, allowing you to experience a variety of countryside and have a good pub lunch.

Most stables offer similar rides at a similar cost, about £20 for an hour, and do half-day pub rides:

- **Babeny Farm Riding Stables** Poundsgate ✆ 01364 631296
- **Cholwell Riding Stables** Mary Tavy ✆ 01822 810526
- **Shilstone Rocks Riding Centre** Widecombe-in-the-Moor ✆ 01364 621281 ⌂ www.dartmoorstables.com
- **Tor Royal Stables** Princetown (also offer luxury B&B – see page 244) ✆ 01822 890189 ⌂ www.torroyal.co.uk

CHAGFORD, CASTLE DROGO & THE NORTH

This is one of the prettiest areas of Dartmoor, with more than its share of river gorges, tors and prehistoric ruins, as well as the delightful **Stone Lane/Mythic Sculpture Garden**, which is close to **Spinsters' Rock**. Chagford makes a perfect base for exploring the region, and you can dispense with your car since this village can be accessed by public transport in both summer and winter. The 173 bus runs several times a day from Exeter, stopping at Drewsteignton and Castle Drogo, and the 178 runs twice a day from Okehampton, so all the places described here can be seen on a 'bus-assisted walk'.

1 CHAGFORD

The first time I came here it struck me as almost too perfect, and a little complacent with it. Perhaps it was the ideal location, sandwiched between the River Teign and Chagford Common, cluttered with prehistoric remains, or the satisfactory shape of the village with a defined centre dominated by the 'Pepper Pot' market house. But now, after many visits, I love its relaxed atmosphere and the mixture of innovation and traditional. In the square is the Devonshire Dairy which sells local cheese, honey and Dartmoor-bred lamb but the town is dominated by the enormous hardware shop, James Bowden, where DIY enthusiasts can disappear for hours. Chagford has a very good vegetarian restaurant, the Courtyard Café, down the hill to the left of the Pepperpot, which specialises in wholefoods.

"The church features include a 400-year-old stone carving of an archangelic St Michael, slaying a 'nasty little demon'."

If you are spending some time here you might like to learn about rush work from Linda Lemieux who runs courses on a variety of traditional crafts using local materials (✆ 01647 231330 🖰 www.woodandrush.net).

This was a stannary town and shows its former tin wealth in its church which has some 'tinners' rabbits' on one of the bosses. Although much restored, with some very modern additions, the church has great appeal; its features include a 400-year-old stone carving of an archangelic St Michael with luxuriant locks, slaying a 'nasty little demon'. The modern carved wood pews and pulpit are especially fine. Look out, too, for the painstakingly done needlework hanging in the south aisle; showing the history of the region, this was made by the Chagford Women's Institute.

Shovel Down

For a total immersion in prehistoric sites, have a walk on to Shovel Down near Scorhill, at the end of tiny lanes west of Chagford. It has a bit of everything, but you need to follow the OS map carefully to locate them – a clapper bridge (Teign-e-ver Bridge), Scorhill stone circle, several stone rows, a standing stone aptly known as the Long Stone and Round Pound (an Iron-Age animal enclosure). Park near Scorhill Farm (❈ grid reference SX661877), walk southwest past the stone circle, then southeast over the clapper bridge to Batworthy Corner and the Long Stone, then head northeast up Kes Tor for a splendid view over the whole area.

TO BOLDLY GO...

If this chapter tempts you to explore Dartmoor, beware! It's a place of many and fearsome hazards. Take the pixies, for a start. They're friendly little beings on the whole, but if you mock or disbelieve in them they turn distinctly nasty. Visitors who are 'pixie-led' can lose all sense of direction and wander alone for days through the mist or be drawn to their death in marshes. Be particularly careful not to trample foxgloves or stitchwort, as these are their special flowers, and don't venture near their cave on Sheepstor. If you do feel threatened, quickly turn your jacket inside out (or your pockets, if you're not wearing a jacket) as this will appease them.

Then there's the Devil. Despite its many churches, Dartmoor is one of his favourite haunts. In 1638 he caused consternation in Widecombe when he tethered his horse to the church tower, bringing it crashing down as he galloped away. Today he and his Wisht hounds, huge and fearsome black creatures with eyes like glowing coals, hunt at dead of night by Dewerstone and Hound Tor; you may hear their ghostly baying in the distance. Should you catch the appetising scent of bacon frying near Mis Tor, don't be tempted to investigate; his frying pan is there and he'll be cooking up his breakfast.

Witches are another risk. To mix her potions, the Witch of Sheepstor uses the water from Crazywell Pool, and Bowerman the Hunter was turned to stone (Bowerman's Nose) because he and his hounds accidentally disturbed a coven of witches when they

were making spells. In fact there's a serious danger of being turned to stone for some inadvertent misdemeanour, so watch your step, particularly on Sundays: it happened to the Nine Maidens at Belstone Tor and The Dancers, because they danced on the sabbath.

If you're driving or cycling along the moor's roads, beware of the Hairy Hands: they'll grab the steering wheel or handlebars and try to force you off the road. Mostly they're on the B3212 near Postbridge, although they've appeared near Exeter too. Making the sign of the cross is said to discourage them. Running to a nearby cottage for help doesn't necessarily work: some travellers near Buckfastleigh were approaching one at dusk, attracted by the lights in its windows, when suddenly it vanished. UFO encounters have been reported on Dartmoor too, so watch out for aliens.

A headless coachman drives Lady Howard's coach and horses across the moor from Okehampton; Benjamin Gayer, a former mayor of Okehampton who was hanged on Hangingstone Hill, appears as a black pony; and the black pig that haunts Lydford Castle is actually the infamous Judge Jeffries. Less threatening are the sad little piglets of Merripit Hill, thin and starving, which trot desperately to and fro in search of food. If you've survived all these, then be careful in Ashburton: the malevolent red-eyed water-sprite Cutty Dyer, who lives by King's Bridge, accosts drunks and other undesirables and throws them in the river. Normally he tolerates tourists, but one never knows....

¶¶ FOOD & DRINK

Gidleigh Park near Chagford TQ13 8HH ✆ 01647 432367 🖰 www.gidleigh.com. Set in its own 45 acres, yet near Chagford, this is a seriously posh hotel with a two-star Michelin restaurant. Come here for that very special treat when you don't care how much you spend.

22 Mill St Chagford ✆ 01647 432244. Top-quality dining at a slightly lower price than Gidleigh Park. Highly thought of by locals and visitors.

Three Crowns High St, Chagford ✆ 01647 433444. A fine thatched inn in the centre of town with excellent food and good accommodation.

2 CASTLE DROGO

Castle Drogo EX6 6PB ✆ 01647 433306; National Trust. Open early Mar to end Oct and winter weekends.

'It looks like a Stalinist gulag!' a visitor remarked. 'And the tapestries look like old bedspreads,' his wife added. Indeed, some find it hard to warm to this monument to 20th-century extravagance and megalomania. But warm I did, and I think it's worth the effort.

Drogo was conceived by Julius Drewe, who retired at the age of 33 and, needing a way to use up his money, decided without any evidence that he was descended from the Norman Baron Drogo de Teign who had given his name to Drewsteignton. Now he needed an ancestral home; so he bought the Drogo estate in 1910 and employed Edwin Lutyens to make his dreams reality. Not a bad commission, even for the most renowned architect of the 20th century.

I never thought that granite could look identical to concrete, but that's the impression given by the precisely cut blocks of stone. Inside, the plasterless walls are the same austere grey and even the furniture is all right angles. The feeling of incarceration is not helped by the muted light. But as you make your way through the house, things soften and brighten, and, coaxed by the enthusiasm and knowledge of the National Trust volunteers, I started to appreciate what I was seeing. The drawing room is almost cosy, for instance, a light, bright room with windows on three sides allowing you to appreciate the castle's magnificent location: ahead lies craggy Dartmoor, and to the side is the Teign Valley. The Dining Room is quite intimate since the Grand Design was never completed. Indeed, the original plans show a castle of, as the brochure puts it, 'heroic size', which must have made Lutyens very, very happy.

The human side of this story is what makes a visit to the castle ultimately rewarding, and this is found in the small room called Adrian Drewe's room.

Fingle Bridge & the Teign gorge

❄ OS Explorer map OL28; start from Fingle Bridge, grid reference SX743899.

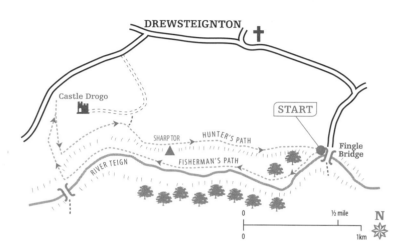

One of the most popular walks on Dartmoor, this 3½-mile 'circular' (oblong really) walk takes you from the picturesque Fingle Bridge, south of Drewsteignton, along the Fisherman's Path which hugs the north side of the River Teign, passing through deciduous woodland and mossy rocks. There are several places where you can swim in the deep pools of the river.

The return is along the high-level Hunter's Path over open moorland, with gorse, heather and stands of silver birch. There are opportunities to access the Castle Drogo estate at the western end of the circuit, and the walk can begin from the Castle's car park instead of Fingle Bridge (where the parking is limited); here you can pick up the National Trust's booklet *Walks in the Teign Valley and Castle Drogo Estate*.

Variations of the walk can be done by taking bus 173 to Drewsteignton and catching it again at Castle Drogo.

Adrian was the first-born son who died in 1917 at Ypres, at the age of 26, having been married for just one year. As the oldest boy he had been involved in the planning of Castle Drogo from the beginning. It's clear from the lovingly displayed memorabilia in the room how deeply missed he was, and one imagines that his father's enthusiasm for the great castle died along with his son. The reduction of the original plan by two-thirds could not have been purely for financial reasons.

Lutyens' ingenuity is found throughout the house. Electricity, for instance, was a relatively new thing, and there are all sorts of electrical gadgets including an electric tablecloth to keep plates warm, and an electric cup-and-saucer warmer. The shower unit incorporated with the bath wouldn't be out of place in a modern bathroom and the loo has a state-of-the-art flush.

The enthusiasm of the National Trust volunteers is infectious. Ginnie Woolfe has been working here for more than ten years. 'I love it not only because the castle is in such a stunning position, but because it's filled with all the interesting items that the Drewes brought back with them from their travels and from their previous home, Wadhurst Hall. Chatting with the visitors is my favourite part of the job. They come from just about anywhere in the world, and I don't think I've ever talked to a visitor who hasn't loved the place.'

The castle is undergoing a five-year, £11 million refurbishment. Basically, it leaks. And it leaks because Mr Drewe specified that there should be a flat roof and no windowsills or guttering. It's a mammoth operation, necessitating the removal of 900 windows. However, the castle will remain open with the opportunity for the public to take a look at how the conservation is progressing – and to learn more from the volunteers. Castle Drogo is served by bus 173 between Exeter and Moretonhampstead (weekdays) or the 274/279 on Sundays and bank holidays.

SIR EDWIN LUTYENS 1869–1944

The home-schooled architect of Castle Drogo was uncomfortable with his wealthy public-school-educated patrons, preferring to sketch ideas for mansions on napkins when seated next to their wives at dinner parties. The commissions that followed were traditional in style but always demonstrated some unique features; Lutyens was as involved in the interiors as with the buildings themselves, including designing furniture. Budgets held little interest for him, and he made it almost a point of honour to exceed them. In 1897 he married Lady Emily Bulwer-Lytton, the daughter of a former Viceroy of India, which must surely have helped him secure his greatest commission: to design the new administrative centre in New Delhi, a task which took him nearly 20 years.

Among Lutyen's best-known designs are the Cenotaph in London and Liverpool Cathedral, but perhaps his most appealing was Queen Mary's Dolls' House which is on permanent display in Windsor Castle and was created as a showcase for the craftsmen of the time. He was knighted in 1918.

¶¶ FOOD & DRINK

Drewe Arms Drewsteignton EX6 6QN ✆ 01647 281224. This 17th-century thatched pub, right next to the church, serves good food and local ales in an assortment of small rooms, and has a history tied to Castle Drogo. It was Drewe (who else?) who persuaded the landlord to change its name from The Druid Arms and provided his coat of arms for the inn sign. The Mudge family took over in 1919 and Mabel Mudge was reputedly the oldest landlady on record, retiring in 1994 at the age of 99 having run the pub for 75 years. She was 101 when she died.

Fingle Bridge Inn Fingle Bridge, Drewsteignton EX6 6PW ✆ 01647 281287. The verdant location by the river is the main draw here.

3 SPINSTERS' ROCK & STONE LANE/MYTHIC SCULPTURE GARDEN

The carved stones in these sites may span 5,000 years, but in their own way they are equally mysterious and appealing. How convenient that they are within walking distance of each other (less than two miles), and accessible by the 173 bus, although of course most people will drive.

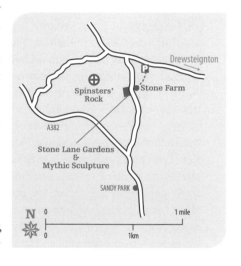

Spinsters' Rock (✻ grid reference SX701907), is a Neolithic burial chamber which stands nonchalantly in a meadow full of buttercups and, occasionally, cows. This chambered tomb or cromlech would once have been visible only as a mound of earth which has either eroded away or been removed to reveal the 'chamber' (now more like a shelter) comprising three upright stones forming a tripod, capped by a huge domed piece of granite. The sign tells us that it was allegedly built by three spinsters one morning before breakfast. Take the A382 off the A30, pass the sign to Venton on the left, and at the next crossroads you'll see it signposted. The gate leading to the site is opposite the yard of Shilstone Farm (a shilstone is the 'lid' of a cromlech). If coming by bus you will need to ask the driver to let you off at the turnoff, half a mile beyond Venton. It's a very pleasant walk up the hill to Shilstone Farm. The lane is shaded by huge beech trees straddling a stone wall, something you often see in Dartmoor. The trees would originally have been a hedge providing additional shelter for livestock, but no one told them to stop growing.

After looking at the tomb, continue up the lane to the T-junction and turn right, then either continue to the car park from where there's a short cut to Stone Farm where you pay your fee and collect your map or, if on foot or disabled, turn right again down the lane to **Stone Lane Gardens** (TQ13 8JU ℡ 01647 231311 🖰 www.stonelanegardens.com; open year round, 14.00–18.00 or dusk if earlier; Mythic Garden Sculpture Exhibition May–Oct). There are some parking places in the Stone Farm yard for disabled visitors. On quiet days an 'honesty box' collects your £5 fee, there are maps to guide you round the woodland paths and a printed list of the sculptures, and you're on your own to enjoy this perfect blend of the work of man and nature. Because what's special here is that this is not just five acres of woods and water, with some intriguing sculptures popping up in unexpected places, but a nationally important collection of birch and alder trees, collected by the late Ken Ashburner from all over the world. There are over a thousand trees, including *Betula ashburneri*, named in memory of Ken. I met June Ashburner up to her neck in shrubbery, yanking out weeds, and learned that 'we've been here since 1962, gradually buying up the land so we could start the garden. We now have 47 species of birch and 33 of alder. I change the sculptures every year. Yes, they're by different artists, and as you can see, there's lots of variety. Have you seen the spiders? They're rather fun – follow that path and you'll see them on the right.'

"What's special here is that this is not just five acres of woods and water, but a nationally important collection of birch and alder trees."

There was no way I was not going to like this place, since I love this sort of secret, woody garden and dabble at sculpture myself, but the Ashburners have made something exceptional here which is recognised by the various awards that they have won. Go and see for yourself.

THE EAST

In the triangle formed by the northern apex of the A382 and the B3212 is one of Dartmoor's few paying attractions, the Miniature Pony Centre, contrasting with some of the most remote-feeling yet accessible valleys in Dartmoor and two of its prettiest villages. Two of the gateway towns to the high moor are also here.

4 MORETONHAMPSTEAD

This pleasant little town sits right in the centre of Devon, surrounded by some wonderful countryside and with the moor on its doorstep. It has a few attractive old buildings (among them arcaded 17th-century almshouses and a fine 15th-century granite church) and a new, artist-led arts and heritage centre, **Green Hill Arts** (✆ 01647 440775 ⏏ www. greenhillarts.org), whose reputation is growing steadily. Details of current exhibitions, largely showcasing Devon artists, are on its website; a permanent display in the foyer traces the history of Moretonhampstead from AD700 onward. For more art, look out for the wrought ironwork outside the Parish Hall opposite the gallery, the sparrowhawk in the central square, and various other small artists' workshops and galleries tucked down side-streets.

The **Tourist Information Centre** in New Street is staffed by enthusiastic volunteers who love their town; it has a comprehensive stock of local information. Here – among the usual maps, lists of accommodation and local guides – you'll find a programme of walks run by the Moreton Ramblers' Club, which welcomes visitors. The main street has small independent shops with some good local produce – baking, meat, cheeses etc – and the area offers a choice of hotels, B&B or self-catering.

What struck us most about Moretonhampstead was its friendliness. Certainly some places are prettier, or richer in visible history, or more spectacularly located; but everyone we spoke to was so pleasant and so ready to spend time answering our questions that we continued on our way afterwards with a great feeling of warmth.

The Miniature Pony Centre

2 miles west of Moretonhampstead, TQ13 8RG ✆ 01647 432400 ⏏ www. miniatureponycentre.com. Open late Mar to end Nov.

This has been a perennial favourite within the Dartmoor National Park. Although aimed at families there is plenty for adults to enjoy here; just the sight of quite small children towering over these dog-sized ponies in the paddock brings a smile. The place is well organised, with a variety of other animals as well as the ponies: kune kune pigs which like nothing more than a scratch behind the ear, rabbits that are surprisingly tolerant of being petted, and pygmy goats. In contrast to the tiny ponies there are two massive heavy horses to remind us of the variety in the equine world.

A friend who lives in Doccombe finds this the ideal place to bring her grandchildren; it has enough child-pleasing attractions inside and out to happily fill a sunny or rainy day. 'The first decision is between seeing the new foals and donkeys in the open barn, or pedalling around on the tractors, then we might go to the outdoor activity area with tunnels, slides, rope climbing frame, and a small climbing wall, and then on to pat the ponies in the large paddock. Whatever the weather the wooden indoor activity area gets them excited with more sophisticated forms of climbing and scrambling apparatuses.' The Transmoor Link (82) bus stops at the Miniature Pony Centre.

5 MANATON & BECKY FALLS

Manaton was once two villages, Manaton Magna and Manaton Parva, which explains its fragmented nature. Upper Manaton, around the church, is perfection: a spacious green sets off the fine church of St Winifred, dressed in traditional Devon white, with a row of thatched houses behind it. One splendid house, Wingstone Manor, was, for a time, the home of John Galsworthy, who wrote *The Forsyte Saga*. The village green was bought in 1928 from its previous owner, Lord Hambledon (who owned a huge swathe of the region in the early 19th century), for £75 collected from parishioners.

The interior of the church has some rather splendid pillars of Devon granite and a fine wooden screen which was literally defaced during the Reformation. Every carved saint and angel has had its face chiselled away. A helpful explanatory sheet tells us what we would be seeing, if we could: for instance St Margaret of Antioch being swallowed by a dragon, with just her red dress visible as she disappears down its throat. She cut her way out of its stomach with her handy sword, so has become the patron saint of women in childbirth. Sadly, I have to admit that I couldn't find her. The view from the churchyard across the moor to Haytor must be one of the best in Dartmoor.

A little over a mile to the southeast are **Becky Falls** (TQ13 9UG ✆ 01647 221259 ᐩ www.beckyfalls.com), a delightful place for pottering although the waterfall itself is pleasant rather than dramatic in the summer. There are three walking circuits of varying difficulty so you can suit your visit to your abilities. It's quite pricey, at £6.95, so it's worth spending half a day here to enjoy the birdwatching (we saw a dipper bobbing about on the

Two Saturday walks to Manaton using the Haytor Hoppa
❋ OS Explorer OL28.

I tested out two Haytor Hoppa walks and found the timings spot on. For the first I did the full bus circuit, for the pleasure of it, and got off at **Parke** (❋ grid reference SX808783), near Bovey Tracey, to walk through the woods and along quiet lanes to **Lustleigh**, and then up to the beautiful mossy woodland of **Lustleigh Cleave** and down to **Manaton**. There's a particularly memorable bit close to Manaton where you cross the river on the boulder stepping stones known as Horsham Steps in the National Nature Reserve of Bovey Valley Woodlands. It would have been a perfect place for a picnic, surrounded by trees and birdsong, and with water to cool off in. This walk took four hours but I lingered over lunch.

The other, shorter, walk is from **Jay's Grave** (❋ grid reference SX733799) to Manaton, via the famous landmark of **Bowerman's Nose** (see page 227). A footpath runs south of the Nose and brings you out to Manaton. Two hours is sufficient for this walk. For both walks you'll need a good map (❋ OS Explorer map OL28 or Harvey's) which shows the footpaths.

rocks) and the mossy quietness (which you won't get during the school holidays). The high cost of visiting is justified when you bring children, with opportunities for boulder scrambling and some little ponies and enormous pigs to pet, along with some organised activities.

The Haytor Hoppa bus runs to Manaton and Becky Falls on Saturdays (summer only), and the 671 makes a single journey on Wednesdays all year. The timing allows you to explore Becky Falls and Manaton and have a meal at the Kestor Inn before catching the return bus.

¶ FOOD & DRINK

Kestor Inn Manaton TQ13 9UF ☎ 01647 221204 ⌂ www.kestorinn.com. This is actually in a little hamlet called Water, a half mile outside Manaton. Nice views from the conservatory area, and a mix of locals and hikers. Serves Otter real ale and home-made bar food.

6 LUSTLEIGH & 7 NORTH BOVEY

Here are two classically picturesque villages of thatched cottages, only a few miles from the A382, but cut off from mainstream traffic by the nerve-rackingly narrow approach lanes. Each has a very good pub and interesting church.

Lustleigh would probably feature in most shortlists of Devon's prettiest villages. It sits at the base of the Lustleigh Cleave escarpment (see page 215) which makes it an excellent place to stoke up on carbohydrates before tackling those hills. The village is best explored on foot, where you can

LUSTLEIGH BLUEBERRIES

The growing season for blueberries on Dartmoor is only six weeks – so how does a rural smallholder specialising in blueberries make a business out of it? 'We had to diversify', Nick Hewison of **Blueberry Bros** told me, standing behind an array of blueberry goodies at a farmers' market: jam, cheese, chocolates, including some wonderfully realistic marzipan blueberries, and a whole range of yummy bakery products. And even beer.

The Hewison brothers (Toby is the other half and, yes, the name is a take on The Blues Brothers) were brought up in Dartmoor. Their mother arrived in Lustleigh as a nine-year-old refugee from France in 1942, having escaped with her parents to Spain and caught a ship to Plymouth. Having grown Christmas trees for years she planted a few blueberry bushes in the 1990s – the acid soil and wet climate on Dartmoor being perfect for this crop. The brothers moved away and did other things. In 2005 they inherited the family house and planted 700 bushes in a part of their three-acre field that had grown the Christmas trees. 'The field was called Yonder, so we called our fruit Yonder Berries. I don't think we'd realised how labour-intensive it would be. We had to contend with badgers crushing 200 bushes, rabbits nibbling the leaves and voles attacking the roots. The fact that netting covered the bushes to protect them from birds was a plus for these animals: they were safe from predators!'

It was a 2009 trip to Maine, one of America's main blueberry-growing regions, which helped give them focus. 'We had realised that growing blueberries in such small numbers in such a location is unviable commercially and we were looking to see how blueberries were farmed and managed in the USA.'

They diversified into other blueberry products, including beer. 'We always have to keep an eye on costs. To begin with I printed my own jam labels, using the computer and a cheap laminator.'

The blueberry part of the Blueberry Brothers' activities will remain small scale, though they plan to grow their business in other areas. 'The blueberries we grow at Yonder remain the heart of the business but not the engine. We cannot rely on this small crop alone if Toby and I are to remain at Yonder. We need to build a business around the much broader concept of all things blueberry; be they bought in from a neighbour, frozen from abroad or in concentrated form from the USA.'

The Blueberry Bros products (www. thebluesbrothers.co.uk) are available at the regional farmers' markets, food fairs, and from Darts Farm (Topsham). In Dartmoor the main stockist is James Mann in the centre of Bovey Tracey.

follow the narrow car-free paths which wind their way around the thatched cottages. May Day is celebrated with aplomb on the first Saturday of the month with maypole dancing in The Orchard, which is reached by keeping the church on your right and going straight ahead at the (road) T-junction past the old post office where there's a display of yesteryear Lustleigh. In the centre of the Orchard is a rock carved with the names of all the May Queens since the 1960s. Continue through the Orchard for the footpath to Lustleigh Cleave.

"In the centre of the Orchard is a rock carved with the names of all the May Queens since the 1960s."

The church is worth a visit for its finely carved screen (though the painted panels have been defaced) and pew ends whose subjects include a rather jolly lion and an elephant. They are by Herbert Read, a fine wood carver who contributed to the beauty of several Devon churches at the end of the 19th century.

If driving here, it's generally quicker to ignore your satnav for the last few miles and follow the signposts.

North Bovey's grassy green is shaded by oak trees of different sizes, all planted to commemorate an event: variously Queen Victoria's Jubilee, George V and Queen Mary's Silver Jubilee, several coronations, and the smallest tree of all – the Millennium. The pub serves food that's good enough to make you want to linger and the church is delightful, with worm-eaten pews and mainly clear glass to let Dartmoor in. There's an elaborate carved pulpit, and a good screen (no painted saints, however). The floor of the nave is almost covered with crudely lettered memorial stones to parishioners who died in the 1700s, and a little harmonium sits waiting to rouse the small congregation to song. Above the approach to the altar are some brightly painted roof bosses; look for the 'tinners' rabbits' (see box, page 196) above the altar rail.

¶¶ FOOD & DRINK

The Cleave Lustleigh ☎ 01647 277223 🖱 www.thecleavelustleigh.com. Meals in this thatched, 15th-century pub are exceptional. John Whitton, who has lived in Lustleigh for 15 years, took it over with his son Ben in 2010 and prides himself on retaining the traditional pub atmosphere (log fires, wooden beams) while providing a reasonably priced, varied and imaginative menu of locally sourced food. In the rear is the renovated old station waiting room (pre-Beeching), London could be reached in about six hours) which gives access to the garden for summer lunches.

Primrose Tea Rooms Lustleigh   01647 277365   www.primrosetearooms.co.uk. Serves classic cream teas in its primrose-yellow, thatched cottage.

Ring of Bells North Bovey   01647 440375   www.ringofbells.net. Another 15th-century thatched inn (they also do B&B), with several small dining rooms and a sunny beer garden. Its restaurant serves high-quality food with an extensive evening menu and very good lunches accompanied by Otter and St Austell Tribute beers plus guest ales.

8   BOVEY TRACEY

Of all of Dartmoor's 'gateway towns', this is where I'd choose to spend a rainy day. Bovey (pronounced Buvvy) Tracey is an absolutely super town, Devon's undisputed leader where crafts are concerned. If you approach from the A38, you'll be able to park next to the helpful **Tourist Information Centre** and near the town's outstanding attraction: the **Devon Guild of Craftsmen** (Riverside Mill   01626 832223   www. crafts.org.uk; open daily). This is seriously good stuff, with all manner of crafts in a shifting exhibition, from jewellery and stained glass to sculpture, pottery and ceramics, as well as fabulous clothing. It also holds events and workshops including some aimed at children.

With all those sheep on Dartmoor, it's not surprising that there are two shops whose business depends on wool. Only some of the wool comes from local sheep. I learned why from Cat Frampton, a farmer

TEMPLER WAY: THE GRANITE TRAMWAY

This 18-mile trail is more than just a long-distance footpath from Teignmouth to Haytor, it is an extraordinary example of using a local material – granite – in hitherto unimaginable ways.

James Templer was born in 1722. An orphan, he ran away to sea and made his fortune in India. On returning to England he bought the Stover estate (see page 156) and built Stover House.

In the 1820s his grandson, George Templer, had bought a granite quarry on Haytor, Dartmoor, and needed to find a way of moving the blocks of stone to a seaport

so they could be transported to London (Dartmoor granite was used for many buildings and even London paving stones). So he built a granite tramway, using grooved granite instead of metal rails. Even the points and sidings were made out of granite. Teams of up to 19 horses pulled the huge, flat wooden trucks. The braking mechanism for going downhill was primitive, to say the least, but history does not tell us about the accidents that must surely have happened.

The granite tracks are still visible along parts of the Templer Way; on Dartmoor you can see them near Haytor and near Bovey Tracey.

(and jeweller – farmers need a second income these days). 'All our wool has to go to the Wool Board' she said. 'And there's almost no money in it. It barely pays the cost of shearing. In the old days the woolclip paid for all of the winter feed. Not any more.' I asked if she resented the Wool Board's control. 'Ha! The Wool Board is a pesky fly compared to DEFRA's charging rhino!' We left it at that. On my latest visit, however, I learned that the price of wool has improved; good news.

The longest established wool-related business is the **Bovey Handloom Weavers** (1 Station Rd ☎ 01626 833424 ⌂ www.boveyweavers.com). Cross the road from the car park and turn left. I spoke to Stuart Gregory who is the weaving side of the business. His wife, Liz, runs the shop. It was Liz's father who started the business over 70 years ago, having learned his trade in Scotland. The two looms that you can see being operated in the workshop are the Harris tweed type – splendid old things that were as interesting as the material being woven: tweed, rugs, and material for ties, headscarves, etc. I asked about alpaca and other fine wools. 'Weaving wool always has to be worked at a greater tension; it has to be twisted much harder so it doesn't pull apart. Knitting wool such as alpaca is too loosely spun to use on a loom.' That's why, I realised, **Spin a Yarn** (26 Fore St ☎ 01626 836203 ⌂ www.spinayarndevon.co.uk) stocks such a huge range of wools. Knitters have far more choice. This shop is a painter's palette of colours, all softly blending with each other. The yarns come from around the world and are enough to make a knitter's mouth water. Or fingers itch. Joyce Mason and her team sell yarn that is not available elsewhere in the country, and attracts visitors from far and wide. She also hosts one-day courses on knitting, crochet, felting and spinning. 'People love to have the opportunity to sit and knit and chat while learning new skills,' she says. 'It's the perfect switch-off from a hectic world.'

"The yarns come from around the world and are enough to make a knitter's mouth water. Or fingers itch."

A few doors before the Handloom Weavers is **Serendipity** (6 Station Rd ☎ 01626 836246 ⌂ www.serendipityquilts.co.uk), which focuses on patchwork and quilting. Myriam Van de Pas and her daughter Sunny sell a huge range of fabrics, patterns, buttons and other sewing supplies as well as finished goods, and run courses. While I was in the shop an old fellow came in for two more yards of material. He told us that a heart attack had put an end to his long walks on the moor so he'd taken up sewing instead. 'I've been making some amazing stuff' he said.

All the delights of Bovey seem to be clustered together near the river at the eastern end of town, but the **House of Marbles** is some way away, near the roundabout on the Newton Abbot road (Pottery Rd, TQ13 9DS ✆ 01626 835285 ⬦ www.houseofmarbles.com). Others may like this place more than I do. I was a bit disappointed; marbles are such beautiful things, and I'd been spoiled by the rest of Bovey so was hoping for more art and less commerce. That said, the marble run – the biggest in the world – is fascinating. I could happily have spent an hour watching the giant marbles progress along an intricate maze propelled by nothing more than gravity. And it's free.

Parke

TQ13 9JQ ✆ 01626 834748; National Trust. Open almost all year round, dawn to dusk.

This peaceful place, about a mile out of town on the B3387, is one of the National Trust's unsung properties, happily free from 'activities'. You come here to stroll in the gardens or walk in the woods, and that's about it, although the Dartmoor Pony Heritage Trust is here, open on Sunday afternoons to visitors, and the Dartmoor National Park Authority has its offices here in the old manor house. The 205-acre estate is open to the public and includes a walled garden in which a variety of fruit trees are being grown to demonstrate different cultivation techniques such as cordons, fans and espaliers. The information board adds: 'In time we hope to add examples of food that could be grown in our changing present climate, such as kiwi fruit, olives, citrus fruit, tea, pepper etc.' This felt optimistic on the chilly July day of my visit, but who knows… and if the experiment succeeds they will supply the cafés and restaurants of Devon's National Trust properties so it will have wide-ranging benefits. Also see Home Farm Café, below.

"This peaceful place is one of the National Trust's unsung properties."

The rest of the estate is given over to a selection of well-signposted woodland and river walks. And it's free.

¶ FOOD & DRINK

My favourite place in Bovey Tracey for lunch is the **Terrace café** at the Devon Guild of Craftsmen. Homemade food in spacious surroundings, inside or out, and those wonderful exhibits close at hand. For dinner in town the Dolphin Hotel is probably best…

Dolphin Hotel Station Rd, Bovey Tracey ✆ 01628 832413. A rather grand old 19th-century coaching house in the centre of town and serving good food.

A DARTMOOR MAN

From an interview with Tony Beard, the 'Wag from Widecombe'. Tony's Sunday lunchtime broadcasts on Radio Devon (www.bbc.co.uk/devon) have a following worldwide.

My mother was in service at a house in Dartmoor, which is where she met and married my father, a local lad. One story she often told was how she was invited to Sunday lunch at Higher Uppacott, the longhouse*. Dinner was cooked in the traditional manner in the huge fireplace, on a covered metal plate surrounded by the hot coals. She said it was one of the best meals she'd ever eaten.

I went to the local primary school in Widecombe and then got a scholarship to Plymouth College. My parents raised dairy cattle and needed help on the farm so for many years I delivered milk in the area. In the early days people would come and collect the milk, then we had a van and sometimes delivered the milk in churns. Bottles with cardboard tops gave way to metal tops. In the end we were supplying virtually the whole parish. When they brought in regulations saying milk must be pasteurised, the equipment was too expensive and we had to give up the dairy and go into beef. Delivering milk was a community service. I think I did everything except deliver a baby! For instance I would change light bulbs and replace a fuse. I would collect 10 or 12 pension books, go to the post office, pick up the pensions and deliver the money the next morning. That's all gone now. People had known me since the day I was born so they trusted me completely. It's been ruined now by red tape and mistrust. I think it's an honour to have lived through those times.

When electricity came to Widecombe in 1963 everybody bought a television. But we soon got fed up with watching that and started a little drama group. We did a pantomime and I used to compère it and sing a few songs. Eventually that led to my slot on Radio Devon. I do a Sunday show from noon to 2.30, chatting about the countryside and nature, and play some requests.

I've got the right voice for radio because of my accent, but dialect goes further than that. There are lots of different words in the Devon dialect, and these can even vary from region to region within the county. For instance that little creature the woodlouse has several different names; round here it's called granfer grigg. A blue tit is an ackermail and a wren is a tit-e-tope. We call a thistle a daishel, and sometimes we swap letters around so a wasp is a wapse.

* Regular escorted visits take place to Higher Uppacott. 01626 832093, or check www.dartmoor-npa.gov.uk or the *Dartmoor Guide*.

Home Farm Café Parke Estate 01626 830016 www.homefarmcafe.co.uk. This is a bustling and popular place, with freshly cooked meals and snacks using around 98% locally sourced produce and 80% organic fairtrade ingredients. Good coffee, too. Open in the daytime plus some weekend evenings.

9 HAYTOR

Four miles west of Bovey Tracey, Haytor is the best-known of all of Dartmoor's tors. Easily accessible from the road, the 1,499ft summit is almost always topped by the silhouettes of scramblers who have reached the top of this huge granite outcrop. Nearly two centuries ago some steps were cut and a handrail provided (now removed) to make the ascent easier, to the disgust of a local doctor who commented that the steps were 'to enable the enervated and pinguitudinous scions of humanity of this wonderful nineteenth century to gain its summit'.

It is no coincidence that the granite tramway (see box, page 218) ran from here; the granite is of exceptionally high quality, although erosion has now reduced Haytor's once single stone to two, with an avenue running between them.

ᵠᴵ FOOD & DRINK

Rock Inn Haytor Vale TQ13 9XP ☏ 01364 661305 ⌂ www.rock-inn.co.uk. A 300-year-old inn standing high on Dartmoor. Run by the same family for over 20 years, it offers convivial surroundings and local produce. Beer garden for fine summer days.

CENTRAL DARTMOOR

With Widecombe-in-the-Moor as its focus, this region offers the most variety and therefore the most appeal to visitors. It has bleak, open moorland, craggy tors, farms and wooded valleys sheltering villages accessible by steep, narrow lanes. Some of Dartmoor's oldest prehistoric sites are here, including **Grimspound** and well-known landmarks such as **Jay's Grave** and **Bowerman's Nose**.

10 WIDECOMBE-IN-THE-MOOR

To most visitors this village is the capital of Dartmoor, with a cathedral to boot. Its popularity as a tourist honeypot stemmed from the traditional song about Widecombe Fair (Old Uncle Tom Cobley and All): it's the one place in Dartmoor everyone's heard of. And once the tourists came they needed to be provided for; Widecombe must, for its size, have more tearooms and car-parking space than any other village in Dartmoor. Despite the coaches and crowds its charm is undiminished, making it an excellent base for exploring the moor and the valleys even without a car. With transport – car or bicycle – all of Dartmoor is within easy reach.

THE SNAILY HOUSE

While researching for this guide I unearthed an old story about two spinster sisters near Widecombe who, long ago, had existed on a diet of snails. Unsurprisingly, their cottage became known as the Snaily House. True or false? My Hercule Poirot instincts twitched. More versions of the story started to emerge as I probed, some brief and others clearly stretched to many times their true length by the teller's or writer's imagination. That's how it is with ancient tales.

It turned out that the sisters' small two-storey cottage, whose proper name was Whiteslade, did exist, and the crumbled lower part of the ruin is still visible today. The vegetation is tangled now, with gorse and nettles growing among the stones, but once it was a working farm. The snail legend seems to date from some time before 1840 and possibly referred to the thick black slugs that thrive in damp areas; locally they are sometimes known as snails. They may have been pickled or salted, as was done long ago in the Hebrides to provide food during the bleak Scottish winters. Probably some snails were involved too, perhaps spiced up with the wild garlic that grows nearby.

As the story goes, the two sisters were negligent farmers and produced poor crops, yet they appeared healthy and well fed even when times were hard; some villagers suspected them of stealing sheep or other livestock, while others whispered furtively of witchcraft. Few visited the isolated cottage. Then one day someone peered through the window as the sisters were sitting at their meal and saw with horror what was on their plates. For the story to have survived over almost two centuries, the discovery must have caused considerable local gossip, and yet it shouldn't have been so surprising: there are records of slugs being eaten in other parts of Dartmoor when food was short. It's a mystery how legends develop. But I leave you with the picture of the two old ladies in their isolated cottage, hunched together over their dining table by the light of a smoky oil lamp, tucking in to something that may or may not have been a greater delicacy than you or I have ever tasted.

The Snaily House lies a few hundred yards from the Bellever Forestry Commission car park, on the opposite side of the river Dart, reached by a rough and sometimes muddy path along the river bank. It's shown on the OS Explorer map of Dartmoor. Bellever is a mile or so south of Postbridge, via a turning off the B3212.

The village sits in a hollow, with the extraordinarily high tower (350 feet) of the church visible from the surrounding hills and giving it the popular name of the Cathedral of the Moor. Much of the **church** dates from the 14th century, but the tower was added later and reputedly paid for by well-to-do tinners. The church is dedicated to St Pancras, and I thought I'd find out something about this saint – partly to get the image

WIDECOMBE FAIR

Widecombe Fair (⌖ www.widecombefair.com), the popular market that enticed Bill Brewer, Jan Stewer, Peter Gurney, Peter Davy, Daniel Whiddon, Harry Hawk and Old Uncle Tom Cobley and all to borrow Tom Pierce's grey mare to transport them from their homes in north Dartmoor to the fun and revelry, is always held on the second Tuesday in September. Originally a livestock show, it has now evolved into more of a tourist attraction, with exhibitions and a funfair. The recently restored Uncle Tom Cobley model with its working parts, which was last exhibited 50 years ago, made its reappearance in 2009.

of a London railway station out of my mind, and partly because I was curious about the significance of the painting of Abraham and Isaac which hangs near the south door. It turns out that this young orphan was beheaded in AD304 as a 14-year-old for proclaiming his faith. He is patron saint of children, which explains the painting, and can also do his bit for headaches – well, he would, wouldn't he? – and cramp. And for perjury, although I'm not sure how that works… Quite a few of his relics ended up in England which explains why there are several churches dedicated to him.

There is plenty of interest in the church; it has a granite pulpit, brought down from the moor, and a good rood screen. The painted bosses on the chancel ceiling are easiest to look at via the information sheet which describes the legends attached to each of them. They include a Green Man and a pelican-in-her-piety, as well as the 'tinners' rabbits' (see box, page 196).

Mixed up with all the legends of Widecombe is the fact that during a dramatic thunderstorm on 21 October 1638, the church was struck by lightning and four people were killed, and many injured, when the tower crashed through the roof. Very little happened in the 17th century that wasn't the work of God or the devil. In this case, an innocuous-looking gentleman had popped into a Poundsgate inn for a glass of ale and asked the way to Widecombe. The landlady remembered afterwards that she heard his drink hiss as it went down his throat. In Widecombe the devil, for it was he, tethered his horse to a pinnacle of the tower while he went about his mischief with some local lads. Some say he was involved in a tussle to gain a soul, others that he simply forgot that his black steed was still tethered, and galloped away, toppling the tower. The pious congregation disregarded the fact that God had, perhaps, selected a time when a service was being held to do a bit of smiting, and the church records their gratitude and praise.

Next to the church is the original **Church House**, which was once an ale house to refresh travellers, and then a poor house. It is now the village hall and headquarters of the local National Trust, with a good bookshop and information centre. On the spacious green is a **Millennium Stone** under which are buried photos of every house and every family in the parish. However, they are on CD/DVD so whether the people who unearth it centuries hence will be illuminated or puzzled remains to be seen.

Time your visit to fit in with a tour by Tony Beard (see box, page 221). He will extend your knowledge and appreciation of his village.

¶¶ FOOD & DRINK

The Old Inn ✆ 01364 621207. Conveniently situated in the centre of the village, it is indeed old (14th century) and has a spacious car park. The food is simple but good, and reasonably priced.
Rugglestone Inn ✆ 01364 621327 ⌂ www.rugglestoneinn.co.uk. Named after a local logan stone (a wobbling stone that has become detached from its base), this small and very popular inn on the outskirts of Widecombe has been a favourite with locals and visitors for many years. The listed building is charming, the food very good and the location sublime. Open all day at weekends. Reservations essential.

11 HOUND TOR, JAY'S GRAVE & BOWERMAN'S NOSE

Northeast of Widecombe are some of the high moor's most iconic attractions. Park at Swallowton Gate, near Hound Tor, reached from either Widecombe or Bovey Tracey. If you visit on a Saturday, the Haytor Hoppa provides the perfect transport, or if you're a keen walker there's a popular three-mile walk from Haytor to Hound Tor which takes in part of the granite tramway (see page 218) and the medieval village (below). This starts at Haytor Information Centre (✱ grid reference SX765772) at Haytor Vale where information on the route can be found.

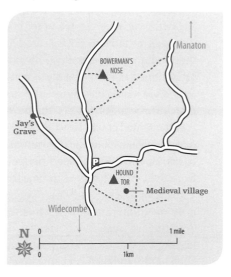

Hound Tor

Hound Tor is a wonderful jumble of rocks, often less busy than Haytor and providing plenty of scrambling for children. It is the starting (or finishing) point of several walks including Manaton (see page 214). It's also – surprisingly – the site of a ruined

"Hound Tor is a wonderful jumble of rocks, providing plenty of scrambling for children."

medieval village, although this is so hidden among the vegetation in summer that it's easy to miss. From Hound Tor car park, walk up the track that runs to the right of the tor and continue to the top of the rise; then as you pass the tor bear slightly left so that you're descending into a valley, rather than heading (to the right) for level moorland. You'll come to the low, broken foundations of around 12 buildings, some showing recognisable features. They're easiest to distinguish in winter or early spring, when there's less undergrowth.

Without a plan or some archaeological knowledge they're hard to identify; a helpful booklet by Lesley Chapman, *Grimspound and Hound Tor*, covers both these sites (for Grimspound see page 227). There's a good description of the village and its history on the English Heritage website (✋ www.english-heritage.org).

Activity on the land pre-dates the ruins: it was farmed for a while at least as early as the Bronze Age, then abandoned after a series of cold wet years when the climate deteriorated. Several centuries later, in about AD500, Saxon farmers on the lookout for good agricultural land began to work it, as it had conveniently been cleared of boulders by its previous inhabitants; they built rough homes of wood and peat, which haven't survived but can be identified archaeologically by post holes. Sometime in the 13th century, these were replaced by more solid stone buildings with wooden doors and thatched roofs. Some were traditional 'long houses', on a slight slope so that the family could live at the higher end and the animals at the lower; drainage channels from the animals' quarters are still visible. They had barns, gardens, ovens – and the people probably enjoyed a healthy diet, from their crops, livestock and nearby game.

The scope of the buildings suggests that it was a comfortable little farming community for a while, but in the 14th century the climate deteriorated again: persistently cold wet weather destroyed crops, leaving both animals and people hungry. Life on Dartmoor will have been hard – and then came the Black Death, sweeping its murderous way across the country. Some families may have struggled on for a time, but almost certainly by the early 15th century the homes were abandoned. Today it's a peaceful place, protecting the memory of moorland farmers from long ago; but any ghosts that flit around the ruins by night could surely spin a few medieval yarns!

Jay's Grave

From the car park take the left fork to walk to Jay's Grave. I first heard about this from my neighbour on the Haytor Hoppa. 'I haven't been there for a while but there always used to be fresh flowers laid there every day.' The grave belongs to Kitty Jay, a girl who took her own life after being seduced by a local lad. As a suicide she was buried outside the parish boundary, but exhumed in 1860 and reburied in a proper grave in its current position at a crossroads. Now I've visited it myself I can confirm that there were fresh flowers there – as well as some coins and an (empty) bottle of whisky.

Bowerman's Nose

From Jay's Grave it's a pleasant and easy walk along a footpath to the lane that runs north of Swallowton Gate, and then over a grassy hill to Hayne Down from where you can take a look at Bowerman's Nose before returning to your car. Despite the misfortune of having been turned to stone when inadvertently disturbing a coven of witches while out with his hounds, the hunter does not look unhappy. Indeed, he has the expression of a twitcher who has just spotted a rare bird. After all, he has an idyllic view of patchwork fields to look out on for eternity, and his faithful hounds are nearby, also turned to stone, on Hound Tor.

12 GRIMSPOUND

Grimspound is the best-preserved Bronze Age pound, or walled enclosure, on the moor and only a short, though steep, walk from the road, about four miles north of Widecombe. The rather fanciful speculations that this massive circle of stones was a Druid temple or Phoenician settlement were quashed when excavations in the late 19th century concluded that the large external wall was nothing more exciting than a corral for cattle, and the smaller stone circles within it the remains of huts, some of them dwellings and others food stores. Considering their age, the huts were quite sophisticated: you can still see the stone beds, which were probably covered with bracken or animal skins.

I had some trouble finding Grimspound by car on my first visit. The road is unsigned and the ruins are not obvious from below. Look for the sign to Headland Warren Farm and park at the lay-by just to its north (❋ grid reference SX808697). Opposite you'll see a couple of stone steps and a path that leads up to the site. Alternatively, walk there from Widecombe, taking the Two Moors Way; it runs above the site, thus giving you the best view of the circle and huts in this wild and desolate place. Imagine the time it would have taken to haul all those stones into position. Then visualise the hillsides covered in trees, providing cover for wildlife and edible plants, and the cattle safe inside the compound. Maybe it wasn't so harsh a life after all.

13 BUCKLAND-IN-THE-MOOR

Heading south from Widecombe, it's the thatched cottages that are the main attraction here, along with the clock on the **Church of St Peter**; the numerals have been replaced by the words 'MY DEAR MOTHER' in gothic lettering. But the church is so much more than the clock. For one thing it is clearly loved. On my first visit in the spring, jam jars containing bunches of wild flowers adorned every available surface and a note rested by a pair of reading glasses: 'Spectacles kindly left by a visitor for the use of other visitors'. And, yes, there's plenty to read here. A framed description of the church suggests: 'The church on its sloping site looks as if it were carved from a natural granite outcrop or perhaps risen over time fully formed from the rock of Dartmoor.'

"Once inside, you can appreciate the contrast between the rough-hewn granite pillars and the intricately carved wooden rood screen."

Before entering, look for the tomb of a soldier who died 'succouring a foeman'. It's touching how proud the community obviously was of this demonstration of humanity. Once inside, you can appreciate the contrast between the rough-hewn granite pillars and the intricately carved wooden rood screen. Its narrow uprights end in fan vaulting – a characteristic of Devon churches. There's a 12th-century font, but no stained glass – it's not needed when the windows look out on to a green and yellow landscape of trees and daffodils. Visitors can buy a tea-towel which provides a sort of poetic mission statement for the church and community, including the fact that they use the King James Bible. This adherence to tradition (and the beauty of the English language) has a historical echo. Up on nearby **Buckland Beacon** are two granite slabs on which are carved the Ten Commandments. These were provided by the same benefactor as the unique church clock: landowner William Whitely of Buckland Manor. Mr Whitely was one of many Devonians who felt strongly about the attempted introduction of a new prayer book (thought by many to have 'popish trends') in 1928. The proposal was rejected, and the Ten Commandments remind parishioners of God's unchanging laws – and landowner Whitely's influence.

The Beacon is not easily accessed from the village. With a car it is easiest to park at Cold East Cross (✳ grid reference SX 740742) and take the southerly track towards rocks which mark the Buckland Beacon (one of many such 'beacon hills' where fires were lit to commemorate the Silver Jubilee of 1935). The walk is level and easy, and from the top you have one of the choicest views on Dartmoor, a mixture of woods, river and moorland. On a clear day you can see the English Channel. The Ten Commandments Rock is just below the Beacon.

14 HOLNE

Holne's attraction is its notable feeling of community, a lively place with plenty happening – and a lovely walk there with an option to cool off in the river. Park or get off the bus at New Bridge and take the footpath south through National Trust property for about a mile. The track initially follows the River Dart through flower-filled woodland and then meanders uphill, crossing a field or two before emerging near the village. As the main track leaves the river you can take a small path to the swimming area where flat slabs of rock channel the stream into deep, cool pools.

Charles Kingsley, who wrote *The Water Babies* and *Westward Ho!*, was born here. His father was vicar, and Charles is commemorated in a stained glass window in the **church**, which is worth visiting in its own right. A splendid lightning-blasted yew stands in the graveyard, so hollow it resembles scaffolding rather than a solid tree. The church entrance is a little wonky – it seems to lean to the left – but inside all is as it should be. A striking rood screen similar to the one in Buckland depicts 40 saints of varying obscurity, and a helpful loose-leaf binder explains who's who and what they were patron of. The pulpit, carved in 1480 from a single block of oak, has recently been restored.

Another nice touch is the leaflet *Walks around Holne*, available in the church. Both Holne and Buckland-in-the-Moor can be reached by the 672 bus, which runs on Wednesdays.

¶¶ FOOD & DRINK

Holne has a 14th-century pub, the **Church House Inn** (✆ 01364 631208 ⌂ www. churchhouseinn-holne.co.uk), and a delightful community-run **village shop and tea room** (✆ 01364 631135). 'It's a struggle to keep going,' one of the volunteers admitted, 'we all lead such busy lives.' But keep going they do, with home baking and bird identification posters to enlighten viewers of the bird table which stands outside the window.

15 WISTMAN'S WOOD

'It's straight out of Tolkien,' a friend remarked. 'You wouldn't be surprised to meet a hobbit there.' Concealed on the western side of the B3212 which cuts across the moor, this small grove of stunted oaks is one of the few remaining examples of the forest that once covered much of Dartmoor, and is not to be missed. Perhaps I'm biased, having visited it on an intermittently sunny day in April, when the banks of the approach track were covered with primroses and the vanilla-scented gorse was in bloom. From the Two Bridges car park (❀ OS Explorer map OL28; grid reference SX609750) it's a two-mile walk north to the grove, first up a farm track and then across the moor where you scan the barren hillside ahead for anything resembling a tree. Suddenly there it is, a green-coated fairyland of gnarled and twisted boughs, festooned in epiphytes, ferns, liverwort and moss, the oaks finding footholds between moss-covered boulders. It's as though some fanatical knitter has been at work with miles of green wool. In early spring the low sun gave the leafless green branches an almost golden outline.

"Suddenly there it is, a green-coated fairyland of gnarled and twisted boughs, festooned in epiphytes, ferns, liverwort and moss."

THE WEST

Much of the western moor, north of the B3357, is used by the Ministry of Defence as a firing range (no doubt under the watchful eye of St Barbara – see page 159). If a red flag is flying, you can't go there. This uncertainty restricts the number of visitors to this part of the moor, which perhaps gives it extra appeal for those who like to be alone. One of Dartmoor's most interesting and popular ancient sites is here, but outside the 'danger area': the **Merrivale stone rows**. The stones are easily accessed from the road; park at the car park just east of Merrivale village. **Tavistock** is the gateway town to the region, with the other villages described here mostly lying to its north, on or west of the A386. The two Tavy villages, **Mary Tavy** and **Peter Tavy**, sound like a cosy married couple. They are named after their church saints, however. Mary Tavy was the centre of a copper boom in the 19th century, leaving Peter Tavy with the rural charm.

16 TAVISTOCK

One's heart lifts on entering this ancient town. There is no urban sprawl, just an arrival over a humped stone bridge with the view of the stately Victorian Gothic of Bedford Square. The first building of significance here was the Benedictine abbey, built about a hundred years before the Norman Conquest on the banks of the River Tavy. *Stoc* is old English for a farm or settlement. The abbey became wealthy, and the town's success was cemented when it was made one of the first stannary towns. Fragments of the abbey wall still remain; some are clustered by the river and one piece is even incorporated into the wall of the Bedford Hotel.

"There is no urban sprawl, just an arrival over a humped stone bridge with the view of the stately Victorian Gothic of Bedford Square."

On the dissolution of the monasteries the abbey's land and the nearby town were bought by the Russell family who later became the Dukes of Bedford. The tin ran out, but a burgeoning cloth industry filled the gap before that too failed. However, just when the town seemed destined for oblivion, large deposits of copper were found at Mary Tavy at the end of the 18th century, and the new wealth of Tavistock was assured.

William Marshall, travelling in 1796, thought Tavistock had the potential to 'rank high among the market towns of the kingdom', adding: 'at present, though meanly built, it is a tolerable market town'. His prediction came true. It is now one of the most architecturally homogenous towns in the West Country, thanks to the money lavished on it by the 7th Duke of Bedford.

The Victorian Gothic architecture is most evident in Bedford Square, which is the centre of the town. Leading from the square is the covered **Pannier Market** (open Tue–Sat) which has been held here since 1105. Though you should forget picturesque visions of shoppers clustered round horses with loaded panniers, this is more than a standard market. There are permanent small shops and temporary stalls selling everything from plastic dinosaurs to organic bread, and a huge range of browsable goods from books, clothing and DIY requirements to vegetables, meat and local honey. These can also be bought at the busy **farmers' market** held in Tavistock on the second, fourth and fifth Saturday of the month. Once a year there is a **Goose Fair** (open second Wed in Oct) along Plymouth Road. You can buy just about anything there – except, possibly, geese. Historically these markets will have been just as their names suggest. The Reverend Stebbing Shaw, writing in 1788, describes the approach road to Tavistock: 'This being market day we met numbers of the people flocking hither with grain, a few sheep, and an abundance of Michaelmas geese. The common vehicles in this country are panniers and horses; nor did we meet a single carriage the whole day.'

> *"There are permanent small shops and temporary stalls selling a huge range of browsable goods from books, clothing and DIY requirements to vegetables, meat and local honey."*

Tavistock has a fine 15th-century church, dedicated to the converted Roman, St Eustachius. It is full of carved beams and angels, and monuments to the town's historic dignitaries. Most notable is Sir John Glanville, a judge, leaning uncomfortably on his elbow. John Fitz is laid to rest under a carved canopy, having survived being lost on the nearby moor where a carved stone with his initials covers the spring that he drank from to protect him from mischievous pixies who might have misled him further.

Sir Francis Drake is said to have been born here in 1542, in the Crowndale area about a mile from the centre. You may well spot his statue in Plymouth Road; it's rather surprisingly classed as a grade 2 listed building. For more about Sir Francis see pages 138–9. The little **Tavistock Museum** (Bedford Sq ✆ 01822 612546 🖰 www. tavistockhistory.ik.com) is open from March to October and has changing exhibits on the town's history.

A weekday bus-assisted walk from Merrivale

✳ OS Explorer map OL28; start at Merrivale car park, grid reference SX553750.

This four-mile walk can be done from Monday to Saturday using the number 98 bus, and takes you through a satisfyingly chronological slice of Dartmoor's history (do of course check the latest bus times, which may differ from those given here). By catching the (currently) 12.40 bus from Tavistock you can explore the prehistoric standing stones by Merrivale, walk along a disused railway line and visit a quarry where stones destined for London Bridge lie cut, but abandoned, and finish at Princetown in time to catch the 15.05 bus back to Tavistock. You will have more time if you catch the earlier 09.20 bus from Yelverton (there are plenty of connections to Tavistock) which gets you to Merrivale at 10.14 giving you oodles of time for the walk, lunch and a visit to the prison museum (see page 234) at Princetown.

Get off the bus at **Merrivale car park**, and get your bearings from the television mast which supplies Princetown. Walk towards it and you should find the stone rows without difficulty. These are thought to date from between 2500 and 700BC and comprise two double rows of stones, with a third single row at an angle to the others. A standing stone, or *menhir*, marks each end of the rows and there's also a small burial chamber.

The second row is just beyond it, running parallel, and the small burial chamber is about halfway along. Next, head to a standing stone adjacent to a wall, then set your sights on **King's Tor** (and the television tower) to the north. This involves a certain amount of cross-country walking, but the disused railway track circles round it, so you can't really go wrong. After that it's easy – just follow the track to **Princetown**. You are walking on a nice piece of history here. The **Plymouth and Dartmoor railway** was built in the 1820s to transport granite from the quarries. When this became uneconomical in the 1880s the route was sold to the Great Western Railway. The last passenger service ran in March 1956. The track passes the disused Swell Tor Quarry, and if you have the time and energy it's worth investigation; look for the stone corbels that were cut in 1903 for the widening of London Bridge but never used.

If you have time to spare in Tavistock, take a stroll along the **canal**. Built to transport copper ore to Morwellham Quay (see page 148) it runs for 1½ miles before going underground. You can also walk across the viaduct, which is such a prominent landmark in the town.

As you would expect for a town of this size, Tavistock is easily reached by **bus** from Plymouth, and also by the 118 and 187 from Okehampton. You can also enjoy the 21-mile scenic cycle ride on the Drake's Trail from Plymouth (see page 130).

¶¶ FOOD & DRINK

Gorton's ✆ 01822 617581 ⌂ gortons-tavistock.co.uk. This is one of the best restaurants in the region. It has two great things going for it: the chef, Peter Gorton, and the dining room which is just that – an elegant dining room in a private house. Peter Gorton used to own the Horn of Plenty, one of the area's best country hotels, and the Carved Angel restaurants in Dartmouth, Exeter and Taunton. He is passionate about locally produced ingredients, and told me proudly 'The lamb comes from the moor, and the fish from around the coast'. His support for the Slow Food movement is shown in his book *Devon's Food Heroes* which profiles the county's food producers. 'When you're young you go chasing awards – like Michelin stars – but as you get older you want to do what you like best, and that's cooking'. He holds international evenings when diners take pot luck on their meals – Italian, French or whatever he fancies. He also runs cookery courses in people's own homes. 'Yes, they clean their kitchen obsessively. It's no good me telling them not to bother!'

17 MERRIVALE

The prehistoric standing stones by Merrivale can be explored on a four-mile walk (see box, page 233).

18 PRINCETOWN

At around 1,340 feet Princetown is the highest settlement on the moor; this and its well-known prison suggest a wild, bleak place with echoes of *Wuthering Heights*, but in fact it's a neat, functional little town geared to the needs of moor walkers and visitors. Rather than chain-gangs and fleeing convicts it has pubs, shops, eating places, B&Bs, its own brewery producing 'Jail Ale' and a small but worthwhile museum.

The town is not particularly old. In 1785 Sir Thomas Tyrwhitt, secretary to the Prince of Wales, leased a large area of moorland from the Duchy of Cornwall, intending to convert it into profitable farmland. The road from Tavistock was built and a settlement gradually grew, named Princetown after the Prince of Wales. The Plume of Feathers Inn, reputedly Princetown's oldest existing building, dates from around this time. When French prisoners from the Napoleonic wars were too numerous for Plymouth jail, Tyrwhitt suggested that a prison be built in his 'new town' to house them; the French were soon followed by American sailors from the war of 1812. The warders and other prison staff needed accommodation, so that was constructed, and in 1812–15 prisoners built the simple granite **Church of St Michael and all Angels**, which is now looked after by the Churches' Conservation Trust

(🖰 www.visitchurches.org.uk). Since then the small town and its prison have coexisted, their histories closely linked. Because of its position Princetown receives large numbers of visitors, many of them walkers; its **High Moorland Visitor Centre** (📞 01822 890414 🖰 www.dartmoor-npa.gov.uk) has a fund of local information (accommodation, routes, weather conditions, etc) as well as interpretive displays and exhibits. It's housed in the former prison officers' quarters, now much renovated; look out for the attractive floor mosaic.

Dartmoor Prison Museum (📞 01822 322130 🖰 www.dartmoor-prison.co.uk), housed in the old prison dairy just past the main prison entrance, has some intriguing exhibits and a gift shop with items made by current prisoners. Officially it's open year-round but times may vary because of staff commitments, so you're advised to check by phone beforehand. Apart from – as you would expect – displays related to the history and running of the prison, there are intriguing tales of individual prisoners and examples of their art and handicrafts. Fingers nimble enough to create duplicate keys from scraps of plastic can also make very fine models (one is of Concorde – perhaps its maker had grandiose dreams of escape?), often from matchsticks. There's some old farm machinery, and items used by the prisoners such as a 'man-hauling belt', with the aid of which they could pull carts around the prison and village. The extremely knowledgeable curator Brian Dingle takes pleasure in developing the displays and helping visitors, and enjoys his job; he told us: 'It's a very exciting place to work – always something to get out of bed for in the mornings.'

"There are intriguing tales of prisoners and their handicrafts. Fingers nimble enough to create duplicate keys from scraps can also make very fine models, often from matchsticks."

Princetown is served year-round (Mon–Sat) by the rather sparse Tavistock/Yelverton bus number 98; for seasonal summer routes – which may be threatened by financial cutbacks – check with 🖰 www.journeydevon.info.

🍴 FOOD & DRINK

Fox Tor Café 📞 01822 890238 🖰 www.foxtorcafé.com. In addition to all-day food, this has a bunkhouse and can arrange guided walks, mountain biking and cycle hire.

Plume of Feathers 📞 01822 890240 🖰 www.theplumeoffeathersdartmoor.co.uk. A busy and popular pub; also runs a year-round campsite and a bunkhouse.

19 PETER TAVY & A WALK TO THE LANGSTONE

Tucked away in a valley with the high moor to its east, Peter Tavy does not feature in most tourist itineraries, but has its own quiet charm, and is a base for some pleasant walks. Its church, with four exceptionally large pinnacles on the tower, is much maligned. W G Hoskins, that respected chronicler of Devon, describes it as 'abominably restored' and indeed it is more notable for what has been removed (such as the rood screen) than for what remains. However, it does have some fascinating carved oak panels, probably former pew ends, which are now fixed to the wall for easy viewing. The lively carvings are of a green man and some Tudor knights with feathers in their helmets, perhaps representing the members of the Drake or Cole families (the grave of Roger Cole, who died in 1632, is in the large and flower-spattered graveyard). All in all this church belies its negative reputation.

An interesting walk is to take the track, Twyste Lane, which runs from Peter Tavy up into the moor, passing the unsanctified grave of John Stephens who, spurned in love, committed suicide in the 18th century. A mile or so beyond is a tall standing stone, the **Langstone** (❋ grid reference SX559786). Over ten feet tall, this menhir is at the head of a stone row, but the stones aren't easy to see. It was used as target practice by American soldiers in the lead-up to D-Day; you can still see the bullet marks.

¶¶ FOOD & DRINK

Elephant's Nest Inn Horndon PL19 9NQ ✆ 01822 810273 ⌂ www.elephantsnest.co.uk. An isolated inn, renowned for its food and wide range of beers.
Peter Tavy Inn ✆ 01822 810348. A 15th-century inn full of charm and locals.

ACCOMMODATION

The places to stay listed in this section have been chosen with an eye to their location, because they are in some way unusual, or because they encapsulate the Slow approach. While prices for hotels vary greatly, most B&Bs in Devon charge around £60–80 per night for a double room. Of course, prices for all types of accommodation reach their peak during school holidays, especially in August. If you want to save money and avoid the crowds, there is much to be said for visiting out of season, when real bargains can be found. Campsites run the gamut from no-frills to luxurious 'glamping' options. The accommodation options listed here are just a small assortment of selected places that we happened to find or hear about.

In Devon by far the most popular accommodation is self-catering, offered by a large number of agencies. We have listed the agencies in the box on page 239, in alphabetical order, and then given an example or two of what they have to offer. Clearly they are just that – an example, chosen for their location – rather than singling out a place as being better than any others on the agency list.

1   THE EXE & TEIGN ESTUARIES

Guesthouses & B&Bs

Church Farm Haccombe, Newton Abbot TQ12 4SJ ☎ 01626 872310 ✆ www.wildlink.org. This elegant Georgian farmhouse, set in a tranquil valley rich with wildlife, is the home of TV wildlife producer Andrew Cooper; he and his wife offer B&B in two luxury *en-suite* double bedrooms (one with bath, one with shower) complete with badger-watching in comfort. There's a choice of full or continental breakfast, also of 'Special Breaks' which include dinner and a guided walk with Andrew around the valley. It's such a beautiful area; for more details see page 42. Visitors can be collected from Exeter Airport or Newton Abbot rail station if necessary.

The Turf Inn Exeter Canal, Exminster EX6 8EE ☎ 01392 833128 ✆ www.turfpub.net. Closed late Nov to Mar. This rambling old pub (see page 25) is wonderfully located, right on the edge of the Exe estuary, accessible only by foot, boat or cycle. It has just two cosy bedrooms, a twin and a double sharing a bathroom between them, up on the first floor looking out eastward across the water: with binoculars you can even birdwatch from your bedroom window. The rooms are generally only available i

A certain amount of basic **camping** – just tents, sharing an outdoor toilet, with a breakfast toastie available – is allowed on the lawn that fronts on to the estuary.

Self catering
Riverside Near Christow, Teign Valley ✆ 01548 202020 🖰 www.toadhallcottages.co.uk. A modern cottage, hidden away by the river in this uncrowded area, with a large garden and small pond for dragonfly viewing. Sleeps four.

2 THE ENGLISH RIVIERA: TORBAY
Hotels
Berry Head Hotel Berry Head Rd, Brixham TQ5 9AJ ✆ 01803 853225 🖰 www.berryheadhotel. com. A listed building in a stunning location on the cliffs close to the nature reserve of Berry Head. Recommended for birdwatchers and wildlife enthusiasts as well as walkers. Six acres of gardens, swimming pool, and ample car parking. Bargain breaks in the off-season.
The Palace Hotel Torquay, TQ1 3TG ✆ 01803 200200 🖰 www.palacetorquay.co.uk. The original, much smaller, building was the Bishop's Palace, built for Bishop Henry Philpotts in 1841. Converted and greatly extended into a hotel in the 1920s, it is notable for its position, within walking distance along lovely Bishop's Walk to Anstey's Cove, and has spacious grounds, golf course, tennis courts, swimming pool, and so on. Good bargains are available off-season. You can also walk across the fields to Babbacombe, with its two bookshops and interesting church.
Redcliffe Hotel Marine Drive, Paignton TQ3 2NL 🖰 www.redcliffehotel.co.uk ✆ 01803 526397. This extraordinary building, the legacy of India-loving Robert Smith, was converted from a private residence, Redcliffe Towers, to a hotel in 1904. Author Dick Francis famously stayed here every year for almost 60 years, so they must be doing something right. A new wing echoing the original style was added in 1986. It is large and very elegant, with an indoor swimming pool and the expected views of the ocean. And by staying here you are experiencing a unique bit of Torbay history. See page 57.

Self catering
Destiny Lodge (The Coffin House) Brixham ✆ 0844 7046518 🖰 www.bluechipholidays. co.uk. Chosen for its history (see page 62) – and clever renaming – this is a two-bedroom maisonette sleeping four, very close to Brixham Harbour.

3 TOTNES & THE RIVER DART
Hotel
rt Marina Sandquay ... outh TQ6 9PH ✆ 01803 832580 🖰 www.dartmarina.com. ...tel in Dartmouth with a riverside location. All the very

comfortable rooms have water views; most have a balcony which is ideal for relaxing and watching the boats and ferry go by. A nice touch in the bathrooms is the provision of House of Elemis toiletries which are also used in the hotel's health spa. The hotel is pricey but for peace, luxury and location it would be hard to beat, and they do offer special deals which include breakfast and dinner in the excellent restaurant. There are also fully equipped self-catering apartments. One more thing: for dog owners the hotel offers ground floor garden rooms with their own entrance.

Guesthouses & B&Bs

Dartington Hall Totnes TQ9 6EL ✆ 01803 847147 ⌂ www.dartingtonhall.com (see page 75). Dartington Hall is proud of its 50 bedrooms, in all shapes and sizes, in the East and West Wings around the beautiful medieval courtyard. Some overlook the courtyard, some the gardens. For meals, there's the refurbished White Hart Bar and Restaurant, just across the courtyard; and the 1,200-acre estate offers plenty of peaceful strolling. As the Dartington website says: 'We're not a hotel or a country house, we're an inspiring destination,' and profits from your stay will support the charitable work of the Dartington Hall Trust.

SELF-CATERING AGENCIES

Blue Chip holidays ⌂ www.bluechipholidays.co.uk. Southwest specialists.

Classic Cottages ⌂ www.classic.co.uk. West-country specialists. See advert, colour page 16.

Coast and Country Cottages ⌂ www.coastandcountry.co.uk. South-Hams-based self-catering holidays.

English Country Cottages ⌂ www.english-country-cottages.co.uk.

Exclusively Dartmoor ⌂ www.exclusivelydartmoor.co.uk. Not just accommodation but other useful bits of information.

Helpful Holidays ⌂ www.helpfulholidays.com. Based in Chagford, Dartmoor, with a huge range of places. See advert, colour page 12.

The Landmark Trust ✆ 01628 825920 ⌂ www.landmarktrust.org.uk. This charitable organisation is quite different from the other accommodation providers listed here. Their role is to rescue historic buildings in danger of dereliction, restore them, and rent them out to holidaymakers. Furnishing is done with an eye for the history and character of the place, and there are no televisions or telephones. A genuine Slow retreat, in fact. Because their properties fit the Slow ethos so exactly, all the places in this region are listed.

Toad Hall Cottages ⌂ www.toadhallcottages.co.uk. West-country specialists who go the extra mile for their clients.

Unique Homestays ⌂ www.uniquehomestays.com. S[...] places such as former barns or summer houses, which slee[...]

Hempstone Park Littlehempston, Totnes TQ9 6LP ✆ 01803 868268 🖰 www.
hempstonepark.co.uk. This Edwardian farmhouse has two comfortable *en-suite* bedrooms
(one double, one double or twin) with views across the garden to peaceful countryside.
Relaxation is the keynote: you can snooze on the lawn, stroll round the orchard and gardens,
tackle a gentle game of croquet or, at night, enjoy the stars in a virtually unpolluted sky.
For more energetic sightseeing you're only two miles or so from Totnes and Dartington Hall.
There are good walks nearby.

Kilbury Manor Colston Rd, Buckfastleigh TQ11 0LN ✆ 01364 644079 🖰 www.
kilburymanor.co.uk. Tucked away in the countryside between Buckfastleigh and Totnes, this
17th-century Devon longhouse is a clean, cosy, peaceful and friendly place, with good-
quality furnishings and lots of thoughtful touches. Hosts Julia and Martin look after their
guests well. Julia is an excellent cook – her breakfasts have won an AA award – and don't
miss her homemade marmalade. The house has four comfortable *en-suite* bedrooms and
a self-catering apartment, set in four acres of gardens and meadow. There are good walks
nearby, and safe parking.

Riverside House Tuckenhay TQ9 7EQ ✆ 01803 732837 🖰 www.riverside-house.co.uk.
A delightful 17th-century cottage with a garden adjacent to the water. Just two double
en-suite bedrooms with river views, and meals are served at the big table in the kitchen next
to the Aga by the companiable Felicity Jobson, an artist, or husband Roger. We love it, but it's
not suitable for those looking for spacious surroundings and formality. Sometimes available
for self-catering.

The Sea Trout Inn Staverton TQ9 6PA ✆ 01803 762274 🖰 www.theseatroutinn.co.uk. This
15th-century inn with an excellent restaurant (see page 75) has ten clean, comfortable and
well-designed *en-suite* rooms in its annexe. Fishing packages are available, which include
accommodation and daily/weekly permits for fly fishing on a nearby stretch of the Dart.

Self catering

Gurrow Point Cottage Dittisham ✆ 01548 202020 🖰 www.toadhallcottages.co.uk.
Exquisitely located at the tip of Gurrow Point, separated from the village by fields and a long,
tree-lined drive. Gurrow Point Cottage is part of a private estate and has beautiful views
of the Dart estuary and surrounding countryside. Guests are free to wander the 80 acres of
woodland and fields of the estate and enjoy over a mile of private river frontage. There are
also pretty gardens, a tennis court and pavillion.

Kingswear Castle ✆ 01628 825920 🖰 www.landmarktrust.org.uk. Surely the most
drama⋯ n. You can watch the stars – or ships – from the
the Union Flag. Sleeps four.

⋯5 268 0788 🖰 www.english-country-cottages.co.uk.
⋯r mill, the centre of commerce in this tiny village. Now

sensitively converted into a holiday complex with swimming pools, gym, tennis courts and so on, it has green credentials, with the pools heated by ground-source heat pumps.

Campsites
Poppy Yurt near Harbertonford, between Totnes and Dartmouth ✆ 01326 555555 ⌂ www.classicglamping.co.uk. A very comfortable yurt set on a raised wooden platform in a wild-flower meadow with woods for children to play in and a small lake. The yurt has an outdoor sink and a gas-fired barbecue; inside there's a loo and shower, and even a wood-burning stove. Sleeps four. No dogs.

4   SOUTH HAMS & DEVON'S FAR SOUTH
Hotels
Buckland Tout-Saints Hotel Buckland Tout Saints, near Kingsbridge TQ7 2DS ✆ 01548 853055 ⌂ www.tout-saints.co.uk. This luxury country-house hotel, tucked away in its own 4½-acre gardens, was once the old Buckland Manor House (see page 112) and the high ceilings, oak panelling and gracious rooms reflect its history. With 16 comfortable bedrooms and surrounded by open country, it's the perfect retreat. It's well worth checking out the off-season breaks and special offers. Food comes fresh from local farms and fishing boats or is grown in the hotel's own garden; menus are of a high standard and dishes (local crab, venison, lamb, duck and the like) are beautifully presented. Even the cream teas are in a class of their own, with champagne available if you feel like an added treat – and there are pleasant walks nearby to counteract the calories.

Burgh Island Hotel Burgh Island ✆ 01548 810514 ⌂ www.burghisland.com. Unique accommodation in a unique hotel (see page 124) Prices are the highest in this book: the most expensive room comes with its own private garden or beach.

Sun Bay Hotel Hope Cove TQ7 3HH ✆ 01548 561371 ⌂ www.sunbayhotel-hopecove.co.uk. A small, family-owned hotel and restaurant overlooking the exquisite Inner Hope village.

Self catering
Gara Rock East Portlemouth ✆ 01647 433593 ⌂ www.helpfulholidays.com. Currently four apartments and two cottages, each sleeping four or five people, are available. This is all about location – if you don't like remote, don't stay here. If you love walking, and want some luxury at the end of the day, this is the place. Unsurpassable cliff-top location, indoor and outdoor swimming pool, jacuzzi and sauna, and all the expected mod cons. The restaurant with its wide sea views is open to the public.

Higher Collaton Cottage near Salcombe ✆ 01548 843773 ⌂ www.coastandcountry.co.uk. A typical Devon thatched cottage with exposed ceiling beams and huge garden with sun terrace. Sleeps six.

Little Noddon Barn Ringmore ☎ 01548 843773 🖱 www.coastandcountry.co.uk. An opportunity to stay in this lovely village, with its access to the South West Coast Path and Bigbury Bay, in a barn conversion that retains many original features including exposed stone walls and cross-beams. Garden and two stone terraces. Sleeps six.

Lower Coombe Royal Kingsbridge, TQ7 4AD ☎ 01548 852880 🖱 www. lowercoomberoyal.co.uk. Luxury self-catering in the grounds of the former Coombe Royal mansion, with a variety of accommodation. They make a real effort to be green, with a biomass boiler and solar panels for water heating. Eight acres of private grounds and woodland for children to play in.

Campsites

The High Nature Centre East Portlemouth TQ8 8PN 🖱 www.high-nature.co.uk. Yurt camping on this organic smallholding, whose aim is to 'promote the protection and preservation of the natural landscape and all those who live and work within it'.

Karrageen caravan and camping park Bolberry, near Malborough TQ7 3EN ☎ 01548 561230 🖱 www.karrageen.co.uk. A small, family-run place surrounded by National Trust land, with terrific views and access to the South West Coast Path. Their website reassures you that 'we do not have a club or bar or children's playground but we do offer a well-stocked shop with freshly cooked baguettes and croissants daily, and plenty of space for children to play happily and safely.'

5 PLYMOUTH & THE TAMAR VALLEY
Self catering

Crownhill Fort Plymouth ☎ 01628 825920 🖱 www.landmarktrust.org.uk. Built in the 1860s to protect Plymouth from attack, Crownhill Fort retains its tunnels, earth ramparts, parade ground and cannons. You stay in the Officers' Quarters and have free run of the Fort once the gates close for the evening. Sleeps eight.

6 THE EASTERN FRINGE OF DARTMOOR
Self catering

Rydon Trusham, Teign Valley ☎ 01637 881183 🖱 www.uniquehomestays.com. A large converted barn in the delightful but untouristy Teign Valley. Heated pool (summer). Sleeps up to six. Dogs welcome.

7 THE NORTHWESTERN FRINGE OF DARTMOOR
Hotels

Lewtrenchard Manor Lewdown, near Okehampton EX20 4PN ☎ 01566 783222 🖱 www. lewtrenchard.co.uk (see page 185). It's not often you can stay in a Jacobean manor, tucked away in its own secret Devon valley and with a restaurant awarded three rosettes by the AA. The house is stunning, dripping with history, standing in several acres of beautifully designed gardens. Each of the 13 luxury *en-suite* bedrooms and suites has its own individual character; they've retained all of their period charm, while period inconveniences have been replaced by modern comforts. This is a grand and gracious house, with oak panelling, ornate plasterwork, stained glass and ancestors gazing down from the walls in their heavy gilt frames, but still it's relaxed and friendly. Food in the restaurant is described as 'flavoursome rather than fussy' and is excellent; herbs and most vegetables come from the walled kitchen garden and it's patronised by locals as well as guests. The energetic can indulge in croquet, hawk walking, clay pigeon shooting and trout fishing on the estate; or you can just relax in the lovely grounds.

Guesthouses & B&Bs

Betty Cottles Inn Graddon Cross, Okehampton EX20 4LR ✆ 01837 55339 ✑ www. bettycottles.co.uk. Inexpensive accommodation with a wide range of options, from standard *en-suite* rooms, to bunk rooms, log cabins and camping.

Coombe Trenchard Lewdown, near Okehampton EX20 4PW ✆ 01566 783179 ✑ www. coombetrenchard.co.uk (see page 186). In this beautiful Edwardian arts-and-crafts country house there are four luxury bedrooms (three doubles and a single) with *en-suite* or private baths/showers, overlooking the extensive gardens and surrounding countryside. They have been modernised for comfort but without losing their period character, which is echoed in the high-quality furnishings. Just walking to your room is a pleasure, through this gracious old house with its many antiques and other treasures. Breakfasts, which can be served either in the morning room or out on the terrace, include eggs newly laid by the owners' own hens. Hosts Sarah and Philip Marsh will look after you well and explain the various local attractions. Evening meals can sometimes be arranged, or you can sharpen your appetite by a ten-minute walk to neighbouring Lewtrenchard Manor (above) with its AA-rosetted restaurant.

The Dartmoor Inn Lydford EX20 4AY ✆ 01822 820221 ✑ www.dartmoorinn.com. Situated near the delightful village of Lydford and near the Lydford Gorge, – there are just three bedrooms.

The Highwayman Pub Sourton EX20 4HN ✆ 01837 861243 ✑ www.thehighwaymaninn. net. This utterly idiosyncratic pub (see page 187) has a few equally unique rooms available: three double and some 'Ships' Cabins' with bunk beds. Its non-identical twin, Cobweb Hall, opposite, has two double rooms. You'll never stay in a place like it!

Self catering

Twelve Penny Barn Lewdown✆ 01637 881183 ✑ www.uniquehomestays.com. A charming converted barn in the somewhat neglected area of west Dartmoor. Sleeps two and one well-behaved dog.

8 DARTMOOR NATIONAL PARK

B&B

Tor Royal B&B Princetown PL20 6SL ☏ 01822 890189 🖰 www.torroyal.co.uk. A luxury B&B in a beautiful old house with its own stables (see page 205). Right in Dartmoor proper, and ideal for walking or riding.

Self catering

The Chapel Lettaford, North Bovey ☏ 01628 825920 🖰 www.landmarktrust.org.uk. A tiny converted chapel, where you live and sleep (maximum two) in one room although the bathroom is separate. Charming and different. Nearby is another, larger, Landmark Trust property, Sanders, a longhouse, which sleeps five.

The Secret Holt Haytor ☏ 01637 881183 🖰 www.uniquehomestays.com. Indeed secret, since this wooden chalet is well off the beaten track at the end of a dirt road, though close to Dartmoor's most popular tor. Sleeps two, plus up to two well-behaved dogs.

Swiss Cottage Endsleigh, near Tavistock ☏ 01628 825920 🖰 www.landmarktrust.org. uk. A delightfully eccentric chalet designed by Jeffrey Wyatville. One of the best surviving examples of that most imaginative and English landscape aesthetic, the Picturesque. Sleeps four. Nearby is Pond Cottage, also designed by Jeffrey Wyatville, which sleeps five.

Campsites etc

Dartmoor is one of the few places in England where you can camp wild. There is also a good selection of campsites, bunk houses and hostels. See 🖰 www.dartmoor.co.uk.

Harford Bridge Holiday Park Peter Tavy, Tavistock PL19 9LS ☏ 01822 810349 🖰 www. harfordbridge.co.uk. Conveniently close to the A386, right on the edge of Dartmoor and adjacent to National Cycle Route 27, this well-kept park is a family-run affair, with two brothers and a sister carrying on what their parents started 30 years ago. 'We're continually enhancing it.' one of them told me, stressing their commitment to sustainable tourism and respect for the environment. There's a peaceful, shaded camping area beside a stream, well-spaced self-catering caravans and holiday lodges, and a lovingly built and cosy 'shepherd's hut'. Facilities are modern, with free hot water and showers. Nature is very close: one visitor mentioned spotting, from the stream-side campsite, kingfishers, dippers, nuthatches, tree creepers, bats and even mink. Only native species of shrubs and trees are planted; and some areas are left untrimmed to protect wildlife. Prices vary seasonally and are shown on the website.

Langstone Manor Holiday Park Moortown, Tavistock PL19 9JZ ☏ 01822 613371 🖰 www.langstonemanor.co.uk. The approach road to Langstone Manor takes you more deeply into Dartmoor than Harford Bridge (above); you feel the park closing in around you as you drive. But the Holiday Park itself, still only three miles from Tavistock, has streamlined modern facilities (including spotless toilet blocks and free hot showers) and a strong commitment to green tourism. There are various interpretation boards (*Life within a Logpile, Butterflies and Moths*...) and rainwater is harvested. Self-catering accommodation includes cottages, an apartment, holiday homes, and dumpy little wooden 'pods' for two or four people if you want to 'camp' without a tent. Camping areas are in an open field with moorland views, in a more sheltered walled garden or among trees; and there's a site reserved for adults only. The Langstone Bar offers a games room, evening meals and a wood-burning stove for chilly Dartmoor evenings, and the small shop has regular deliveries of fresh local baking. Prices are on the website; open Mar–Oct/Nov.

PHOTOGRAPHERS

Age footstock: Craig Joiner (CJ/AF); Alamy: PAUL SHADDICK (PS/A), Wig Worland (WW/A); AWL images: Travel Pix Collection (TPC/AWL); Andrew Cooper (AC); Blackpool Sands (BS); Dreamstime: Nomadimages (N/D); Go Plymouth (GP); Hilary Bradt (HB); Kents Cavern (KC); Lewtrenchard Manor (LM); Otters and Butterflies (OAB); Pennywell Farm (PF); Shutterstock: Erni (S/E), Helen Hoston (S/HH), ian woolcock (S/IW), Ron Ellis (S/RE), Sue Robinson (S/SR); South West Coast Path: Nick Shepherd (NS/SWCP); Tamar Valley AONB: Ted Giffords (TG/TV); The Art Café (TAC); Totnes Town Council (TTC); Visit Britain: David Clapp (VB/DC), Joanna Henderson (VB/JH)

INDEX

Page numbers in **bold** refer to major entries.